E. Pauline Spencer

German Literature

As Known in England

1750–1830

German Literature as Known in England

1750–1830

By

V. Stockley, M.A.

George Routledge and Sons, Ltd.
Broadway House: Carter Lane, London
1929

PRINTED IN GREAT BRITAIN BY
BILLING AND SONS LTD., PRINTERS, GUILDFORD AND ESHER

Contents

Contents

Contents

Contents

Preface

THIS book is in the main the result of research work done when the writer was a research student of Newnham College, Cambridge, and holder of a Travelling Studentship from the National University of Ireland (1916-1918). Dr. Karl Breul, Schroeder Professor of German in the University of Cambridge, suggested the subject and directed the work, and I gladly take this opportunity of thanking him for his help. The University of Cambridge granted the dissertation a Certificate of Research in 1919.

It treats of the slow introduction of German literature into England, from the beginning of the modern classical period, about 1750, until 1830, a couple of years before Goethe's death; by which time the literature of Germany may be said to have established itself in England as worthy of serious interest and study. Special reference is here made to translations from German: to the choice of works translated, how these were done, and by whom, and how received by English critics and the English public. No pretence is made to estimate the influence of these German works on English writers of the time. This has been done recently by Mr. F. W. Stokoe in his interesting book, *German Influence in the English Romantic Period* (Cambridge University Press, 1926), to which frequent reference will be made in these pages. The general remarks in his Preface on the whole question of "influence" in literature are particularly interesting. In closer connection with the subject here treated is his general survey of periodical literature in Chapter III (pp. 43-49); which makes it unnecessary to give another such survey here. But although this study would, perhaps, have appeared more appropriately before Mr. Stokoe's work, it is hoped that it may not be entirely without value, though appearing later. It is an attempt to give a complete survey of the actual translations from German between 1750 and 1830, a subject treated only incidentally by Mr. Stokoe and over a less wide period. The whole work has been recently revised and reconsidered in the light of any publications of the last ten years bearing on the same subject; and it is hoped that nothing of importance has been overlooked.[1] The intention was, at first, to include in this survey all branches of German literature. But restriction was found necessary, and so lyric poetry has been omitted throughout. Thus, the translations of Goethe's and Schiller's lyrics are not treated of: neither are the translations from writers almost exclusively known as lyric poets—*e.g.*, Bürger, the Stolbergs, Claudius, Matthisson, etc.[2]

The chief sources of information have been: ordinary books of reference, specially Goedeke's *Grundriss der deutschen Dichtung* (not always accurate as to translations); catalogues of the principal libraries of Great Britain and Ireland; modern German and English periodicals with articles treating of comparative literature; and books and articles already written on the subject of German literature in England by German,

[1] Reference will be made to a valuable compilation of *all* translations from German into English recently made by a painstaking American scholar, Mr. Bayard Quincy Morgan: *A Bibliography of German Literature in English Translation* (Madison, 1922). Mr. Morgan, however, worked under the disadvantage of not being able to consult English libraries on the spot and so he has sometimes mistaken American reprints for original editions. But he gives much useful information about American editions. Critical notes are added only in a few cases, and not apparently at first-hand.

[2] For list of articles on Bürger's *Lenore* and for Goethe's Lyric Poems, see Appendix C.

English, or American scholars. Where such books or articles treat exhaustively of the translations made from a particular author or of a particular work, I have not attempted to repeat the information already given, but have merely referred to the work in question, adding any necessary comments. Full references will be found in the footnotes and in the list of works consulted, and it is hoped that the new material now added, taken in conjunction with these references, will provide a complete survey of translations within the given period.

The compiler has worked in the British Museum; in the Bodleian, Oxford; in the University Library, Cambridge; and in the Library of Trinity College, Dublin; and has consulted by correspondence the Advocates' Library, Edinburgh. She can testify to the existence of all translations mentioned, with the exception of those marked *, of which she could find no copy. As to these, the evidence has been stated for or against their existence, where such might be doubtful. (Unless expressly stated otherwise, the translation may be found in the British Museum.) In all cases, criticism of the translations has been given after a firsthand acquaintance with the work in question, and after careful comparison with the original. But because of their length it has been found impossible to give all the examples and extracts which were collected. For the same reason are omitted the German originals of the extracts from well-known authors whose works are easily to be had.

The lists of works in the Appendices are meant to provide an easy means of reference to anyone interested. Appendix A gives the works translated from all the more important writers under the authors' names. Appendix B, works (with the exception of a few from obscure authors, or anonymous) in chronological order. Thus is shown, at a glance, the ebb and flow of the interest taken, in England, in German literature;

also the curious mixture of good, of mediocre, and of quite worthless, in the works chosen for translation.

It is hoped that the information here collected may prove of some interest and may be of use to others, who are studying from various points of view the interrelations between the literatures of England and Germany.

V. STOCKLEY.

1928.

GERMAN LITERATURE
AS KNOWN IN ENGLAND
1750–1830

INTRODUCTION

The *Edinburgh Review* in 1816[1] thus spoke of German literature in England: "The astonishing rapidity of the development of German literature, has been the principal cause both of its imperfections, and of the enthusiasm of its warmer admirers. About five-and-twenty or thirty years ago, all we knew about Germany was—that it was a vast tract of country, overrun with hussars and classical editors; and that, if you went there, you would see a great tun at Heidelbergh; and be regaled with excellent old hock and Westphalian hams; the taste for which good things was so predominant as to preclude the slightest approach to any poetical grace or enthusiasm. At that time, we had never seen a German name affixed to any other species of writing than a treaty, by which some Serene Highness or other had sold us so many head of soldiers for American consumption, at a fair and reasonable market-price; or to a formidable apparatus of critical annotation, teeming with word-catching or billingsgate in Greek and Latin."

Much other evidence bears out that this—allowing for journalistic high-colouring—fairly represents the state of affairs about 1770. The growth of English interest in things German was slow and precarious; and though isolated German works had English

[1] XXVI. 305.

readers before 1790, yet not until after that date was there in England anything like a real appreciation of the general development of German literature.

For this ignorance there were many reasons.

First: All through the seventeenth and the first half of the eighteenth centuries, when France was at the height of her literary fame, Germany had no literature worth international notice. Politically, she had been weak and divided since the Thirty Years' War; her arms had fallen into disrepute, and also indirectly her language: indeed German, it must be remembered, was long despised in Germany itself by the scholars who wrote in Latin, and the courts which spoke French. There was a general prejudice against Germany and things German in England during the reigns of the first two Georges—little lessened by the ways and manners of these two monarchs whose court language was French though they spoke German in private. This prejudice took time to overcome, and was too deep-seated to be removed at once, when the rapid development of German literature began.

Second: As far as foreign literatures were concerned French literature and style were dominant in England, and French opinion was accepted without question in most branches of literature. In regard to German works this opinion was very often prejudiced and unjust.

Third: Ignorance of the German language, commonly regarded as presenting almost insurmountable difficulties to a foreigner. Few even attempted to learn it. In 1813 the *Edinburgh Review*[1] says: "Thirty years ago there were probably in London as many Persian as German scholars." Towards the end of the eighteenth century as commerce with Germany increased, some merchants indeed sent their sons to Germany to learn the language; but for

[1] XXIII. 198.

purposes purely utilitarian and commercial. In Edinburgh as late as 1806 Gillies had great difficulty in finding one competent teacher of German.

From the general ignorance of the language followed the want of competent interpreters of the literature. With few exceptions—such as John Richardson's versions of Lessing's *Fables* (1773) and of several of Wieland's works—the translations before 1790 were very bad. Eschenburg—who took much interest in the spread of German literature in England—wrote from Weimar in 1793: "Weder die Wahl der Originale noch die Geschicklichkeit des Dolmetschers war immer von der Art, dass wir Deutsche grosse Ursache fanden, zu dieser ihr geschenkten Aufmerksamkeit uns Glück zu wünschen oder einen sonderlichen Grad ihrer Verbreitung zu hoffen." And even long after 1790 bad or mediocre translations of worthless originals far outnumbered good ones. We often feel amazed at the translator daring to translate from a language of which he obviously knew so little. Very few were the interpreters of German literature with any real knowledge and understanding of the subject—such as the pioneer, William Taylor of Norwich.

Fourth: The scarcity of German books. The great expense of printing in England hindered reprints; and the exorbitant duty on foreign books hindered importation.[1] A writer in 1823 says: "One cause of this neglect of important books is undoubtedly the enormous expense of printing in this country, which deters publishers from risking their capital. While the Germans publish re-prints and translations of the best English works at a fourth of the price we pay for the originals, we cannot afford to do the same with theirs; and even those who understand the German language are not able to purchase as they would gladly do, on account of the high prices charged by the

[1] For details of the tariff *vide* Hauhart, *Faust in England*, Introduction, p. 1.

London booksellers, which are partly ascribed to the heavy duties on importations."[1] Scott in 1796 found it impossible to obtain a copy of Bürger's works without sending to Hamburg.[2]

Among the influences which aided the introduction, however slow, of German literature into England were: First: The number of German officers in the English army during the American War (1775-83), who spread some knowledge of their language and literature among their English comrades. Second: A certain amount of court encouragement for German works. George III. married a German Princess, Charlotte of Mecklenburg, in 1760, and several early translations—*e.g.*, Mrs. Collyer's *Messiah* (1763)—are dedicated "to the Queen." Others were accomplished under her Majesty's direct patronage, *e.g.*, an anonymous translation of Haller's *Usong* (1772). Third: The growing interest in France for German literature. French literature had such prestige in England, that any German work introduced into England through French, came with a special recommendation to English readers. And the first translations of several German works were made, not from the originals, but from French translations—often from a bad one, the German author faring very badly in the double metamorphosis. Thus the first translation of *Werther* (1779), of Lavater's *Physiognomy* (1789), of Zimmermann's *Solitude* (1791), of *Dichtung und Wahrheit* even as late as 1823, came through French. The number of these translations from French has, however, sometimes been exaggerated; some critics speaking as if scarcely any German work became known in England except through French. Yet English translations of Klopstock's *Messiah* (1763), and Wieland's *Abraham* (1764), *Don Silvio von Rosalva* (1773),

[1] *London Magazine*, VIII. 210; 1823.

[2] See F. W. Stokoe, *German Influence in the English Romantic Period*, p. 66 *ff.*

Dialogen des Diogenes von Sinope (1771) and *Göttergespräche* (1795) appeared earlier than any French translations; while many other important translations, such as *Agathon* (1773), Gellert's *Schwedische Gräfin* (1752), Gessner's *Abel* (1761), etc., were made directly from the German. Fourth: The activity of Germans resident in England.[1] Some were mere literary hacks, and their translations bear much internal evidence of their origin besides the German name. A few are better known. R. E. Raspe (1737-1794), famous as the author of *Baron Münchhausen*, is said to have known English well; but his translations of *Nathan* (1781) and of Zachariæ's *Tabby im Elysium* (1781) are poor enough. Dr. W. Render, German born, in England from about 1790, "teacher of German" at Oxford, Cambridge and Edinburgh, published, besides several translations,[2] a number of educational manuals for learners of German—probably the earliest of such books in English. His *Concise Practical Grammar of the German Tongue* (1799) is said to have been very successful. G. H. Egestorff, the translator of the *Messiah*, also taught German in England some years later.

The earliest translation of a work of the "New High German Literature" was Gellert's *Swedish Countess* (1752); followed by Rabener's *Satirical Letters* (1757); Gessner's *Death of Abel* (1761); the *Messiah* (1763); Wieland's *Abraham* (1764); and Bodmer's *Noah* (1767). Among the writers thus early translated none was so widely known or so much thought of as Gessner. His *Death of Abel* was found on all the bookstalls in London, and is said to have been even more popular in country districts, taking

[1] For a fuller account of these see Stokoe, *German Influence*, etc., pp. 22-26; and K. H. Schaible, *Geschichte der Deutschen in England*. Strassburg, 1885.

[2] Schiller's *Robbers*, *Don Carlos*, *Maria Stuart*, *Ghost-Seer*, 1800; Goethe's *Werther*, 1801.

its place beside the *Bible* and the *Pilgrim's Progress* among the "sacred classics" of the people.[1] His Idylls were also much translated; and two separate translations of his works were made in 1802 and 1805 with illustrations and fine engravings.

After Gessner, Wieland was probably the most popular. He pleased by his wit and his light, graceful style. These writers were specially popular with women readers, who, at that time, having much more leisure, read much more than men. It is worth noting also how many of the early translators were women—Mrs. Collyer, the "Lady" of Gellert's *Swedish Countess* (1776), Mrs. Howorth, Anne Plumptre, etc. It was Mrs. Barbauld who read W. Taylor's translation of Bürger's *Lenore* in MS. in Edinburgh in 1794 and indirectly brought the poem to the notice of Scott.[2]

In the last decade of the eighteenth century, the years of "the revival of Gothic romanticism," the popularity of German literature was at its height, and the numbers of translations increased each year. The novel-reading public threw themselves eagerly on translations and adaptations of German novels—the sentimental novel, with *Werther* as its great prototype, the "Familienromane" of La Fontaine and others, and above all the "Schauer- und Ritterromane," which provided English writers with rich materials for their own tales of horror and mystery.

Kotzebue's dramas drew ever-increasing crowds to the theatres. Also many German plays were freely adapted to the English stage, and given without any mention of their source. A French writer, Lamartelière, writes in his preface to his *Théâtre de Schiller* (1799): "Nous allons puiser chez ces insulaires ce qu'ils ont emprunté eux-mêmes aux allemands, et nous ajoutons ainsi à l'orgueil d'une nation rivale et dédaigneuse un titre de gloire et de supériorité dont

[1] *Quar. Rev.*, II. 78; 1814.

[2] See F. W. Stokoe, *German Influence*, etc., pp. 65 *ff.* and 176.

elle se pavane et qui ne lui appartient pas. . . . Une pièce de théâtre, intitultée le *Spectre du Château*,[1] qui depuis six mois fait courir tout Londres, est tirée de l'allemand. Il en est de même d'un grand nombre de romans traduits en Angleterre, et que nous traduisons ensuite comme originaux."

With novels and dramas, some German ballads also found their way into England. No less than six translations of Bürger's *Lenore*[2] were published in 1796; four of *The Wild Huntsman* before 1801;[3] and various ballads were translated and imitated by Lewis and others. Scott translated Goethe's *Erlkönig* probably in 1797.

Unfortunately it was not the best of contemporary German literature which became most popular in England. As H. C. Robinson wrote from Weimar to the *Monthly Register*[4] in 1801: "I have for the present but one observation. You know nothing of German literature. Kotzebue's and Iffland's plays are not German literature. Though popular German works, they are not considered classical here." In the flood of poor translations, works of real merit such as Taylor's *Nathan* (1791) and *Iphigenia* (1793), Scott's *Götz* (1799), Coleridge's *Wallenstein*, and T. Churchill's translation of Herder's *Ideen* (1800), were passed over with comparatively little notice. Only Sotheby's *Oberon* (1798) received its due recognition.

It may be interesting to quote here the impressions of a German traveller (C. A. G. Goede) in England in 1802, as to the attitude of the English towards foreign,

[1] *The Castle Spectre*, by M. G. Lewis.

[2] V. W. W. Greg, *English Translations of Lenore*, *Mod. Q. of Lang. and Lit.*, V., August, 1899.

[3] (1) *The Chase*, by W. Scott, 1796. (2) *The Wild Hunter*, by W. Taylor (printed in *Hist. Surv.*, II. 25). (3) *The Wild Huntsman's Chase*, Anon., 1798. (4) *The Wild Hunter*, by "J. C.," *German Mus.*, III. 16; 1801.

[4] I. 327.

and particularly German literature:[1] "Of foreign literature, except French, little is known in England. Translations are very fashionable among the English and are too often cruel distortions of the original design, and this is the only medium through which German literature is at all known in England. It has been asserted, but certainly without truth, that German literature was in high repute among the English. It is a fact, indeed, that Kotzebue's plays, having been well-received, herds of wretched translators introduced a heap of ridiculous German novels to the attention of the public. A few good works followed; but they were so dreadfully mutilated that the rage died away. . . . Many English consider German literature immoral and dangerous, but they have formed this hasty opinion on some trifling German novels, which too easily find their way from circulating libraries to the toilet of beauty." Of German works he says: "Pitt's admiration of the *Robbers* gave it celebrity, but *Werther* is the only work really popular." Speaking of the difficulty of obtaining any foreign publications in London, he says that in the whole metropolis he found only three German booksellers, and these not worthy of notice. Outside of London there was apparently nothing. He continues: "German works in the original are scarcely read by anyone. The natural pride of the English and their dislike of foreigners makes it almost impossible for them to comprehend the peculiarities of a strange people. This affects their study of languages and makes it very difficult for an Englishman to acquire a perfect knowledge of a foreign language; for what is absolutely required for the study of languages, a deep insight into the genius of those who speak them, he cannot attain without the most severe application. . . . Moreover, there is perhaps no country where the ordinary science of

[1] *A Foreigner's Opinion of England*, London, 1802, Vol. II., chap. vii. See Chap. IX.

geography is so little cultivated. In their daily conversation they constantly utter the most ludicrous absurdities about foreign parts. They are, in particular, strangely perplexed in forming an adequate conception of Germany."

Thus we see that, in the last decade of the eighteenth century, little serious interest in German literature accompanied the popular rage for German plays and novels. A reaction against their popularity set in about 1800. With the progress of the anti-revolutionary wars and the strengthening of the Tory party in England, the "Sturm und Drang" literature of Germany came to be regarded as synonymous with all that was revolutionary in politics and free-thinking in philosophy. Its popularity was looked on by many as marking a decline of true taste and of sound morals. This reaction was led by the *Antijacobin*, begun in 1797 by Canning and others with the express purpose of combating everything liberal in literature and politics ; also by *The Meteors* and other Conservative journals. A paper[1] read by W. Preston before the Royal Irish Academy in 1802 on "The Peculiarities of Style and Manner of the late German Writers Whose Works have appeared in English, and of the Tendency of their Productions" is significant of this change of feeling. Preston criticises severely not only Kotzebue, but also Schiller and Goethe, "who by his *Goss* [*sic*] *of the Iron Hand* had established a reign of terror and of blood."

There followed during the first fifteen years of the nineteenth century a period of comparative apathy towards German literature. It was fostered by the hampering of intercourse with the Continent resulting from the Napoleonic wars. Carlyle writes in 1824: "After a brief interval of not too judicious cordiality, the acquaintance on our part was altogether dropped; nor in the few years since we have resumed it, have

[1] Trans. of R.I.A., VIII., p. 15-79.

our feelings of affection and esteem materially increased."

The notices of German works in English periodicals grow rarer and rarer during those fifteen years. There are also much fewer translations than in the preceding decade. Yet there are a few of importance: *e.g.*, Gessner's *Works* by Rose Lawrence (1802), and another and much better translation of the same by F. Shoberl (1805); Wieland's *Peregrinus Proteus* (1804); *Hermann und Dorothea* (1805); several plays in Holcroft's *Theatrical Recorder* (1805), the *Messiah* (extracts) by Egestorff (1811), and by Raffles, 1814; Kleist's *Frühling* (1814); as well as numerous works of Kotzebue and La Fontaine. These sufficiently show that the acquaintance was not "altogether dropped," as Carlyle puts it.

The revival of interest in German literature was brought about largely by Madame de Staël's *de l'Allemagne*, translated into English in 1813,[1] while a French edition was printed in London in the same year. It was reviewed at length in all the leading periodicals,[2] and attracted much attention. Carlyle—speaking perhaps in too great forgetfulness of W. Taylor and others of an earlier generation—in translating Jean Paul Richter's review of *de l'Allemagne* in the *Annalen*, said: "The work indeed, with all its vagueness and short-comings must be regarded as the precursor, if not the parent, of whatever acquaintance with German literature exists among us." After 1815 the conclusion of peace facilitated the renewal of literary intercourse with the Continent, and while a certain prejudice against French literature followed on the

[1] *Germany*, by the Baroness Holstein, translated from the French, in three vols. (London, 1813).

[2] *Gent.'s Mag.*, LXXXIII. 461; 1813. *Brit. Crit.*, I. 504; 1814. *Crit. Rev.*, V. 67; 1814. *Edin. Rev.*, XXII. 198; 1813. *Month. Rev.*, LXXII. 431; 1813. See R. C. Whitford, *Madame de Staël's Literary Reputation in England*, University of Illinois; *Studies in Language and Literature*, IV. 1; 1918.

long political enmity of the two countries, the alliance in arms between the Germans and the English helped to bring them closer together.

Blackwood's Magazine was begun in 1815, with Lockhart as editor, and opened its pages freely to German literature. Gillies, by his translations in the "Horæ Germanicæ" (1819-1828)—which also included many other works—introduced the "Schicksalsdrama" into England. The *Edinburgh Review* (though often very unjust), the *Literary Gazette* (begun 1819), and later the *Foreign Quarterly Review* (1817) also brought German literature prominently before the notice of their readers. Besides this, several translations of serious German works were made, *e.g.*, A. Schlegel's *Lectures on Dramatic Art* (1815); F. Schlegel's *Lectures on the History of Literature* (1818); Goethe's *Wilhelm Meister* (1824); Schiller's *Thirty Years' War* (1828). Also the first verse translation of the *Messiah* (1821); *Undine* (1821) and other of Fouqué's works by G. Soane; Grimm's *Märchen* (1823); and the five collections of "German Stories" in 1826, followed by Carlyle's[1] *German Romance* in 1827. With a few exceptions—*e.g.*, the miserable *Memoirs of Goethe*, translated through French in 1832—the translations of this later period are incomparably superior to those of the period ending about 1813. Gillies, Soane, Lockhart, Carlyle etc., all knew German well, and all had literary ability, and had enough respect for their originals not to substitute their own ideas for their authors'. One very good translator deserving mention here is Sarah Austin, authoress of *Characteristics of Goethe* (1832). She made some contributions to *Blackwood* before 1830; but most of her work was done later.

[1] For Carlyle *vide* W. Streuli, *T. Carlyle als Vermittler deutscher Literatur und deutschen Geistes* (1895) and Kräger, *Carlyle's Stellung zur deutschen Sprache und Literatur*, *Anglia*, Vol. XXV.; and before all, J. M. Carré, *Goethe en Angleterre*, Paris, 1921.

In this later period (*c.* 1813-1830) French influence is much less strongly marked than between 1780 and 1813. Again, with the above-mentioned exception of Goethe's *Memoirs* (which did not avow its French origin), no translations were made through French, and several German writers—*e.g.*, H. von Kleist and Heine—were known in England before they became known in France. Madame de Staël[1] wrote even in 1813: "German literature is much better known in England than in France. In England the foreign languages are more studied and the Germans are more naturally connected with the English than with the French. Nevertheless, prejudices do exist, even in England both against the philosophy and literature of Germany." These prejudices she attributes chiefly to the differences in the temper of mind between the English and the Germans, the English taking more pleasure in the real, the Germans in the ideal.

Between 1820 and 1830 the lyric poetry of Germany at last received some attention in England. Up to this time it had, in comparison with other branches of German literature, been much neglected. The only collection of lyrics was that by Beresford, printed in Berlin (1801), most of them of no literary worth. A few German poems were well translated by the Hon. W. Herbert in his *Miscellaneous Poetry* (1804); but most were ballads rather than lyrics. Occasional translations in periodicals were mostly very poor, with a few exceptions, *e.g.*, Schiller's *Ideale*.

Between 1820 and 1830 we have several collections of lyrics. In 1821 Beresford's translations, with some additional and much better ones by Mellish, were reprinted as *Specimens of German Lyric Poetry*. This reached a second edition in the following year. In 1823 and 1824 Lord Leveson Gower translated Schiller's *Song of the Bell* and many other German poems;

[1] For her remarks as to the reception of German literature in England *vide* Part II., chaps. i. and ii.

and in 1827 he appended several more to his translations of *Tasso*. In 1827 John Macray published a volume of poems, including many German lyrics entitled *Stray Leaves*, and in 1828 Robert Robinson another—*Specimens of the German Lyric Poets*. Of these translators the best is John Macray.

Thus by 1830 we see German literature in all its branches, if not widely popular, or fully appreciated, at least firmly established in England; and the way was open for a more serious understanding of the Idealism of the best German poetry and philosophy—an understanding completely absent during the late eighteenth century rage for German dramas and novels. Carlyle in 1831 writes of German literature as rapidly growing in favour: " This favour is now more hopeful because it grounds itself on better knowledge, on direct study and judgment. Our knowledge is better, if only because more general. Within the last ten years independent German readers have increased a hundredfold. . . . With independent readers, the writer ceases to be independent, which is in itself a considerable step. Our British translators for instance have long been unparalleled in modern literature, . . . but now there are symptoms that even in the remote German province they may not roam at will. . . . We regard this renewal of our intercourse after twenty years of languor or suspension as among the most remarkable and even promising features of our recent intellectual history."[1]

[1] Essay on W. Taylor's *Historic Survey*, *Edin. Rev.*, 1831 ; reprinted in *Miscellaneous Essays*, III. 283.

CHAPTER I

A.—Early Prose Writers

GELLERT; RABENER; ZIMMERMANN; LAVATER.

The early developments of the new German literature in the first half of the eighteenth century attracted practically no attention in England.[1] The magazines of the time, though replete with notices of German philosophical, theological, legal and scientific works, contain but one review[2] of a work, purely literary in character, *i.e.*, Brocke's *Irdisches Vergnügen in Gott* (1748), an imitation of Thomson's *Seasons.*

Gottsched is occasionally mentioned[3]—as for instance in connection with the translation of the *Arminius* of his disciple Schönaich—but none of his critical works were noticed; nor were those of his opponents, Bodmer and Breitinger. It might be thought that this famous dispute between the Leipzig and Zürich schools would have roused some interest in England, since it ended in the decisive victory of English models over French, but no echoes of it seem to have carried across the Channel.

From early in the second half of the century, however, isolated works of German writers travelled to England, and the very earliest of those who thus became known were Gellert and Rabener.

[1] An article by G. M. Baker in *Mod. Lang. Notes,* XXIV. 111, 1909, on *Some References to German Literature in English Magazines of the Early Eighteenth Century,* gives interesting information on this subject.

[2] *Republic of Letters* (November, 1731).

[3] *The Literary Journal,* Dublin (September, 1746) gives a list of some twenty "living Muses of Germany," mostly imitators and emulators of Gottsched and his wife.

German Literature

C. F. GELLERT (1715-1769).

Gellert's novel, *Das Leben der schwedischen Gräfin von Guildenstern* (1748), modelled on the English novels of Richardson, was the first work of the new epoch to be translated,[1] and for many years Gellert was regarded in England as one of the principal founders of the new German literature.

From the preface of the anonymous translator it seems that the translation of the work was suggested to him by a Dr. Luther, eminent in the law in Frankfurt. He admits that he was doubtful at first about translating the work into English " because of the prevailing talent of an Englishman, namely, that narrow admiration of the works of his own country, for which he is censored all over Europe," and also fearing that its didactic spirit would not suit English taste. But it is just this characteristic which specially attracted the translator himself. According to the title-page, the work is " specially calculated to recommend an early Attachment to Virtue in young Ladies of no affluent Fortune; also a becoming Fortitude in Adversity and a spontaneous Resignation to our Destiny."

The translator was probably a foreigner resident in England. In the preface to the later translation " by a Lady " his work is criticised in no very flattering terms, concluding thus: " the whole exhibits a miserable daubing copied without art from a fine original." *The Monthly Review*[2] gives cooler praise to the work itself while also condemning the translation. " The work is the first of the kind from Germany which has vivacity enough to recommend it to nations less phlegmatic, and it contains more real merit than many similar English works of this life-writing age, yet in

[1] *The History of the Swedish Countess of G——*, in two parts, by C. F. Gellert, M.A. Translated from the original German (London, Smith, 1752).

[2] VI. 231 ; 1752.

its English dress it appears to such disadvantage that few readers will find patience to read it through." It must, however, have found some readers, for a second edition was published in 1757.[1] The translation certainly deserves most of these harsh criticisms. The choice of words is bad, the sentences stiff and awkwardly turned, the style heavy, and the whole reads as if the writer was expressing himself with difficulty in a language not his own.

Twenty-four years after this early translation, two more appeared in one year, apparently quite independently of each other.

The first is by a clergyman, the Rev. Mr. N.[2] His foreword is short and betrays no knowledge of either of the other translations. His own is somewhat better than that of 1752. It is rather more literal than that "by a Lady," and occasionally brings out the meaning of a particular passage more clearly; but on the whole it is poor, and the style flat and heavy. The *Monthly*,[3] calling it "a vile translation of a beautiful work," makes the mistake of thinking that it may be the old translation re-printed.

The third translation "by a Lady"[4] is undoubtedly the best of the three, even if it does not quite deserve the high praise given it in the Advertisement which was written by the translator's husband, she herself having died before the publication of the work. He says that she had made herself proficient in the German language under his tuition, and translated the *Swedish Countess* by way of amusement in hours of relaxation. She was induced to publish the book by the approba-

[1] The only copy of the First Edition I have found is in the Bodleian, and of that, Part I. is missing.

[2] *The Life of the Swedish Countess of G——.* Written in German by the late ingenious Professor Gellert. Translated from the German by the Rev. Mr. N—— (London, 1776).

[3] LV. 157; 1776.

[4] *The Life of the Countess of G.* Translated by a Lady (London, 1776).

tion of friends. The translator has taken a good many liberties with the original, and has sometimes introduced moral dictums of her own. But it is the only one of the three translations which reads at all like a piece of original prose. The *Monthly*[1] gives the work in this version warmer praise than in 1752, calling it "a very elegant work, which exhibits fine pictures of human nature." But the *Gentleman's Magazine*,[2] disclaiming any knowledge of Gellert's fame, thinks the incidents of the novel "too uncommon in life and too common in fiction to cause either interest or surprise." A more telling bit of criticism of the novel is given by John Richardson in his preface to *Agathon* where he says: "Some parts of the *Swedish Countess* abound with true pathos and well-imagined scenes of affecting distress; but the incidents are perhaps not sufficiently diversified, the moral reflections are tedious, and he seems rather unfortunate in his attempts at humour."

One only of Gellert's comedies was translated into English. It is *Die zärtlichen Schwestern*, which appeared as *The Tender Sisters* in the first volume of Holcroft's *Theatrical Recorder*[3] (1805). He appends a short account of Gellert, taken mostly from Van Veterlein's *Handbuch*.[4] He has translated rather freely than literally, giving English equivalents for German names, and making slight changes in the descriptions of manners, etc. He does not think the play would be successful on the English stage. Nor does it appear that it was ever produced.

W. Taylor speaks of Gellert's *Fables* as perhaps the first poetic work of the modern Germans to become decidedly and nationally popular. He gives a pleasing translation in verse of one of them—*The Nightingale*

[1] LV. 66; 1776. [2] XLVI. 570.

[3] *The Tender Sisters*, a Comedy in three Acts, translated from the German in T. Holcroft's *Theatrical Recorder*, Vol. I., 1805.

[4] *Handbuch der Poet. Lit. der Deut.*, Koethen, 1800.

and the Cuckoo—in the *Monthly Magazine*, 1819.[1] I found no other translations of any of the Fables before 1830. (A collection of Gellert's *Fables and Poems* appeared in translation in 1850.)

There is again an interval of nearly thirty years between the translations of the *Swedish Countess* and the next appearance in England of a work by Gellert. It is a translation of Moral Lessons delivered by him to students in Leipzig, preceded by an account of his life. It is the work of a lady, a Mrs. Douglas, and was published in 1805.[2] The book bears throughout a religious character and was translated with a purely religious and didactic purpose. "May it prove useful and my end will be answered," says Mrs. Douglas in her Preface. Of the German language she admits herself "wholly ignorant." She translated the *Moral Lessons* from a French version[3] of Gellert's *Moralische Vorlesungen*.[4] The Life of Gellert she took partly from the *Réflexions* which preceded the French version (which are a translation from the German of Garve) and partly from an account of Gellert prefixed to a French translation of his letters by Madame de la Fite. From the same work, Mrs. Douglas also translated two of Gellert's *Essays on Religion and Devotion*, which, with the *Life*, occupy the first volume. The other two volumes contain the twenty-six *Moral Lessons*, *the Instructions from a father to his son*, and the *Moral Characters*. The *Life* is a fairly detailed one and gives many extracts from Gellert's letters. With regard to the translation of the rest of the work it must

[1] XLVII. 398; *Hist. Surv.*, I. 220.

[2] *The Life of Prof. Gellert, with a course of moral lessons delivered by him in the University of Leipzig*, taken from a French translation of the original German in three vols., by Mrs. Douglas of Ednam House, Kelso, 1805.

[3] *Leçons de Morale . . . par M. Gellert. On y a joint des réflexions sur la personne et les écrits de l'auteur, le tout traduit de l'allemand.* Utrecht, 1772.

[4] Published after his death. Leipzig, 1770.

naturally suffer from being done at second hand. The *Monthly*[1] calls it "the shadow of a shade." Mrs. Douglas says herself that she suspects the French translator of having sometimes rendered Gellert very imperfectly. It is impossible without a detailed comparison to give a definite judgment in a case like this; but from comparing several passages in the French and English and these with the original I judge that the French version is on the whole faithful and accurate, and that Mrs. Douglas in her turn followed this carefully and accurately, so that her translation is a very fair presentation of the original. In style, too, it is quite readable. The *Moral Lessons* was warmly welcomed by the *British Critic*,[2] which compares Gellert to Cowper, and considers that Mrs. Douglas has conferred a benefit on the public in bringing to its notice the life and writings of "so truly amiable and Christian an author." But both this review and one in the *Critical*[3] warn readers not to expect anything very original, new or profound in Gellert's *Lessons*—nor again vigour of thought or brilliancy of wit; they will find, however, purity and tenderness of sentiment and chaste and elevated piety. The comments of the *Annual Review*[4] are less favourable. It considers that it was wise to select for translation the devotional writings of Gellert, for provided books "abound with pious aspirations and conscientious apprehensions, the religious public care little how feeble the eloquence or how trivial the truisms." Other people would be less easily satisfied. It then passes in review the other works of Gellert "all of a secondary or tertiary value." On each it comments, saying little that is favourable.

[1] XLIX; 1806.
[2] XXV. 654; 1805.
[3] VII. 358; 1805.
[4] IV. 516; 1805.

Early Prose Writers

WILHELM RABENER (1714-1771).

Rabener's *Satirische Briefe* was one of the earliest German works translated; but I was unable to find a copy of the translation. One can, however, learn a good deal about it from contemporary reviews and criticisms.[1] It was noticed and criticised by Lessing[2] in 1758, the year after its appearance. He expresses gratification at Rabener's works becoming known in England, but regrets that it should be through the medium of a translation full of mistakes, of which he gives several examples. He believes, however, that in spite of all these blemishes, the translation will have a great success in England; "an einem Rabener muss man sehr viel verderben, wenn er gar nicht mehr gefallen soll." The English critics were not so hopeful. The *Critical*[3] thinks the *Letters* may be proper for Germany, but are little calculated to please in England. The *Monthly*[4] says that any translation, even a good one, must place a foreign humoristic writer in a disadvantageous light, while these letters have still more to suffer from a bad translation. From the extracts given here and in the *Critical*, the translation certainly seems very poor, stilted in style and full of English idioms only half understood and wrongly used. *E.g.*, Christmas boxes "are quite against my grain," the daughter is required to "have a little snatch of her catechism," and the son "has all his paces." The translator was obviously a German. Still, the *Monthly* concludes by saying that "nothing can quite destroy the humour of these letters, and English readers will only regret that they cannot read them in the original." John Richardson in his Preface to *Agathon* (1773)

[1] **Satirical Letters, translated from the German of G. W. Rabener, First Secretary to the Treasury at Dresden* (London, A. Linde, 1757). (Morgan, *Bibl. of Ger. Lit.*, p. 413, mentions a copy in the Lib. Con.)

[2] See Lachmann-Muncker ed., VII. 104.

[3] III. 499; 1757.

[4] XVII. 104; 1757.

alludes to the *Satires* as follows: "Rabener's *Satires* have indeed appeared in an English dress, but in so loose and negligent a one, that the author, were he now living, and could read and understand his translation, would have some difficulty to know himself under this disguise. In any case the local character of his satires necessarily makes them less interesting to an English reader. These, perhaps, are the true reasons why he is so little read amongst us, and has not met with that applause which his genius so deservedly claims."

A short piece, *Traum von den Beschäftigungen der abgeschiedenen Seelen*, was twice translated. First in 1762 under the title *The Employment of Souls after separation from the Body: A Dream*, as a supplement to a series of tales from the French, called *The Country-Seat or Country Evening Entertainments* (Lownds, 1762). Herzfeld[1] thinks it was made from a French version, which appears probable. From a short extract given in the *Monthly*[2] the translation seems poor. (The work itself I could not find.) A second translation of the same piece as *A Dream upon the Occupation of departed Souls* appeared in the first volume of the *German Museum* (1801). The introduction and concluding paragraphs are omitted, and the translation is pretty free, but correct and in good English. In volume xxvi. (381) of the *Monthly* there is a review of *Briefe von den Herrn Gellert und Rabener*. The reviewer translates one letter of Rabener, telling of the burning of his house.

In Tooke's *Selections from Foreign Periodicals*[3] there is one piece from Rabener—*The Life of a Martyr to Truth*.

[1] *W. Taylor*, p. 4.

[2] XXVII. 71; 1762.

[3] I. 517.

Early Prose Writers

J. G. ZIMMERMANN (1728-1795).

English interest in Zimmermann was largely due to his position as doctor to the English Court at Hanover. Several of his medical and other works were translated, and a French biography by Tissot was frequently reviewed and twice translated (1797).

The medical works do not concern us here. Of the others the first appeared in 1771—*An Essay on National Pride* (London, Wilkie), reviewed in the *Monthly*[1] with many extracts and a long discussion on Zimmermann's estimate of the English character; also in the *Critical*[2] as "a very entertaining work." A later translation of the same work was made by S. H. Wilcocke in 1797.[3] Wilcocke does not mention the earlier translation; it was probably forgotten by this time.

A religious tract—*The Influence of the Knowledge of Jesus Christ*, translated by Moses Browne (1772)—was called in the *Monthly*[4] "a heavy lump of German enthusiasm" (*i.e.*, fanaticism).

Zimmermann's writings about Frederic the Great did not pass unnoticed in England, where a lively interest was taken in the great monarch. *Conversations with the King of Prussia* appeared in 1791, and *Select Views of the Life of Frederic the Great* in the following year.

But the work of Zimmermann's which obtained the greatest popularity in England was his treatise *Über die Einsamkeit* (1773). The first translation[5] was made in 1791 from a French version by Mercier, an abridgment in four chapters of the German original. It is reviewed at length and very favourably in the *European*

[1] XLV. 484; 1771. [2] XXXIII. 361; 1772.

[3] *Brit. Crit.*, XI. 164; 1798.

[4] XLVI. 401; 1772.

[5] *Solitude considered with respect to its influence on the mind and heart*, written originally in German by M. Zimmermann. Translated from the French of J. B. Mercier (Dilly, 1791).

Magazine[1] and the *Monthly*.[2] The reviewer in the first recommends Zimmermann's work as "the best preservative against suicide, which is denominated throughout the continent as 'the Englishman's malady,'" and he beseeches his countrymen "to blot out this foul national reproach." It has been suggested that the frequency of the discussion of suicide in English periodicals of this time is very likely due to the popularity of *Werther*, regarded by many as an apology for suicide. There is frequent mention of the lady who committed suicide and under whose pillow was found a copy of *Werther*. By 1798 *Solitude* had gone through six editions. In 1797 another version in seven chapters was published by the "Associated Booksellers."[3] The first four chapters are a refashioning of the former translation; the last three are taken from other parts of the original. It is accompanied by a life of the Author, notes and engravings. A note in Dilly's edition of 1798 warns the public against this "Imposition by the Associated Booksellers, a mutilated Piracy of my own." This edition of Dilly's[4] is a sequel to the former volume (1791). Mercier had only chosen the parts dealing with the salutary effects of solitude, and thus given a very one-sided view of the original. This aims at presenting a good idea of the real development of the views and sentiments of the author, and concludes with a retrospect and comparison of the arguments on each side. A review in the *Monthly*[5] does not consider that Zimmermann deserves quite as high praise as this translator

[1] XIX. 184; 1791.

[2] VII. 376; 1792. Also *Crit. Rev.*, III. 14; 1791.

[3] *Solitude considered with respect to its dangerous influence upon the mind and heart*, selected and translated from the original German of M. Zimmermann (Dilly, 1798).

[4] *Solitude or the Effects of Occasional Retirement on the Mind, the Heart, in General Society, in Exile and Death*, etc., written originally by J. G. Zimmermann.

[5] XXIX. 176; 1799.

gives him. The "Associated Booksellers" (who had published a second edition of their *Solitude* in 1798) in 1799 published another with a second volume on *Solitude or the Pernicious Influence of a Total seclusion from Society upon the Mind and Heart*—in obvious imitation of Dilly's sequel (1798). This version was much more popular than Dilly's and went through numerous editions.[1] A "new translation" in 1827 is only a reprint of it.[2] In all the reviews of *Solitude* Zimmermann is praised as not being an extravagant Misanthrope, who would advise men to live as monks and hermits, but a wise philosopher who would give men a just sense of the value of social duties and lead them to make proper use of occasional retirement.[3]

Two collections of Aphorisms by Zimmermann appeared in English. The first—*Reflections on Men and Things* (1799)—was made from the French and taken from a manuscript of Zimmermann's found among the papers of a French officer, a friend of the author's, who had died in Guernsey. Zimmermann had written these *Reflections* early in life, but never published them. The second—*Aphorisms and Reflections* (1800)—purport to be taken from a German manuscript of the Author, entrusted to an officer in the Mortimer Regiment, who after Zimmermann's death gave it to the Editor for publication. The French manuscript cannot have been a translation of the German one, for both collections are entirely different. The only explanation seems to be that Zimmermann wrote two collections of *Reflections*, one in French and one in German, both of which first appeared in an English translation.

In 1804 Alexander Campbell compiled a volume

[1] 1800, 1802, 1804, 1805, 1808, 1811, 1819, 1824, 1827.

[2] Only one new edition of Dilly's first volume (1799); the second was never reprinted.

[3] Vide *Anal. Rev.*, XI. 319; 1791.

of *Beauties of Zimmermann* (Tegg) with a biographical Memoir. It consists of extracts from his works under alphabetical headings according to subject.

The *Monthly*[1] in 1809 reviewed a booklet by a Mrs. Bayfield: *Gleanings from Zimmermann*, to which are added occasional observations and *An Ode to Retirement* (Lindsell). She reduces Zimmermann's work to the size of a "pocket companion." The reviewer hopes she will thereby "increase the diffusion of his beautiful sentiments." These little books are interesting merely as showing the popularity of Zimmermann's works in England.

J. C. LAVATER (1741-1801).

Lavater's *Physiognomische Fragmente* (1775-8), a work almost forgotten now, roused much interest in its own day, being the first monumental work on Physiognomy—a study which many people in the eighteenth century thought might be developed into a regular science. In England the *Fragmente* attracted much attention, and several translations (two from the French and one from the German) and abridgments appeared between the years 1789 and 1800. The different editions of Lavater's original work are not all procurable in England, nor are all the translations; so I have not been able to make a detailed comparison of them. But I have endeavoured to put together as clearly as possible the principal facts to be found out about them.

The *Monthly* of February, 1775, announced the publication of the original work;[2] and in 1782[3] gave a long account of it from the French translation,[4] calling it "ingenious, singular and entertaining." The *New*

[1] LIX. 219.

[2] Leipzig, 1775. This text was not used by any of the English translators.

[3] LXVI. 491 *ff*.

[4] *Essai sur la Physiognomie* . . ., par Mme. de la Fite, Caillard, et Renfer (La Haye, 1781-1803).

Review[1] also gave an account with many extracts from the same translation—apparently not yet published.[2] The first English translation was made from this French version by the Rev. Henry Hunter († 1802), a Scottish clergyman.[3] He visited Lavater himself in Zürich in August, 1902, in order to secure his assent to the publication of the English translation. The three volumes were published separately in 1789, 1792, and 1798. Lavater must have been flattered to see his works appear in English in such magnificent form. It was called " the finest printed book which has ever appeared in this or any other country."[4] The cost price of each copy is said to have been £30. The cngravings are splendidly done. It was published by private subscription, and we find the names of W. Taylor and " Monk " Lewis among the list of subscribers. The French translators' Preface is given, stating that their translation was made from a manuscript of the Author, which was not quite identical with the German printed edition. The English text is taken unaltered from the French, but it has been rendered more complete by the addition of many more plates and vignettes. The Advertisement gives a few words on the value of Physiognomy and a short account of Lavater, which was furnished to Hunter by Lavater's friend, the painter Fuseli, who lived for some time in England. Fuseli praises Hunter's translation as scrupulously faithful and exact. It reads quite well. The *Monthly*,[5] in noticing this " splendid publication,"

[1] I. 305; 1782.

[2] G. Herzfeld (*A.S.N.S.*, V. [neue Folge] 30; 1900) makes the mistake of taking this to be a projected English translation by Mme. de la Fite from the French.

[3] *Essays on Physiognomy, designed to promote the knowledge and love of mankind*, by J. C. Lavater . . . illustrated by more than 800 engravings, . . . executed by or under the inspection of Thomas Holloway. Translated from the French by Thomas Hunter, D.D., three vols. (London, 1789–1798).

[4] *Monthly Magazine*, IX.; 1800.

[5] XXXIV. 11; 1800.

remarks that Lavater's opinions have attracted considerable attention in Europe.

About the same time as Hunter's translation there appeared another done from the German by Thomas Holcroft.[1] I have not been able to find a copy of this. In the *Dictionary of National Biography* the date of it is given as 1793. This appears to be a mistake, as in the Memoir of Holcroft[2] the date given is 1789; and the work was reviewed several times in that year. From Holcroft's Preface (quoted in the *Monthly*)[3] we learn that he made his translation from the abridgment of Lavater's work by his friend Professor J. M. Armbruster,[4] in which the order of the Fragments is changed, many passages omitted and some new parts added. These alterations, however, were revised and sanctioned by the Author and met with his entire approval (*vide* his letter to Armbruster, April 7th, 1783). The *Monthly* commends the translation, saying that Holcroft's reputation stands too high to admit of any doubt as to its fidelity or elegance. This translation met with much more attention from the critics than Hunter's. It was noticed at length in all the principal reviews. The *European Magazine*[5] gives long extracts, admires the beauty of manner and force of reasoning of Lavater and praises the translation. In an earlier number[6] it had translated Lavater's own account of the history of the *Physiognomy* and his characterisation of himself and given his portrait. The *Critical*,[7] giving an outline of the work and many extracts, speaks of it as the first complete English version of Lavater's well-known work: "in it Mr. Armbruster has only lopped off the too luxuriant

[1] **Essays on Physiognomy designed to promote the knowledge and love of mankind*, from the German of Lavater, by T. Holcroft. Three vols.

[2] *Memoirs of the late Thomas Holcroft* . . . 1816. Re-published in "Traveller's Library," 1852.

[3] X. 583; 1793.

[4] Winterthur, 1783–7.

[5] XVII. 273, 343; XVIII. 40.

[6] XV. 5, 275; 1789.

[7] LXVIII. 285; LXIX. 194, 265; 1789.

branches." The *Analytical*,[1] on the contrary, gives a very severe criticism, which led to some disagreeable altercation between Holcroft and the reviewers. It disapproves altogether of the abridgment, saying that from the title the reader would expect a translation of the German work in four volumes; while in reality it is only an imperfect epitome in three. It then gives extracts with notes giving the text of the original where it differs from that given by Armbruster. It admits that the translator was faced with exceptional difficulties arising from the novel subject-matter and Lavater's self-created style, but points out examples of wrong words and perverted phrases. As far as one can judge from various extracts, serious inaccuracies are not frequent; but all Holcroft's translations bear some traces of hurried and careless work.

The next version of the *Physiognomy* bears the name of one Samuel Shaw.[2] It is not dated, but was reviewed in 1792. It is an abridgment in fifty-two chapters. From the title-page, and from the Preface which declares the aim of the work to be "to present English readers in a small compass with everything that is interesting in the work of Lavater, . . . to preserve the spirit of his reasoning and the Sublimity of his Conceptions . . . while arranging it with more order and method," one would naturally take the translation to be a new and independent one. In reality, it is merely extracts from Holcroft's translation with many errors in the transcribing and printing, and put together with little understanding of Lavater's theories. The *Analytical*[3] calls it "one of those contemptible catch-pennies, which cannot be too severely reprehended." The proprietors of Holcroft's translation were much

[1] V. 454; VI. 426; 1789.

[2] *Physiognomy, or the Corresponding Analogy between the Conformation of the Features and the Ruling Passions of the Mind.* Translated from the original work of J. C. Lavater by Samuel Shaw. London, Symonds (17—).

[3] XIII. 427; 1792.

incensed at "these literary pirates, who with the utmost effrontery and without any acknowledgment have appropriated to themselves with a pair of scissors a great part of our work and disgraced it by their mutilated and inaccurate copy." The proprietors avenged themselves by publishing—with a preface from which we have just quoted—a carefully revised and edited abridgment of their own,[1] with three chapters added. The *Critical*[2] concludes an account of this reprint by saying that it is certainly the business of literary journals to expose and detect such frauds on the public as Shaw's "translation." But this fraud had a long life, for a new edition of it was published as late as 1827[3] (though with some mistakes corrected) when the more authentic versions of the *Physiognomy* were probably forgotten.

The third translation[4] of the *Physiognomy* is one to which I found no allusion in any reviews, nor is there a copy in any of the big libraries. Nor is it given by Goedeke. I came across a copy of it quite by chance on a bookstall in Cambridge, and it is now in the Beit Library there. It is a fine edition in four volumes with numerous engravings. The translation (1797) is again done from the French, and by another clergyman, the Rev. C. Moore. There is a good deal of likeness between his work and Hunter's, though the arrangement of chapters and volumes is not the same. But particular passages are almost identical, and make one

[1] *Essays on Physiognomy*, abridged from Mr. Holcroft's translation (London, Robinson).

[2] VI. 105; 1792.

[3] New and improved edition with engravings, printed for T. Tegg (London, 1827).

[4] *Essays on Physiognomy, calculated to extend the knowledge and love of Mankind.* Written by J. C. Lavater . . . translated from the last Paris edition by the Rev. C. Moore, Ll.D, illustrated by several hundred engravings (London, 1797). I do not know what this "last Paris edition" can be unless he refers to Mme. de la Fite's as such. This was the only French translation before this date, and no edition was published at Paris till 1806–9.

wonder whether the two translators can have worked quite independently.

In a London periodical entitled *The Conjuror's Magazine or Physiognomical Mirror* (1791-3) continued as *The Astrologer's Magazine and Philosophical Miscellany* (1793-4), the title-page says there is included "a superb edition of Lavater's *Physiognomy* in monthly portions." But in the numbers of this Magazine bound together in the British Museum Lavater's *Physiognomy* is nowhere to be found, except in the table of contents. Perhaps it was published on separate sheets, which are now lost. It seems unlikely that this was a new translation. It was probably extracts put together either from Hunter's or Holcroft's translation. But it is interesting as showing the popularisation of the work. A note at the beginning says that, whereas no edition of Lavater's *Physiognomy* is sold for less than five guineas, subscribers will here have the whole work presented to them nearly gratis in the course of two years. The *Lady's Magazine* (XX.; 1789) also printed long extracts from the *Physiognomy* (Hunter's).

Another example of the popularisation of the *Physiognomy* is a work with a curious title: *Lavater's Looking-Glass.*[1] It consists of thirty-four Essays on physiognomical subjects. It is partly a compilation from Lavater's work and partly a translation from a French *Essay on Living Creatures*, by a Dr. Sue. Hence the names on the title-page. Sue's is a more systematic study than Lavater's, but less characteristic and original. There are no illustrations.[2]

In 1802 there was published a book of engravings illustrating Lavater's work.[3] Under each drawing is

[1] *Lavater's Looking-Glass, or Essays on the Face of Animated Nature, from Man to Plants*, by Lavater, Sue and Co. (London, 1800).

[2] Reviewed in *Monthly*, XXV. 214; 1801.

[3] *Physiognomical Sketches by Lavater*, engravings from original drawings by John Luffman (Westley, 1802).

a short observation from Lavater and as introduction there is a short sketch of his life.

We find a good many articles on Physiognomy in periodicals about this time[1]—all probably due to the interest aroused in the subject by Lavater.

The *Physiognomy* can scarcely rank as a piece of literature, and the other works of Lavater which were translated into English have also but small literary importance. A collection of his *Aphorisms*[2] taken from *Vermischte unphysiognomische Regeln für Selbst- und Menschenkenntnis*, published anonymously in 1787, appeared in 1788, translated, it is said, by Fuseli. It went to several editions and was reviewed on the whole favourably in the *Analytical*[3] and the *Monthly*.[4]

Lavater's *Geheimes Tagebuch von einem Beobachter von sich selbst* was translated in 1795[5] by the Rev. Peter Will,[6] and originally intended to be circulated in manuscript only. The translator was induced to publish it "by the consideration of its great utility in propagating piety and religious prudence." Strictly speaking, it is not a piece of "literature" at all; but it is interesting to note that such a work was translated and found favour. Works of moral and didactic tendency were very popular among a certain section of the public about the end of the eighteenth century, and many of them were taken from German originals. The *Secret Journal* was noticed by most of the leading reviews;

[1] E.g., *The History of Physiognomy*, by T. Cowper. *Europ. Mag.*, XIX.; 1791.

[2] *Aphorisms on Man*, translated from the original MS. of Rev. J. C. Lavater (2nd ed., 1789; 3rd ed., Dublin, 1790; 5th ed., 1793). First vol. A second vol., published in 1788, was not translated. Several editions appeared in America, 1790–93.

[3] II. 286; 1788.

[4] LXXX. 536; 1789.

[5] Date given in *Brit. Mus. Catal.*; there is no date on title-page.

[6] *Secret Journal of a Self-Observer or Confessions and Familiar Letters* of the Rev. J. C. Lavater, author of *Essays on Physiognomy*, *Aphorisms on Man*, *Views of Eternity*, etc., by Rev. Peter Will (London, Cadell and Davies).

by the *British Critic*[1] and *Analytical*[2] very favourably, by the *Monthly*[3] rather less so. The *Critical*[4] doubted the usefulness of publications of this kind at all. A translator's note[5] refers to Lavater's *Views of Eternity* as a work of great value, and says that he has himself attempted an English version, which he hopes to publish, if it receives the sanction of some learned friends. Apparently it did not receive it, for no translation appeared. Mr. Will, however, did not let his interest in Lavater end here. In 1805 he published a translation of a short religious tract by Lavater, *On the Nature, Excellence and Necessity of Faith*, and in the Preface to this he announces his intention of publishing some more tracts from Lavater's works, and then a larger volume containing Gessner's Account of Lavater's Life, which account he is at the moment engaged in translating. There is no evidence of the publication of these.

One other religious tract by Lavater was translated anonymously in 1805—*Letters of St. Paul the Apostle written before and after his conversion*—but was not well received by the critics, who thought the attempt of such a fiction "very presumptuous."

Lavater's political Pamphlet, *Remonstrance addressed to the Executive of the French Republic against the Invasion of Switzerland*, was translated and printed over and over again in 1798 and 1799. We find frequent mentions of Lavater in periodicals and books of travel, etc., between the years 1790 and 1800.[6] In the *Monthly Magazine* of April, 1801, there is a notice of his death, followed by an account of his life and character, the latter taken from that drawn by Professor Meiners in his *Letters on Switzerland*. But this

[1] VII. 421; 1796. [2] XXII. 274; 1795.
[3] XIX. 581; 1796. [4] XV. 149; 1796. [5] Vol. II. 5.
[6] *A Tour in Switzerland*, by Miss H. M. Williams (1798) gives a long account of him.

already speaks of a decline in Lavater's reputation in England, saying that the " well-executed translations " of his *Physiognomy* by Hunter and Holcroft were much applauded at the time of their first publication, but are now treated in England with a disregard that does injustice to their actual merits.

An Imitation of Lavater.—In 1800 Miss Plumptre translated a work on Physiognomy by J. Musaeus—*Physiognomische Reisen, voran ein Physiognomisch Tagebuch.* It is really a skit on Lavater's work, representing a man acting in practical matters of daily life on judgments of character from Physiognomy, and thereby involving himself in all kinds of difficulties and disasters. It is a work of entertainment rather than instruction. The translation[1]—a rather free abridgment of the original—probably amused many English readers. But it did not receive much praise from the reviewers. The *Monthly* finds the satire over-strained and the whole work too long and diffuse.

A. VON HALLER (1708-1777).[2]

Haller became early known in England as a physician and physiologist. His scientific works were much praised in the medical journals of the day, and many of them were translated. A French life of Haller by Tissot was frequently noticed in the leading English reviews, and an English *Memoir* compiled chiefly from French sources by a well-known English doctor, Thomas Henry, appeared in 1783, only six years after Haller's death; it was probably the first English life of a contemporary German writer.

[1] *Physiognomical Travels, preceded by a Physiognomical Journal*, from the German of J. Musaeus, by Anne Plumptre. To which is prefixed a short sketch of the life and character of the author by his pupil, Kotzebue (London, 1800).

[2] G. Herzfeld, *A.S.N.S.*, gives the date incorrectly as 1776.

Haller did not become known in England as a poet until 1794,[1] but a couple of his prose works had been translated many years before. With these alone we are concerned here.

The first, *Usong, an Eastern Narrative*, owed its translation, in 1772, only one year after the original had appeared in Germany (according to the *Gentleman's Magazine*),[2] to Queen Charlotte of Mecklenburg. The anonymous translator was probably connected with court. The book is beautifully bound, with a monogram of George III. on the cover. This accurate translation, one of the best of the time, well reproduces the simple and direct style of Haller. Nevertheless it was hardly a work likely to become popular in England; it is dull, and it is an apologia of royal absolutism. The *Critical*[3] found it "a happy imitation of *Télémaque*." But the *Monthly*[4] called it "the laboured effort of a cold and slow imagination." A reader wrote[5] protesting vigorously against this judgment, saying he was ravished with *Usong* in the translation and warmed again in reading the original. But the reviewer held to his opinion.

In 1780 was translated a religious work of Haller's —*Letters of Haller to his daughter on the truths of the Christian Religion*; fourteen letters which the translator considers "the completest defence of Christianity, in our judgment, which has yet been offered to the world." The letters must have been fairly popular, for new editions were published in 1803 and 1807. The *Gentleman's Magazine*[6] gave them very high praise;

[1] *The Poems of Baron Haller*, translated into English by Mrs. Howorth (London, 1794). *The Alps*, translated by Henry Barrett (1796). W. Taylor's *Hist. Surv.*, I.

[2] XLIII. 189; 1773.

[3] XXXV. 195; 1773.

[4] XLVIII. 160; 1773, and LXIII. 515; 1780.

[5] XLVIII. 248.

[6] LI. 281; 1781.

the *Critical*[1] also, but thought Haller was unnecessarily diffuse. The *Monthly*[2] was much colder. The translation is fair, but heavy in style.

MOSES MENDELSSOHN (1729-1786).

Mendelssohn's *Phædon* (1767) was a work much noted in its own day. Three German editions appeared in two years; and it was soon translated into other languages, among them into English in 1789 by Charles Cullen, Barrister at the Middle Temple.[3]

In *Phædon* Mendelssohn aimed at adapting the ideas of Socrates to the eighteenth century. And in this an English reviewer in the *Critical*[4] considers he has been successful. Cullen prefixed to his translation an account of the life and death of Socrates. His translation is faithful, but his translation not always good.

No other works of Mendelssohn's were translated before 1830. But his name was not forgotten, and in 1825 M. Samuels published an original Memoir,[5] with a translation of the famous correspondence between him and Lavater, on the occasion of Lavater's dedication to Mendelssohn of *Bonnet's Enquiry into the Evidences of Christianity*. (This Dedication and the ensuing letters had already appeared in English, though Samuels was evidently ignorant of the fact. H. Crabb Robinson had sent a translation of them to the *Monthly Magazine* as early as 1801.)[6] Samuels' *Memoir* gives an interesting account of the Jewish philosopher's

[1] L. 151; 1780. [2] LXIII. 515; 1780.

[3] *Phædon, or the Death of Socrates*, by Moses Mendelssohn, a Jew, late of Berlin. Translated from the German (London, printed for the author, 1789).

[4] LXVIII. 472; 1789.

[5] *Memoirs of Moses Mendelssohn, the Jewish Philosopher, including the Celebrated Correspondence on the Christian Religion with J. C. Lavater, Minister of Zurich*, by M. Samuels (London, 1825).

[6] XI. 390; 1801.

life and character; also a list of his works (Hebrew and German), and short biographies of T. Abbt, Nicolai, Lessing and Lavater. The *Memoir* is said to have been reviewed and recommended by fourteen of the principal literary journals[1] and presumably found readers. Samuels translated Mendelssohn's *Jerusalem* in 1838.

A. VON KNIGGE (1752-1796).

Baron Knigge was known in England not only by his two novels, mentioned elsewhere, but also by a little didactic work which became rather popular. The English translation—*Practical Philosophy of Social Life or the Art of conversing with Men*[2] (1799) is really a compilation of ideas and observations taken from Knigge's *Über den Umgang mit Menschen*, with additional remarks gathered from the works of Bahrdt, Zollikofer, Reinhard, Zimmermann and Fessler, together with a few remarks of the translator's. This was the Rev. Peter Will, a German, many years resident in England as minister of the German church, whose name is frequently met with as author of translations, mostly of a like didactic kind.[3] The Preface gives an account of the life and works of Knigge. The *Monthly*[4] recommends the book as "useful and suitably adapted to English taste."

[1] *Lit. Gaz.*, 1826, p. 160; *Month. Mag.*, LIX. 351; 1825; *Europ. Mag.*, LXXXVII. 122, etc.

[2] *Practical Philosophy of Social Life, or the Art of Conversing with Men*, after the German of Baron Knigge, by P. Will, Minister of the Reformed German Congregation in the Savoy (London, 1799).

[3] Lavater's *Secret Journal*; and many translations in the *German Museum* (1801).

[4] XXXII. 31; 1800.

B.—Some Early Translated Poems

SCHÖNAICH'S ARMINIUS.

This anonymous prose translation[1] of C. O. von Schönaich's *Hermann oder das befreyte Deutschland; ein Heldengedicht* dates from 1764. The most interesting thing about the work is the Preface by Gottsched, apparently the only bit of Gottsched's critical writings translated into English. In it he compares *Hermann* to the *Iliad*, the *Æneid* and to the *Henriade* of Voltaire. The *Monthly*,[2] in a review of *Arminius*, takes great exception to these extravagant comparisons and specially to some remarks of Gottsched's as to *Paradise Lost*, but says the Baron has based on the old story, "a well-conducted, pathetic and interesting fable." The translation is judged to be "execrable." The *Critical*[3] finds the poem "on the whole a tame performance, well-suited to the tastes of such critics as Gottsched and Voltaire."

The translation shows at least great industry, for the poem is a long one in twelve Books. But as English it could not be much worse, being often incomprehensible. It is obviously the work of a foreigner.

BODMER'S NOAH.

Bodmer's most celebrated poem was translated into English in 1767 by Joseph Collyer.[4] There had been several German editions of the book[5] before this, and Collyer does not say which he used. It seems to have

[1] *Arminius, or Germany Freed*, translated from the third edition of the German original, written by Baron Cronzech, with an historical and critical Preface by Professor Gottsched of Leipzig (London, 1764).

[2] XXII. 15; 1765.

[3] XVIII. 353; 1764.

[4] *Noah, attempted from the German of Mr. Bodmer in Twelve Books*. Printed for J. Collyer (London, 1767).

[5] See Goedeke, IV., ii., p. 8.

been that of 1752, or possibly the slightly different one of 1757.[1] Collyer takes a good many liberties with his text. These he excuses in his preface saying he has aimed at "correcting some trifling blemishes in a work filled with beauties." But he has "always endeavoured to do justice to the sweet and tender, the bold and animated strokes of his author." He lays great stress on the moral tendencies of the work, and hopes that his translation of it may afford "a source of pure and sublime entertainment to the English reader." It is curious to find W. Taylor[2] calling this "a good prose translation." It is in the affected, bombastic style so common at that time, with grandiloquent phrases and long, pedantic words. One critic[3] characterises it rather well: "The nauseous affectation of expressing everything pompously and poetically is nowhere more visible than in this performance. . . . We wish Mr. Collyer would endeavour to avoid this tawdry style if he ever attempts another work of this kind." Mr. Collyer does not aim at accuracy, often adding quite unnecessary epithets of his own invention, and omitting or changing whole sentences of the original. Here is one example of his style at its worst: "How sweet the rapture which drew thy soul into thine eye, where it beamed collected and there with rapture gazed insatiate"! But it is not all as bad as this. A short passage from the beginning of Book X. gives an idea of the translation at its best and of the style of a now almost forgotten work:

"Beasts, birds and insects, destroyed by one blow stopped not the greedy jaws of Death, who hasted to the deep to gratify his insatiate appetite on the finny race, and multitudes who lived in the water

---

[1] I could not verify this as the 1757 edition is not in the English libraries.

[2] *Hist. Surv.*, I. 186, where he attributes the translation to Mrs. Collyer, but everywhere else it is attributed to her husband. The title-page bears neither name.

[3] *Critical*, XXIII. 280; 1767.

dy'd in the foaming waves. Some perish'd in the slime, entangled as in nets, hence their teeth, their bones, their skeletons are found in flaky state or bury'd in lands far distant from the shore. Others escaped not the concussions that tore up the bottom of the watery deep; or were dashed to pieces in the eddies of circumvolving whirlpools."[1]

Noah did not attract much attention in the critical journals. The only serious notice is that quoted above from the *Critical*, which thinks that sacred history and romance, Scripture and fiction make a very unnatural mixture. The *London Magazine* gives an extract without comment.[2] The *Monthly*[3] exclaims: "Had the author of these volumes been with Noah in the Ark, the good old antediluvian would have certainly tossed him overboard and left him to shift for himself on the mountains of Ararat"!

Yet *Noah* found some readers, for another edition was printed in 1767 (in Dublin) and another in 1770. *Noah* appealed to Southey because of the subject; but he read it in the original. He wrote to W. Taylor on May 30th, 1799, thanking him for the present of the *Noachide*, which he is going to plod through with dictionary and grammar. He adds: "It is nine years since a schoolfellow's account made me desirous of reading it, and luckily the translation has never fallen in my way." He appears himself to have considered the idea of a poem on the same subject, but never carried out the project.

[1] "Thier und Vögel und Menschen mit einem Schlag zu verkümpfen
Stopfete nicht den Rachen des Todes; er stieg in die Tiefen
Auch an dem Wasserwieh den ewigen Hunger zu speisen,
Mengen verdarben im Wasser, das doch ihr' eigene Luft ist.
In dem Schlaume verstrichten sie sich wie in Rensen und Netzen.
Und wir finden oft ihren Geripp und Knochen und Zähne
Zwischen den Schliefern, die aus dem schlaumichten Wasser entstanden.
Andere die diesem Tode entgiengen, entflohn nicht den Stössen
Die vom Bersten der irdischen Rund in Wasser entstunden
Oder vom reissenden Strudeln erwürgt, die unter sich kreuzten."

[2] XXXVI. 193.

[3] XXXVI. 235; 1767.

W. Taylor[1] translated twelve lines of the close of the eighth Book into the hexameter metre of the original, *e.g.*:

"Now on the shoreless sea, intermixt with the corses of sinners,
Floated the bodies of saints, by the side of the beasts of the forest."

In the same place he gives a short analysis of Bodmer's unfinished Epopea of the *Voyage of Columbus*, suggesting that it might be translated in abridged form. Apparently no one carried out his suggestion.

In 1794 the *Critical*[2] gave a long account of Bodmer's life, works and character, taken from a Swiss book, but added no extracts from his writings.

SOLOMON GESSNER (1730-1788).

Gessner's *Death of Abel* was first translated in prose by Mrs. Collyer in 1761. Five other translations appeared between that and 1811, three in prose and two in blank verse. But the first version was the best known and went through innumerable editions. *The Death of Abel* was to be found upon all bookstalls and became specially popular in country districts. It rivalled *Robinson Crusoe* and the *Pilgrim's Progress* in popularity, and took its place among the "sacred classics" of the people. It also led to numerous imitations beginning with *The Death of Cain*, by a Lady, 1789. A short extract from this will give some idea of the style:

"For each successive tear with its saline clearness stole from the beauteous orb which was its productive fount, as a gem of the most curious workmanship, and quickly increased their distilling powers so as to cause the dropping flow to be a spontaneous flood of pearly liquid which overflowed the most charming visage nature e'er beheld."

Scott speaks of reading *The Death of Abel* with the *Bible* and the *Pilgrim's Progress*. Byron read it at the age of eight. Coleridge early took an interest in it

[1] *Hist. Surv.*, I. 187.

[2] XI. 492 *ff*.

and imitated it in his fragmentary *Wanderings of Cain* (1798).

A collection of *Works* translated from Gessner appeared in 1802 and again in 1805. The *Idylls* were also very popular, and translations from them appeared in nearly every literary magazine of the day.

But the subject of Gessner in England has been already dealt with by Miss Berta Reed in *The Influence of Solomon Gessner on English Literature* (Philadelphia, 1905). She may "attribute influence with a recklessness unusual even in this branch of research" (Stokoe, p. 131); but her facts are accurate and her discussion of the translations usually adequate. So we merely refer the reader to her work; and to Mr. Stokoe's *German Influence in the English Romantic Period* for many interesting evidences of the interest taken in Gessner by English writers.

F. W. ZACHARIÆ (1726-1777).

Zachariæ's most famous work, *Der Renommist*, though written in imitation of Pope, found no English translator. A less well-known poem, *Murner in der Hölle : ein scherzhaftes Heldengedicht in fünf Gesängen*, was translated in 1781 by R. E. Raspe,[1] with the title *Tabby in Elysium*.[2] Raspe announced his intention of publishing other works of the same author. This translation is in prose; it is too slavish an imitation of the original to be idiomatic English and it bears many traces of being the work of a foreigner. The *Monthly*,[3]

[1] *Rudolf Erich Raspe* (1737–1794). Born at Hanover; studied at Göttingen and Leipzig; 1774 secretary of the University Library at Cassel; 1775 was pursued for abstracting valuable coins committed to his care and fled to England and later Ireland; had already translated Ossian into German; wrote *Baron Münchhausen* (1785); translated *Nathan* in 1781 and several German books of travel; died at Muckross, Co. Donegal, 1794.

[2] *Tabby in Elysium*. A mock poem from the German of F. W. Zachariæ, by R. E. Raspe (London, 1781).

[3] LXV. 236; 1781.

none the less, praises the translator as having acquired a more idiomatic knowledge of English than foreigners usually arrive at, but does not think the work will have much success in England, where readers are more critical of works of this kind than in Germany, " where humour is still in its infancy."

No other reviews noticed the work.

CHAPTER II

F. G. KLOPSTOCK (1724-1803)

Messiah.—It might be expected that Klopstock's *Messiah*, so closely related in subject to Milton's epic, would have made an impression in England. But it did not; one reason probably being that for years it was known only in one bad prose translation.[1] Again, the choice of subject shocked some religious people, and many who were quite indifferent to the defects of the translation (they had gone into raptures over the *Death of Abel* by the same translator) disapproved of a poem which they considered a profanation of sacred history. It was, however, fairly widely read and Klopstock[2] was known in England chiefly as the author of the *Messiah*.

The later and better metrical translations of the *Messiah* did not become very generally known. Some appeared only as fragments in periodicals, while several complete versions were not published till a time (about 1820) when the *Messiah* was already out of date. Allusion will be found to several translations carried out but never printed and not now to be found. This is specially unfortunate in the case of two, carried out under Klopstock's auspices. One of them (H. E. Lloyd's) is said to have been preferred by him to all others he had seen. They would be interesting at least from this connection with the author.

[1] It is worth noting that no *good* prose translation of the *Messiah* has ever been made.

[2] *E.g.*, three translators of Goethe's *Werther* translate the allusion to Klopstock's *Frühlingsfeier* as " die herrliche Ode " by " the divine ode."

Klopstock

The first, and for many years only, English translation of the *Messiah* is by Mr. and Mrs. Collyer. Mrs. Mary Collyer had translated Gessner's *Death of Abel* in 1761, and, according to her husband, the extraordinary success of this work rendered many people desirous to see the *Messiah* attempted in the same manner and by the same hand. So Mrs. Collyer began her translation. She died, however, soon after (1763), and the translation was continued and published by her husband.[1] The name of David Garrick appears among the list of subscribers. The first two volumes (containing the Introduction on Divine Poetry and the first ten Books) appeared in 1763[2] with a dedication to the young George III.; the third volume with six more Books in 1771. Before 1784 this *Messiah* had gone through four editions and was out of print. A writer in the *New Review*[3] (1784) says he could not procure a copy and that many of his friends of taste did not even know of the work. A new edition was published in 1799.[4] In 1811 these sixteen Books were re-published with three more translated in the same style by a Mrs. Meeke.[5] The twentieth canto was not considered by the editor to be necessary to the poem, so this translation[6] was never really completed. Collyer's Preface is not of great interest. He

[1] *John Collyer*, the elder; son of a bookseller; compiler and translator. Besides the *Messiah* he translated Bodmer's *Noah* (1767), and the *History of Lady Sophia Sternheim* (1776). Died 1776.

[2] *The Messiah*, attempted from the German of Mr. Klopstock, to which is prefixed his introduction on Divine Poetry (London, Dodsley, 1763).

[3] VI. 321.

[4] *Month. Mag.*, XI.

[5] *The Messiah*, from the German of Klopstock. The first sixteen Books by Mrs. Collyer, and the last three by Mrs. Meeke. To which is prefixed an introduction on Divine Poetry (London, 1811).

[6] *Mary Meeke*, probably the wife of Rev. Francis Meeke, Christ's College, Cambridge. She wrote poems and many novels, popular at the time, and made many translations from the French. This is the only one from the German. Died 1816. There were several later editions, 1819, 1821, etc.

makes the usual comparisons between Milton and Klopstock, " who has completed what that favourite son of the British Muse had left unfinished." But he considers the *Messiah* to be far superior to *Paradise Regained* both in plan and in beauty of execution. He hopes that his translation will arouse in the breasts of his readers the same "sublime sensations" he himself felt during the prosecution of the work. Unfortunately, whatever may have been his feelings, his translation has attained the unenviable distinction of being, in the opinion of many competent critics, the worst translation of the *Messiah* in any language. A testimony to its contemporary reputation in Germany is given by W. Taylor in an Italian letter from Detmold, December 26th, 1782: " Molti quì si lagnano orribilmente de questa traduzione, poichè come si dice, non spiega le sublime bellezze dell' originale."[1] It certainly deserves most, if not all of the hard criticism given to it.[2] It has not the first essential of a prose translation — faithfulness to the original. Collyer constantly seeks to improve on Klopstock by adding ideas of his own and all his changes weaken and cheapen the effect. His language is stilted and affected and totally lacking in simplicity and dignity. Many of his expressions are quite meaningless. He has sometimes, however, been unjustly accused of mistranslations, through a comparison of his version with later German editions.[3] But the divergences

[1] *Memoir*, I. 24.

[2] J. M. Good in *Month. Mag.*, XI. (1800), thinks it probable that neither of the Collyers were acquainted with German, and only acquired their knowledge of the works from a bombastic and inflated French version. But this is impossible. The only French translation before this date was one of the first three Cantos only by Tscharner, 1750. The first complete French translation was *Le Messie*, Paris, 1769–75 (Goedeke, IV. ii., p. 88).

[3] For instance, Shumway accuses him of translating " der Allbarmherzige " (I. 8), wrongly by " the Omnipresent." But it was " Gott Allgegenwärtig " in the earlier editions of 1751 and 1755, and it must not be forgotten that Collyer must have used one of these.

among the various editions are only slight; and it is easy to see where Collyer has "improved" on his original. We have a good example already in the opening lines, "Inspired by thine immortality, rise, O my soul, and sing the honours of thy great Redeemer: honours obtained in hard adversity's rough school—obtained by suffering for the sins of others himself sinless," for:

> "Sing, unsterbliche Seele, der sündigen Menschen Erlösung,
> Die der Messias auf Erden in seiner Menschheit vollendet."

Two other short examples: (1) "Thither he now went to offer up his supplications to the Eternal Father and once more to declare his full, his free resolution to sanctify the favoured sons of men," for "Nach dem Gebirg begab er sich jetzt." (2) "The sincere are rewarded; their involuntary errors receive forgiveness," for "Einige werden belohnt; die andern werden vergeben." These will suffice to give some idea of Collyer's method of work and to show that he has not been always unjustly accused of mistranslation. All through he amplifies the original in the same way.

The contemporary criticism of the *Messiah* in the English periodicals was on the whole unfavourable. The *Monthly*,[1] though it had given high praise to the original *Messiah* in a former article, now objects to this "medley of prose and verse, where the poet shows himself the greatest enemy of religion by incorporating with it the fables of his own imagination." In a notice[2] of the third volume it again expresses disapproval of compositions like this, the *Noah* and the *Abel*, as "doing honour neither to the Christian religion, nor to the judgment of those who admire them." But it says the *Messiah* has met with great success in England, and calls Collyer "a worthy and ingenious translator"! The *Critical*[3] (taking *Abel* also to be

[1] XXX. 69; 1764. [2] XLVI. 467; 1772.
[3] XVI. 417; 1763.

by Klopstock) considers that he has here attempted a work of very different character, and has failed most miserably. "When Klopstock steps out of the limits of mortality we find nothing in him but the enthusiastic (fanatical) raptures of an idle visionary, carrying us out of this terrestrial into an ideal world, and talking a language which we do not understand." But it also approves of Collyer's translation, which it refers to as "just and elegant." In a notice of the third volume the *Critical*[1] again regrets the introduction into English of such works, only calculated to pervert public taste. It condemns "the improbable fictions, affected sentiments and turgid style, and the entire lack of that noble and majestic simplicity which characterises all the true classic writers." It never seems to occur to this critic how far his remarks, based only on a translation, may or may not apply to the original. But it is obvious that many of these critics were men of not much literary judgment.

In one curious pamphlet: *Thoughts upon some late pieces, particularly the Death of Abel and the Messiah* (London, 1766)[2] we find, on the contrary, exaggerated laudation. Speaking particularly from a religious point of view, the writer recommends these two pieces, not only as the best reading after the Bible and the Book of Common Prayer, but almost as an infallible means of salvation. The passage is worth quoting as throwing some light on the popularity of works of this kind. (Yet it is scarcely probable that any young person ever carried out these precepts to the letter!)

"Whoever is acquainted with these pieces early in life and acquaints herself with them thoroughly, and reads them over at least once a year; and is never tired of them, but still resumes them, and still reads them, till she is perfect mistress of each of these pieces, and has a full comprehension of them; so that she can readily call to mind, or lead into discourse any material circumstance in them. Such a young person

---

[1] XXXIII. 393; 1771.

[2] Ascribed to a John Whitfield (Goedeke, IV. ii., p. 90).

will be timely instructed in true piety and virtue; will scarce ever be at a loss for any point of conduct, great or small ; will have a competent store of real knowledge ; and will find herself gradually enabled to write and to discourse, to live and to die like a Christian."

The *Messiah* in particular the writer cannot praise too highly. He takes both pieces to be really English originals, though given to two German masters with hard names ! "It is probable," he says, "that the names are only mentioned as a trial of the taste of the times, and for a stroke of raillery on that nation, which was never eminent for epic poetry." The *Critical*[1] calls this little pamphlet "A puff to recommend the heavy dung-carts of German poetry which are daily perfuming the metropolis." And the *Monthly*[2] comments on it satirically as "the work of a profound and curious critic."

Collyer's version of their greatest epic poem did not pass unnoticed in Germany. It was censured in no unsparing terms. A critic in the *Bibliothek der schönen Wissenschaften und der freyen Künste* (1764)[3] writes:

> "So sehr wir uns erfreuen wenn unsere guten Dichter zur Ehre unsers Vaterlands in auswärtige Sprachen übersetzt werden, so unangenehm ist es uns, wenn sich poetische Pfuscher einfallen lassen, uns bei den Ausländern entweder durch elende oder ungetreue Übersetzungen von unsern Originalwerken zu Schande zu machen. Dies ist der Fall bei der Übersetzung des Herrn Collyer. Sie weichet so sehr von der Urschrift ab, dass man hin und wieder ganz fremde Gedanken, Ausdrücke und Einkleidungen findet. Wir wünschten dass ein anderer guter Übersetzer uns bei einer Nation rechtfertigte, die in ihren Urteilen gegen die Ausländer so streng ist."

An article in the *Briefe der neuesten Literatur betreffend*[4] discusses Colyer's translation at great length. The writer especially objects to Collyer's free treatment of his original, his emendations and additions, and the vanity which made him think that by these changes he could enrich and beautify such an original. He

[1] XXI. 315 ; 1766.
[2] XXXIV. 399 ; 1766.
[3] XI. 196.
[4] *Briefe*, 267, 268. Said to be by Resewitz, not Lessing.

adds: " Muss man sich nicht ärgern, dass ein solches Gedicht als der *Messias* ist, zu Auswärtigen und noch dazu Englandern in solchem Aufzuge vorgestellt wird ?"

Klopstock himself deeply regretted that his *Messiah* had been presented to the English in such an unsatisfactory form. He expressed his opinion on the subject to Coleridge, who tells us of the incident in his account of the visit he and Wordsworth paid to Klopstock during their stay in Germany, 1798:

" He spoke with great indignation of the English prose translation of his *Messiah*. All the translations had been bad, very bad—but the English was no translation—there were pages and pages not in the original and half the original was not to be found in the translation. W. told him that I intended to translate a few of his odes as specimens of German lyrics—he then said to me in English, ' I wish you would render into English some select passages of the *Messiah* and *revenge* me of your countrymen.' It was the liveliest thing he produced in the whole conversation."[1]

In Wordsworth's journal, October 2nd, 1798, he tells of showing to Klopstock another translation of the *Messiah*:[2]

" Klopstock wished to see the *Calvary* of Cumberland,[3] and asked what was thought of it in England. Went to Remnant's (the English bookseller) where I procured the *Analytical Review*, in which is contained the review of C's *Calvary*. I remembered to have read there some specimens of a blank verse translation of the *Messiah*. I have mentioned this to Klopstock, and he has a great desire to have a sight of them. I walked over to his house and put the book in his hands."

The above-mentioned number of the *Analytical Review* is Volume XIII., ii. (1792). The critic is led to speak of the *Messiah* by the likeness in subject to the work under review. Klopstock, he says, is the only

[1] *Biographia Literaria—Satyrane's Letters*, III.

[2] See W. Knight's *Life of Wordsworth*, I. 171 (1889). Also given by Coleridge in same letter as above.

[3] *Calvary, or the Death of Christ*, by R. Cumberland, 1792. In spite of identity of subject it does not appear that the author imitated, nor even knew, the *Messiah*.

name which may be mentioned near Milton; but he is known in England only through "an execrable prose translation." He proceeds to give a translation of his own in blank verse of Book II. (427-735) and Book IV. (110-171). These few lines are noteworthy as being the earliest attempt at a metrical translation of the *Messiah*. The translation too, though in parts somewhat laboured, is on the whole fair and often happy in expressions, *e.g.*, "and anger winged his flying words" for "mit zorngeflügelter Stimme." He is clever in giving the sense of the hexameter, line for linc, in the shorter English pentameters, as in the following passage:

"And thus with thunder armed
Went forth his voice: 'If yon tremendous host
Be still the same, who on ethereal plains
That treble day of horror stood, then hear
Triumphant what of my exploits on earth
I shall relate; nor that alone, but hear
The great design against Jehovah's self.'"
(II. 248-433.)

Before going on to the nineteenth century we must return a moment to mention two earlier fragments of prose translations.

In the same year as Collyer's *Messiah*, a correspondent "A. B." sent a prose translation of part of the seventh Book[1] to the *Gentleman's Magazine*.[2] He worked on the same plan as Collyer—"improving" on the original, *e.g.*, "Jesus replied only by a look of divine serenity, or grandeur without pride, and meekness without fear" for—

"Der Gottmensch sah, mit einem Blicke
Seiner Hoheit ihn an."

A notice in the *New Review*,[3] 1784, has been already mentioned. It is a review of an Italian translation

[1] LI. 301-591. [2] XXXIII. 570-5; 1763.
[3] VI. 321.

of the *Messiah* by Giacomo Zigno, giving an analysis of each Canto with extracts in Italian, with an appended literal English translation. It is an accurate and faithful, if not always idiomatic, rendering of the Italian—a translation evidently much superior to Collyer's. Among the many German works which came to England through French, it is interesting to note this fragment coming through Italian.[1]

The *Messiah* figures several times in the *Monthly Magazine* for 1800. A letter in the August number[2] from a John Mason Good shows a fair knowledge of German literature and some sound criticism. He regrets that the English public, while being burdened with works of questionable merit and ephemeral duration, are not supplied with any "sufferable translations," except Sotheby's *Oberon*. He gives faint praise to the translations of *Iphigenia* and Gessner's *Idylls*; but Goethe, he says, has much reason to be dissatisfied with the translations of his *Werther*, and Gessner and Klopstock still more so at the injustice they have suffered from "the crude and inadequate attempts of the late Mrs. Collyer." After criticising Mrs. Collyer's *Messiah* at some length, he concludes: "Thus this admirable poem, by far the first in the German language, and probably superior to every modern epic, except *Paradise Lost*, is merely rendered into English in one individual and wretched prose version alone, and that not even complete." He then alludes to a projected translation in hexameters by a Sir Herbert Croft, announced three years before as being done under the eye of the author himself, with whom Croft was intimately acquainted. But Good presumes the design has been dropped. He does not

[1] This same critic refers to a projected English translation of the *Messiah* in blank verse by a Mr. Eton, an Englishman, consul at Constantinople, for the Court of St. Petersburg, as soon to be published. I have not found any further mention of it.

[2] X. 1.

himself approve of the hexameter metre, and gives a few passages translated in heroic couplets.

In the November number (and continued in December and January, 1801) appeared another Letter on the *Messiah*. The correspondent is W. Taylor. He also refers to Croft's projected translation, and to his having been enabled to consult the author on some obscurer passages;[1] but he speaks of it as a "prose translation, line for line." Taylor takes a directly opposite view to Good and considers the heroic couplet "fatal to the majestic simplicity of style and tending to become flat and featureless." He pleads for the use of the hexameter as no less possible in other Gothic dialects than in German, and as better adapted to transfer with faithfulness the manner of Klopstock. Why, he asks, should not a translator convert the English nation to hexameters as Klopstock did the German? He doubts, however, whether the work in the most fortunate translation would find the same national recognition in England as in Germany: "It will appear dull in English because it really is so in German." The detailed criticism of the *Messiah* which follows is not without interest even today; but it is too long to quote from here. It will be found in full in the *Historic Survey* (I. 15) where the whole letter is reproduced, with some changes and omissions.[2] (The allusion to Croft's translation is omitted.)

[1] Another translation of the *Messiah*, also done under Klopstock's auspices, by H. E. Lloyd (1771-1847), was never published (*D.N.B.*, XXXIII. 421). A notice of Lloyd in the *Gentleman's Magazine* (II. 324; 1847) also refers to this translation, and says it was the only one, which came to his notice, with which the author was really satisfied. See also Chap. VII.

[2] Carlyle thought this Essay on Klopstock the best chapter in the whole *Hist. Surv.* "Perhaps there is no writing in our language that offers so correct an emblem of him as this analysis." But he accompanies this compliment by the remark, "The sphere of Klopstock's genius does not transcend Mr. Taylor's scale of poetical altitudes" (1831).

I found but one other mention of Croft's[1] translation, and that in his own *Letter from Germany to the Princess Royal of England on the English and German languages, Hamburg*, 1797. There he gives a few specimens from the *Messiah*, translating very closely line by line. He accompanied his translation with copious notes, justifying the use of certain words etc. Modern scholarship would disprove most of his philological theories, but even the attempt at such a study at that date is interesting. Croft does not mention that he ever intended translating the whole *Messiah*, either in hexameters or literally, as here. His specimens are taken from Cantos III. and XIV. He certainly gives an exact reproduction of the original, but the whole poem translated in this style would be very wearisome. Good's heroic couplets read more pleasantly.

To return to Taylor. His analysis of the poem is interspersed with translations in hexameter, a verse for which he always had a special predilection. His first attempt in that line—*English Hexameters exemplified*, a transversion from Macpherson—had appeared in the same magazine in June, 1796.[2] Taylor maintained that the hexameter, modified as in German by the substitution of the accentual for the quantitative principle and the use of trochees instead of spondees, could be used with as good effect in English as in German. In Schipper's[3] opinion this is the only successful method of adapting the hexameter to English use. It was under the influence of the study of German poetry, and largely owing to Taylor,[4] that English

[1] *Sir Herbert Croft* (1751–1816); matriculated University College, Oxford, 1771; took orders 1797; went to Hamburg 1780; again went on the Continent in 1802 and spent the remainder of his life in France; wrote much, but his *Life of Young* is his only important work. Was a good classical scholar and spoke French, German and Italian.

[2] *Cf.* Robberd's *Memoir*, I. 157-166; G. Herzfeld, *W. Taylor*, 37-39.

[3] *History of English Versification*, p. 264.

[4] Southey chose this form for his *Vision of Judgment* (1820) at Taylor's suggestion. See Preface to the poem.

hexameters began to come a little into favour about this time.

As an example of Taylor's hexameters we quote a few lines which he gives purposely as a contrast to Good's heroic couplets:

"Like huge islands uptorn from their deep seats,
Came loud, rushing, resistless, the princes of darkness to Satan,
Countless as billows advancing to burst on a mountainous sea-shore
Followed the rabble of spirits in thousands of thousands successive.
Stalking, they sang of their deeds, to endless infamy sentenced;
Proudly striking their splitten, by thunder splitten and hoarse harps
Now dishallow'd and vocal to death-tones only."

(II. 403-411.)

Taylor has succeeded better in the *Messiah* than in his other hexameter pieces. Many of the passages are good. One common fault is an adjective in the last foot, getting by the verse accent a stronger accentuation than its norm, *e.g.*, hígh friends; péle gleams; gréat deed, etc.

A couple of later attempts to render the *Messiah* in its original metre will best be mentioned here.

The first is an undated translation of part of the second Book,[1] by F. W. Cronhelm.[2] The British Museum catalogue suggests 1820 as the probable date. The Preface says this fragment is intended as "a metrical specimen of an intended version of the poem," which, however, did not appear. The author calls it an imitation, but it is really a fairly close translation. His hexameters are not as good as Taylor's, and it is often involved and complicated in expression.

Finally, there is an hexameter translation of Book I. in the *London Christian Instructor and Congregational Magazine*[3] for 1821 and 1822. The anonymous

[1] I. 239-end.

[2] *Poems, with an hexametrical Translation of Part of the Second Book of Klopstock's Messiah*, by Frederic William Cronhelm (London, Longman).

[3] IV. 248, and following numbers.

writer states that some years before he studied for a while at a German university, chiefly from a desire better to understand and appreciate the writings of Klopstock. He was induced to translate part of the *Messiah* both from the religious and poetical value of the work and from a wish to attempt English hexameters; feeling encouraged therein from the publication of Southey's *Vision of Judgment*. The translation is accompanied by detailed metrical notes, showing careful study. It avoids the fault, pointed out in Taylor's hexameters, of an accented adjective in the last foot; and also his translation preserves more of the poetic spirit of the original.

In the volume for 1822[1] the same writer gave a translation of the beginnings of Books II. and III., but this time in blank verse, thinking it more acceptable to the majority of readers. His verse is generally harmonious and fluent. It is a pity this translator did not undertake a complete version of the *Messiah*.

In 1810 G. E. Egestorff published some prose extracts from the *Messiah*. These will be considered later in connection with his metrical translation of 1821.

1811[2] saw the re-publication, already mentioned, of Collyer's translation with Mrs. Meeke's additions.[3]

In 1814 the whole twenty books appeared for the first time in English,[4] edited by the Rev. Thomas

[1] V. 194.

[2] In 1811 a letter to the Editor of *Monthly Magazine* (XXXII. 332) from a K. Pedestal announces a translation of one canto of the *Messiah* "by a young native of Germany, eleven years resident in England, who speaks English with fluency and accuracy, and who has devoted much time to literary studies." The translation, which was to have been accompanied by a preface, does not appear to have been published.

[3] Morgan, *Bibl. of Ger. Lit.*, p. 292, gives a partial translation which appeared in America. *The Messiah*, a poem, attempted in English blank verse by Solomon Halling, Georgetown, S.C., 1810 (a versification of Book I., apparently made from Collyer).

[4] *The Messiah*, by Klopstock. A new translation from the German. The five last Books prepared for the press by the Rev. Thomas Raffles (London, 1814).

Raffles.[1] The volumes, well brought out and elegantly bound, are dedicated to Queen Charlotte. Though entitled a new translation, the first fifteen Books are merely a re-print of Collyer's translation. The last five, Raffles says in the Advertisement, were faithfully and literally translated by a German Gentleman and given for revision to Raffles, who found the translation had been made without any regard for English idiom. He was therefore obliged to re-compose the whole, with the assistance of a foreigner intimately acquainted with German. From this it does not appear that Raffles knew much German himself. No mention is made in his *Memoir*[2] of German studies; and his visits to the Continent were all made long after this date, and not for purposes of language study. His interest in the *Messiah* was probably mainly religious, for he does not seem to have taken any further interest in German literature. His translation is on the whole better than Collyer's, the original being less unrecognisably changed, and the language simpler, *e.g.*, for Mrs. Meeke's "The chilly dews of night fall on his exhausted frame; he was dead to all sensations of corporeal inconvenience," Raffles has "the cool dew of evening distilled itself upon his weary limbs; he felt it not." But it is still far from good.

In 1815 an episode from the twelfth Book—"The Death of Mary, the Sister of Lazarus," was translated by Sarah Candler, and transmitted to the Editor of the *Monthly Magazine*[3] by her brother. The translation was evidently suggested by Madame de Staël; for the passage from *de l'Allemagne* on the *Messiah* is prefixed to the piece. Miss Candler translated with care,

[1] *Thomas Raffles* (1788–1863), Minister of the Wesleyan Methodists in Liverpool, 1811–1862; a very popular preacher there. He published sermons and many works on Biblical subjects. A friend of Collyer.

[2] *Memoir of the Rev. Thomas Raffles, LL.D.*, by T. S. Raffles (London, 1864).

[3] XXXIX. 235.

and her version is accurate except in a few small points. But her blank verse has neither ease nor fluency.

In 1821 appeared the first complete metrical translation of the *Messiah* by G. H. Egestorff,[1] a German schoolmaster who lived in England from 1800 to 1817. Already in 1810 he had published a volume of prose extracts from the first fourteen Books of the *Messiah*.[2] Never, he says in the preface to these Extracts, was a work so maimed as the *Messiah* in Collyer's translation; and he wishes to present the public with a new and literal translation of some detached passages, before carrying out the larger design of translating the whole into blank verse. Unfortunately Egestorff's prose translation, though in point of faithfulness an improvement on Collyer's, is in other ways no more satisfactory. It is "literal" with a vengeance. The English is still more than half German in construction, *e.g.*, "Art thou preparing, God, over one of the worlds judgment to hold?" or "dare at a distance and in obscurity the muse to sing thee venture." And it is often quite ungrammatical. It has also many curious expressions, *e.g.*, Adramlech's "exprobating eyes" for "in dem hohen Auge." And the picture of Adramlech "loitering on condensed clouds" is rather comical.

Egestorff's *Elegant Extracts* seem to have been little noticed, and they did not replace Collyer's version in public favour. The London publishers were also

[1] *G. H. C. Egestorff*, born in Hanover, 1783; lived in England 1800–1817; on his return to Hamburg he taught music and English; he translated Kleist's *Frühling* in 1818, and Schiller's *Jungfrau von Orleans* in 1836; returned to London in the forties and lived by teaching German; published many works on German language. For a full account of Egestorff's translation, see article by Daniel B. Shumway: *Egestorff's Translation of Klopstock's Messiah compared with other Early English Translations; Americana Germanica*, III. 284 (1899), from which above facts as to Egestorff's career are taken.

[2] *Elegant extracts from Klopstock's Messiah, selected and translated from the German by G. H. Egestorff, master of the German language. To which is added, never before translated, an Ode on God* (Brighton, 1810).

quite contented with what they already had, and when Egestorff offered them his completed blank verse translation, not one would accept it. So on his return to Hamburg in 1817 he took his work with him, still in manuscript. In 1820, fearing it might never be published, he presented the manuscript to the library at Göttingen, where it can still be seen. Soon after, however, several friends, German and English, interested in the work subscribed and had it printed in Hamburg in 1821.[1] The edition was limited and did not receive a wide circulation. None of the English periodicals noticed it and it was probably little known in England. Shumway mentions one German review of it in the *Leipziger Literatur Zeitung*. Egestorff naturally felt much satisfaction, seeing his work in print at last. The translation bears witness to much industry, perseverance and zeal. Before publishing Egestorff made a most careful revision with numerous corrections and expansions; and the autograph copy in the British Museum has copious manuscript notes and corrections in his own hand. He had certainly made much progress in English since the earlier prose translation. But after allowing that the work is creditable for a foreigner, and that Egestorff was fully justified in considering it much superior to its predecessors, one must add that it has many serious faults. Shumway rates it rather too highly. The passages he quotes are good, but there are others which would mar any poem. Some sentences are very long and involved; a few are completed by no verb; sometimes, as in the prose extracts, the translator makes too free with the word order, *e.g.*:

> "Into the wilderness attending him
> Remote, at his seducing miracles,
> Astonished gazing."

[1] *Klopstock's Messiah*, a poem in twenty cantos; translated from German into English verse by G. H. Egestorff (Hamburg, published by and for the author, 1821–2).

He is too much influenced by German constructions and his metre is often faulty. His manuscript changes—as far as they are still legible—are generally improvements.

Egestorff's most serious fault in the opinion of a German reviewer was not keeping within the same number of lines as the original. In some cases he might certainly have condensed more, but the iambic pentameter line being so much shorter than the hexameter, a translator is often obliged to choose between adding another line or ignoring part of the text.

The following lines show Egestorff at his best:

> " And soon his foot the sacred gate attained
> Which opened softly like the rustling wing
> Of Cherubim ";

for

> " Und stand des Unsterblichen Fuss an der heiligen Pforte;
> Welche vor ihn wie rauschender Cherubim Flügel sich aufthat."

Shumway gives this, and some longer specimens of what is best. In spite of its faults Egestorff's work certainly deserved more recognition than it received from his contemporaries. His translation of a shorter and easier work, Kleist's *Frühling*, is less uneven, and as a whole more successful than his *Messiah*.

In 1823 was published a poem called *Gethsemane*,[1] an imitation or rather abridgment in six Books of the first eight Books of the *Messiah*, made from the English prose translation. The authoress, a Mrs. Montolieu, by her own admission " totally ignorant of the German language," used the prose version of the *Messiah* as her basis throughout, introducing little new matter of her own. From " Motives of Reverence " she condensed several passages relating to the Saviour's sufferings and death. As metre she chose the heroic

[1] *Gethsemane, a Poem, founded on the Messiah of Klopstock*, by Mrs. Montolieu, authoress of the *Enchanted Plants*, etc. (London, 1823).

couplet; and she expresses the hope that by giving the *Messiah* this "more pleasing dress" some distinguished poet may be led to do it more justice.[1] Her version is perhaps "pleasanter" than Collyer's, but it is equally far removed from the spirit of the original. Klopstock would hardly recognise himself after this double metamorphosis. A few lines from the opening of Book II. will give an idea of the whole:

> "Morn o'er the woods her roseate colours spread
> And waving cedars choicer fragrance shed,
> As if to welcome from his short repose
> The blest Messiah, who refreshed arose.
> Him, now earth's vapours rising beams dispelled
> The spirits of the just from far beheld:
> Chief, the first pair, in heavenly charms arrayed
> The awakened Jesus with delight surveyed,
> And to seraphic harps enraptured lays,
> Alternate hymned to his immortal praise."

The last translation of the *Messiah* within our period is (according to the catalogue of the British Museum, for no name appears on the title-page) also the work of a lady, a Miss Frances Anne Head;[2] but it is of much more merit than the foregoing. She published first Cantos I.-VIII., which were very favourably noticed by the *Literary Gazette*,[3] the critic declaring that Klopstock has had to fight in England against the prejudice of ignorance; the average Englishman who can read German, objecting to the metre, gives it up as "confoundedly difficult"; while the more the *Messiah* is known in the existing English translation [*i.e.*, Collyer's] the less it can be appreciated. And yet, says this critic, the *Messiah*, though inferior in the original to Milton, nevertheless has a far greater hold on the pious mind; and its obvious faults should

[1] She evidently knew nothing of Egestorff's translation. Nor did the reviewer of her translation in *Lit. Gaz.*

[2] *The Messiah : A poem.* Translated into English verse. Two vols. (London, 1826).

[3] April, 1826, p. 216.

not be allowed to hide its beauties. He gives the opening lines in this "new and admirable translation":

> "Oh! sing, immortal soul, the glorious theme
> Of sinful man's redemption! that great work
> On earth accomplished by the Incarnate God
> Whose sufferings, death and resurrection raised
> The fallen sons of Adam to the love
> Of His Almighty Father."

He pleads for the encouragement of the work by the public; an encouragement evidently forthcoming, for the whole work appeared that same year, in fifteen Cantos, covering the ground of the twenty of the original, long passages being omitted, while towards the end two or three Cantos are abridged into one. A list of the omitted passages with a short summary of their contents is given at the end.

The translation is in blank verse, and decidedly the best metrical version which had yet appeared. Miss Head had the advantage over Egestorff of writing in her mother-tongue. She appears to have known German well, and there are few inaccuracies.

Her verse is not that of a poet, but it is usually correct and reads with ease. The following passage, describing the assembling of the Devils, is good translating:

> "Huge and tall
> Like islands from their ocean seats uptorn
> Proudly they mov'd. With them flocked countless hosts
> Of meaner rank who round the rebel throne
> Pressed like the circling waves which beat the foot
> Of some high rock-bound shore. Thronging they came,
> Millions on millions; and advancing sung
> Their own exploits of shame and lasting scorn,
> To the harsh cords of broken harps, deep split
> By Heaven's red thunder, whose discordant tones
> Hoarse and unhallow'd were but tuned to breathe
> Death's dismal cries." (II. 403-411.)

Miss Head's translation received, however, but scant attention from the reviewers. The time of popularity of such poems was long past.

Imitations.—Before leaving the *Messiah* there remains to be said a few words on its imitations in English. Several poems with the same or an analogous title and showing a certain similarity of plan and treatment were published in the latter half of the eighteenth century. Possibly some were suggested more or less by Klopstock's epic, or rather by Collyer's version of it—but none as a direct or avowed imitation. The subject seems to have been generally popular. R. Cumberland's *Calvary* has been already mentioned. A *Messiah—a Sacred Poem* by Beecroft was reviewed in the same number of the *Critical* as Collyer's *Messiah* (1763) and also absolutely condemned.

Another *Messiah* (1788) is the work of a lady, a Miss Scott. It aspires to be a " national epic "!

A *Messias* by Samuel Goodwin is not in the British Museum, but from a few lines quoted in the *Critical* it seems to be very different in style from Klopstock's.

Another *Messiah*, without date,[1] but apparently written before 1780, is the work of a Rev. John Cameron,[2] a Scotsman who came to Co. Antrim to preach to the Covenanters about 1752. His *Messiah* was composed, " with a design to amuse and instruct." It opens with an assembly of Devils on Mount Hermon, which recalls Book II. of Klopstock; though the course of the action is different, the same Devils speak. Assembling of Devils is a feature, however, of most of these poems. Cameron nowhere mentions Klopstock, yet it is quite possible that Collyer's *Messiah* penetrated to the North of Ireland and that Cameron had seen it.

[1] A second edition dated Dublin, 1811.

[2] Died 1799.

Dramas.—Two of Klopstock's sacred Dramas were translated into English. The *Death of Adam*[1] appeared anonymously the same year as the *Messiah*. The translator was a Robert Lloyd.[2] In a long preface he praises Klopstock as a worthy imitator of the Ancients. Lloyd finds particular resemblancc between the *Adam* and Sophocles' *Œdipus Coloneus*, proving this by parallel passages. It is interesting to note beside this far-fetched comparison W. Taylor's judgment on the *Adam*: "Except the *Athalie* of Racine, this is probably the best sacred drama extant; at least, it is not rivalled by the author's subsequent efforts: it is not surpassed by the *Samson Agonistes* of Milton." Few today would concur with either judgment.

Lloyd's version is rather a free paraphrase in blank verse of the original in rhythmic prose than an actual translation. He often expands a short phrase to several lines or even adds four or five quite new lines. There are some mistranslations, *e.g.*:

> "Wäre sie länger geblieben, so hätte ich ihren
> Anblick nicht aushalten können."

> "A little while
> And those fond eyes shall ne'er behold her more."

In some passages the verse is pleasing enough, but on the whole it is mediocre.

[1] *The Death of Adam*. A Tragedy in three Acts, from the German of Mr. Klopstock (London, 1763).

[2] *Robert Lloyd*, educated at Westminster and Trinity, Cambridge; wrote dramatic pastorals, comic operas, etc., and did literary hack work; an accomplished scholar, friend of Garrick etc., but led an irregular life and died in the Fleet at thirty-one; *Poetical Works*, 1774. This is the only translation he made from the German. A second edition of *Adam* was published at Portsea, 1810. Lloyd was editor of *St. James's Magazine*, 1762–1764, and included one scene of *Adam* (II. 2) in the number for March, 1763. G. Colman (the elder) inserted this scene in his *Prose Writings and some Pieces in Verse* (1787) without mentioning Lloyd's name.

The *Critical*[1] preferred *Adam* to *Messiah*, praising it as a work of great merit, written according to the spirit of Greek tragedy, and abundantly proving the untruth of the assertion that German literature is without taste, spirit or genius. It also praises the translation. A reviewer in the *Monthly*[2] continues the comparison with *Œdipus Coloneus*. He wishes the translation were as correct as it is spirited and pathetic [*sic*].

Klopstock's other sacred drama, *Solomon*,[3] was not translated till 1809. In his Preface the translator, Robert Huish, regrets that the great poet Klopstock should be so much neglected in England, and specially that his greatest work, the *Messiah*, should be known by a translation which resembles it only in name. But he acknowledges the difficulties it offers to a translator and indeed, he adds, even to a reader, "since it requires an uncommon share of perseverance and industry even to peruse the twenty volumes without ennui." The Dramas of Klopstock, he considers, rank next to the *Messiah* in sublimity of thought and excellence of design. The translation is in blank verse as the original; it also imitates the change in Act II., Scene 3, to free rhymed verses, though not exactly of the same type. The verse of the translation is fair, but it gives no idea of the style of the original, which is direct and concise. Huish is fond of making quite unnecessary amplifications, *e.g.*:

"Wenn auch mein Leib mir nicht die Müde Seele Belastete"

becomes

"Were not my soul, now weary of the world,
Lab'ring beneath its cumbrous load of clay
Eager to wing its flight to realms of joy."

---

[1] XVI. 38; 1763. [2] XXIX. 95; 1763.

[3] *Solomon, A Sacred Drama*, translated from the German of Klopstock, by Robert Huish (London, 1809).

Solomon received contradictory reviews. The *Gentleman's Magazine*[1] says the reader will find much interest in the story and be repaid by many beauties; if he can once conform to the inharmonious versification. The *Critical*[2] says the translation is executed with great ability, no easy task, because of the "tumid, obscure and inverted style of the German poet." (Perhaps this critic had a somewhat inadequate knowledge of German!) The *British Critic*[3] speaks of the fine scenes and passages in this, the most interesting of Klopstock's dramas. But he blames a general want of harmony in the versification of the translation. A critic in the *Monthly*, with no high opinion of German literature in general (he condemns Schiller and Kotzebue together as both "wanting in taste"), judges *Solomon* to be "dull beyond toleration, and although Solomon himself had written it none but Job could have perused it throughout with a certain command of temper." The only virtue he will allow the translator is that of patience.

Klopstock's historical dramas, as might have been expected, did not find a translator. These somewhat artificial representations of ancient German history could have had no interest whatever for foreigners. Taylor gives a short analysis of the Hermann trilogy in the *Historic Survey*,[4] and a close translation of a couple of choruses from the second and third scenes of the *Hermannschlacht*.

Not only Klopstock's works but also his personal history received its share of attention in England. A small volume of *Memoirs*[5] was published in 1808 and seems to have been very popular.[6] There are copies

[1] LXXIX. 45; 1809.
[2] XVIII. 218; 1809.
[3] XXXVII. 299; 1810.
[4] I. 295.
[5] *Memoirs of Frederic and Margaret Klopstock*, translated from the German by the Author of *Fragments in Prose and Verse* (1808).
[6] Third edition published already in 1809 at Bath. Other editions: Bath, 1810, 1811, 1812; London, 1814, 1818, 1824–6, 1842.

of it still in circulation. The translation was made by a Miss Elizabeth Smith[1]—a young woman keenly interested in linguistic studies—and edited by a friend after her death. The *Memoirs* are compiled from papers communicated to her by a Dr. Mummson of Altona;[2] to which are added extracts from Cramer's *Klopstock ; Er und über ihn* (1780) and from a Life of Klopstock in the *Monthly Magazine*. They contain an account of his life, many anecdotes, criticisms of his works translated from German, remarks on his character, etc. The collection of letters includes nine Letters to Bodmer, Letters between Klopstock and Meta, four Letters from Klopstock to his departed Meta, etc., also some of Meta's posthumous writings, with an introduction by her husband, and Meta's Letters to Richardson, already published in Richardson's correspondence. The little Memoir is compiled

[1] Born at Durham, 1776. She was a clever and bookish child. She received, or indeed mostly gave to herself, an education quite exceptional in a woman of that day. She was specially interested in linguistic studies. At eighteen she knew French, Spanish and Italian, and began German with the encouragement of a friend. During a short visit to Ireland in 1795 she picked up an Irish grammar and began to study it. Later she learned Latin, Arabic, Persian, and Hebrew, and we are told that she had philological collections with lists of words in Welsh, Chinese, African dialects and Icelandic. She does not appear, however, to have had any creative talent, and her original verse is without merit. A reviewer in the *Monthly* (LXIV. 67) accuses her of being wanting in genuine poetic taste, and mistaking any display of pious feelings for real poetry. The estimate of her literary powers by her biographer (see *Fragments of Prose and Verse*, 1809) is a good deal exaggerated. But this does not take from her merit as a diligent and enterprising linguist at a time when linguistic studies, especially among women, were by no means common. She died in 1806 at the early age of thirty.

[2] Dr. Mummson writes, September 7, 1804 : "Very willingly I will look out for such materials as you desire. . . . Klopstock certainly deserves to be more known to the English, not only for his extraordinary genius as a sublime poet, but also for his private virtues and amiable character." And July 2, 1805 : "I am charmed to find that you are pleased with materials I have sent. Go on in your laudable endeavour. . . ."

with great care and with genuine and even exaggerated admiration for the subject of it. Klopstock is called "the Milton of Germany, the pride of his country, whose piety and virtue, still more than his talents, make him an honour to human nature." The authoress hopes by her book to increase the number of those who study Klopstock's works with the attention they deserve, and by so doing to counteract the mischief caused by the corrupt German literature which is inundating the country. Miss Smith seems to have had a good reading knowledge of German, though she could not speak it. Her prose translations are carefully and correctly done, but somewhat stiff in style. The *British Critic*[1] reviewed her work favourably. The *Critical*[2] criticised it more severely. The Letters it thought well translated, but not at all worth the doing; "those of the poet and his wife are the merest uxorious dotage." At the end of the work Miss Smith translated several odes. These will be referred to again later.

In spite of adverse criticism, Klopstock's Letters evidently found favour with the public. Only a few years later a much larger collection of them was published; again translated by a lady.[3] They are taken, with a few omissions, from the German collection *Klopstock und seine Freunde*, by Klamer Schmidt (1810). Miss Benger alludes to the interest aroused in Klopstock by Miss Smith's *Memoir* and the publication of Meta's letters to Richardson, and praises Klopstock's letters as possessing in supreme degree the charm of confidence, so commonly wanting to English letters. She gives a sketch of his life and a short account of each correspondent.

[1] XXXV. 59.

[2] XXIII.; 1811.

[3] *Klopstock and his Friends, a Series of Familiar Letters, written between the Years* 1750 *and* 1803. Translated from the German with a biographical introduction by Miss Benger (1814).

Klopstock

Odes.—The earliest translator of Klopstock's Odes was W. Taylor in his article in the *Critical*[1] (1804), later incorporated with the same translations, in the *Historic Survey*. Taylor says: "In his Odes Klopstock does not lose himself in those mazes of description, nor cluster together that bewildering variety of imagery, which normally constitutes the essence of an English Ode: but his feelings are strong, his images lofty and his diction bold." Their form has no parallel in modern literature. On the whole they constitute Klopstock's strongest claim to fame. In this Taylor's opinion concurs with that of most modern critics.

These Odes present many difficulties to a translator. Klopstock avowedly advocated classical rhythms as opposed to modern rhyme, and not only adopted Horatian forms, but freely invented new and elaborate metres constructed on the same principles. Many critics think that he carried his theories too far, but they had some measure of success. English is, however, much more unsuited than German to such experiments, and the translator is bound to sacrifice the peculiarities of the form if he wishes to make a readable English poem.

Taylor has translated several of the Odes in prose. Here the task was comparatively easy, and Taylor has accomplished it successfully. One can only criticise a few small points. I only noted one case in which he has not quite caught the meaning of the German. This is the word "*Volksbühnisch*" in the fifth line of *Das Neue*:

"Singen den Ton Volksbühnisch, am Fest der Sansculottiden" which he translates as "in tones that abuse the people" instead of "in such a tone as is found in the lower and more common theatres."

These prose translations give an exact idea of the

[1] II. 473. *Die Choren* had already appeared as *Sacred Music* in the *Monthly Magazine*, II. 49 (1796); and *Die Genesung* in the same, VII.; 1799.

matter of the originals, and, as Taylor says, are more instructive, if less gratifying to the reader, than looser metrical renderings.[1] A few lines will give an idea of their literal simplicity:

"Behold, Jehovah comes no longer in storm; in gentle pleasant murmurs comes Jehovah, and under him bends the bow of peace."

> "Siehe, nun kommt Jehovah nicht mehr im Wetter,
> In stillem sanften Säuseln
> Kommt Jehovah,
> Und unter ihm neigt sich der Bogen des Friedens."

In the four Odes translated in verse (the *Lake of Zürich*, *To Young*, *My Recovery*, *The Choirs*) Taylor has not attempted an exact reproduction of the classical metres used by Klopstock, but has adopted in all a uniform measure of two iambic trimeter lines. He translates as simply and literally as possible: as for instance the second verse of *My Recovery*:

> "Had I not heard thy gentle tread approach,
> Not heard the whisper of thy welcome voice,
> Death had with iron foot
> My chilly forehead prest."
>
> (II.5-8.)

Miss Smith in her translation, on the other hand, endeavoured to give an exact reproduction of Klopstock's rhythms.

It can be seen from Miss Smith's remarks in her Preface that she had not a very clear understanding of Klopstock's system of versification, the result of much care and elaboration; and she had not herself enough metrical skill to imitate it with any success. Her odes have neither the merit of being always an *exact* reproduction of the form of the original—for instance, in *To Ebert*[2] she quite changes the character

[1] Carlyle thought the prose translation of the *Two Muses* perhaps the finest passage in the whole book (1831).

[2] *To Ebert*, also translated in fairly good blank verse by "N. R.," of Trinity College, Dublin, in *Black. Mag.*, III. 416; 1818.

by adopting an ascending for a descending rhythm—nor of being harmonious English verse. So they are unsatisfactory from either point of view. Most of the critics thought her method of versification mistaken.[1] Her work, however, is done with great care and her self-acquired knowledge of German seems to have been very thorough.

The *Ode to Fanny* is more freely translated than the others, and better. It seems to me superior to Egestorff's translation (given at the end of his *Messiah*) both in choice of expressions and in the swing of the verse.

The little poem *Das Rosenband* has been simply and pleasingly translated both by Miss Smith and Egestorff. Miss Smith's (except for one line inexactly rendered) gives the closest reproduction of the original.

The best translation of Klopstock's Odes comes just at the end of our period in a long review of Klopstock's Life and Odes which appeared in the *Foreign Review*[2] for 1829. Many appeared here for the first time in English.

Of Klopstock's place in literature the reviewer speaks as follows:

> "Literary men in Germany esteem themselves members of a great spiritual priesthood, which pretensions may seem rather extravagant or presumptuous in England; but the idea is certainly elevated, and to Klopstock is due some of the praise for having given this direction to the mind of the country."

It would take too long here to make a detailed study of each ode. Suffice a few general remarks, and allusions to a few of the most important Odes.

They are all translated in unrhymed verse, and keep fairly closely to the form of the originals. In one or two cases German idioms are too literally rendered, and there is sometimes obscurity (*e.g.*, *To Wingolf*);

[1] *Crit. Rev.*, LXIV. 67; 1811. *Brit. Crit.*, XXXV. 59.
[2] III. 340-377.

but they give more of Klopstock's spirit than do any former attempts. The *Ode to God* is, he says, "one of great beauty and pathos, but it is not the beauty of holiness, nor has it the purity of spiritual emotion." A couple of verses will show how closely he reproduces the character of the original.

> "God! Let this life pass like a fleeting breath
> Ah no!—But her who seems designed for me
> Give—easy task for thee to accord me—
> Give to my trembling tearful heart!
>
> * * * * *
>
> "With the same effort dost thou grant and take
> From the poor worm, whose hours are centuries,
> His brief felicity—the worn man
> Who blooms his season, droops and dies."
>
> (II. 93-96, 105-8.)

Egestorff also translated this Ode in free unrhymed lines, but without strophic division. It begins literally, but afterwards becomes freer.

In his note to the *Lake of Zürich*, the translator in the *Foreign Review* refers to Taylor's critique of the same "in his excellent work, the *Historic Survey*." Comparing the two translations (Taylor's and the *Foreign Review*) we find that they are made much on the same plan, giving the impression of the original metre, without exact reproduction of it. Both are faithful and accurate, except for one small mistake of Taylor's, pointed out by the Foreign Reviewer. Both make readable verse, but on the whole the *Foreign Review* version is more poetical. Here are the three last verses in both versions:

> "Full of affection, in the airy shades
> Of the dim forest, and with downcast look
> Fixed on the silver wave,
> I breath'd this pious wish:
> 'O were ye here, who love me though afar,
> Whom singly scattered in our country's lap
> In lucky hallowed hour
> My seeking bosom found:

Here would we build us huts of friendship, here
Together dwell for ever! The dun wood
A shadowy temple seem'd
Elysium all the vale.'"

(Taylor.)

"In tender thought, within the airy shades
Of the dim forest, mutely, with sunk gaze
Fixed on the silver wave,
I mused the pious wish:
'Were you with us, who love me though afar,
Whom on the bosom of our fatherland
    Lone-cast, my seeking soul
    In happy hour once found.
Oh, we would build us huts of friendship here,
And here for ever dwell! The shady wood
To temple changed; the vale
Into Elysium.'"

(*For. Rev.*, II. 55-56.)

Der Frühlingsfeier—translated by W. Taylor in prose—is here for the first time rendered in verse as the *Solemnisation of Spring*. It is in a free metre, the long lines of the German being given in two or even in three shorter lines. Of all these Odes it is that which most fully gives the tone and spirit of the original. Here are a few lines:

"Airs! that about me blow and breathe
Soft coolness on my glowing brow,
    The Lord, the Infinite
    Sent you, ye wondrous airs!
But now they hush, they scarcely breathe—
More sultry grows the morning sun—
    Clouds stream on high and visibly
    He comes—th' Eternal comes!
Now swoop the winds, they rush, they whirl—
How bows the wood, how swells the stream!
    Visible as thou canst to mortals be,
    Oh! Visibly thou comest—Infinite!
The forest bends, the stream recedes, yet I
    Fall not upon my countenance
    Before the coming Deity."

(II. 53-66.)

None of the other Odes translated in the *Foreign Review*—*The Sea-Course*, *My Fatherland*, *The Omnipresent*—had ever been done before. The last is translated in rhyme, in order to enable readers to judge of the effect likely to be produced by such a mode. One verse will enable us to do so here:

> "This mortal lot, this earthy weight
> Enthrals my soul else free,
> When she herself would elevate
> Thou Infinite to Thee."

> "Dieser Endlichkeit Loos, die Schwere der Erde
> Fühlet auch meine Seele
> Wenn sie zu Gott, zu dem Unendlichen
> Sich erheben will."

I think all will be agreed that unrhymed verse is the only possible form for these Odes. Their whole character is lost by the "jingle of rhyme"—as Klopstock called it. Also, the necessity for finding rhymes obliges the translator so far to alter the German expression that often the originality and force of Klopstock's thought is completely lost.

A later translator[1] adopted rhyme in all cases, much weakening the originals.

[1] *Odes of Klopstock*, translated from the German by William Hind (London, 1848).

CHAPTER III

A. Lessing; B. Wieland

G. E. LESSING (1729-1781).

The question as to how far Lessing's works were known in England, and what influence they had on English thought has, within the last few years, been made the subject of independent research by two scholars, one in Germany and one in England: Wilhelm Todt in *Lessing in England*, 1767-1850 (Heidelberg, 1912), gives a detailed study of the various translations; Sidney H. Kenwood in *Lessing in England* (1914)[1] covers a good deal of the same ground, but adds information on many points. The two works together treat so exhaustively of the subject of Lessing in England, that it is not necessary here to do more than refer the reader to them.[2] Both rather tend to exaggerate the influence which Lessing exercised in England. But I have found no reason to question any of their facts, nor have I come across any new ones of importance.

A few small points may be mentioned. A translation, or rather free imitation, of one of Lessing's early poems, *Die Küsse*, as *The Kiss* by J. Macray in *Stray Leaves* (1827), has not been noticed before. Nor has a translation of a Fable, *The Furies* in the *German Museum* (III. 276), 1801.

Lord Leveson Gower's translation of the *Faust* Fragment (appended to his translation of Goethe's

[1] *Mod. Lang. Rev.*, April, 1914, IX., No. 2. Later reprinted separately by the Cambridge University Press.

[2] For list of translations see Appendix A.

Faust, 1823) deserves perhaps more than the passing mention by Kenwood.[1] Lord Gower gives as his reason for presenting Lessing's *Faust* besides Goethe's, a remark of Madame de Staël in *de l'Allemagne* to the effect that Goethe had borrowed "the idea of Faust's insatiable curiosity, the origin of his perdition" from Lessing. He translates the first scene—Satan demanding of the Devils an account of their various performances—as given by J. J. Engel.[2] The narrative of the third spirit is condensed into a few lines. Otherwise the translation follows the original closely, and is free from any serious inaccuracies.

A few of Lessing's early letters to his father are translated by W. Taylor in the *Historic Survey*;[3] also part of Lessing's letter[4] on Gebauer's *History of Portugal*. Taylor writes to Southey, April 27th, 1806: "I have been translating forty pages of Lessing's Letters on Gebauer's *History of Portugal*, because I had a fancy you should read; and now I am contriving to weave them into a critical survey of the writings of Lessing for the *Monthly Magazine*." (They appeared in his survey of Lessing's works, 1809.)

Taylor's translation of *Nathan* is discussed at length by Todt and Kenwood. One might add a few words about his translation of J. G. Pfranger's sequel or "Gegenstück" to *Nathan*: *Der Mönch von Libanon* (1782), which for a time passed as being by Lessing himself. As such it is regarded by Taylor in the *Monthly Magazine* (June, 1809), where he gives an account of it with a translation of the interview between Saladin and Nathan (Act I.). In the complete version in the *Historic Survey*[5] it is attributed to its rightful author and called "the forged sequel to *Nathan*." Taylor praises it as a close imitation of Lessing's

[1] P. 212.
[2] *Deut. Nat. Lib.—Lessing's Werke*, III. ii., p. 171.
[3] I. 338 *ff.* and 359 *ff.*
[4] *Literaturbrief*, XXXII.
[5] II. 121-232.

manner, but admits that it is "a work already nearly forgotten." That over a hundred pages of the *Survey* should be devoted to a work of so little permanent interest is the most noteworthy example of the lack of proportion and unity in Taylor's work. As Carlyle remarks in 1831: "When we have conscientiously struggled to peruse an entire sequel to *Nathan* the author turns round, and without any apparent smile, tells us it is by a nameless author and worth nothing."

Nathan Drake, in his *Memorials of Shakespeare* (1828), included one chapter translated from the *Dramaturgie—Shakespeare and Voltaire compared, as to their use and management of preternatural machinery*. It is a rare example of interest taken in England in this important work of Lessing, which was practically unknown there at this time.

B. Wieland

C. M. WIELAND (1753-1813).

In a review of Wieland's *Werke und Leben* by Gruber (Tübingen, 1818-28) in the *Foreign Quarterly*[1] (1828) it is said that there are few names of equal eminence in literature, of which so little is known in England, as Wieland. This statement, though perhaps true of the years immediately before 1828, gives a somewhat false impression of the earlier period. In the second half of the eighteenth century no German writer except Gessner was as popular in England as Wieland, and many of his works were translated earlier into English than into French. Between 1770 and 1775 almost each year brought a translation; again 1787, 1795, 1796, and 1798 *Oberon*. About 1795 began, too, the

[1] II. 403-461.

series of reviews of Wieland's works contributed to the *Monthly*, the *Monthly Magazine* and the *Critical* by W. Taylor,[1] whose extravagant admiration of Wieland is often cited as an example of the want of discrimination in his criticism. In the *Critical*[2] he calls Wieland "in every sense the greatest writer of the Germans." In the same article he passes shortly in review the translations made up to that date. It is true that Wieland's popularity declined as the nineteenth century advanced. The older translations were mostly forgotten; few new ones appeared, and these all either by W. Taylor or due to his influence. In Madame de Staël's *de l'Allemagne* (1811), which contributed so largely to the re-awakening of interest for German literature in England, the chapter on Wieland is one of the most sketchy and least satisfactory. The writer in the *Foreign Quarterly* (1828) strongly recommends Gruber's *Life*, and gives from it a long account of Wieland; he also translates extracts from his letters, a description of him in his old age from the pen of Sophie de la Roche, and his own account of his interview with Napoleon. The article concludes with a very good summing up of Wieland's literary character. The writer shows very clearly that Wieland was not one of those original, creative minds which strike out new paths for themselves, but that he was an improver rather than a discoverer, an eclectic philosopher rather than an original thinker. This judgment is more measured than W. Taylor's and more in accordance with Wieland's place in German literature.

That Wieland was in so many ways not typically German was probably one of the chief reasons of his popularity in England. He imitated English writers,

[1] These articles afterwards put together to form chapter on Wieland in *Hist. Surv.*, II.

[2] II. 543; 1804. In same article is a long passage translated from *History of Apollonius* (Bk. V., Sec. 5).

specially Sterne, and was also much influenced by contemporary French philosophy, as the whole character of his writing in his second period bears witness. He soon became popular in France,[1] and this also facilitated his introduction to English readers. The ease and lightness of his style obviated the prejudice against the proverbial dullness and heaviness of German works, and showed that "the German Muses are no longer remarkable for their awkward carriage, but for elegance and grace." As remarked a reviewer in the *Critical*[2] speaking of the earliest translation from Wieland—that of his Biblical epic, *Der geprüfte Abraham*, a product of his early Pietistic period, when he was a disciple of Bodmer. *The Trial of Abraham*[3] (1764) will have taken its place in England beside *Noah*, *Abel* and the *Messiah*, and been popular with the same readers. Judging from the few extracts given in the *Critical* and the *Monthly* the translation is in much the same style as Collyer's *Abel* and *Messiah*, though the *Critical* which praises these, condemns *Abraham* as "a very imperfect translation of a work abounding in striking beauties." It calls the language "affected and unintelligible," giving as examples such words as tenebrous, ecstasied, uberous, emaning, solaceful, etc. Such are also to be found in Collyer. The *Monthly*[4] compares "the poor Prose bleeding beneath the merciless hands of the high-inhabitating translator" to Isaac beneath Abraham's knife. *Abraham* was also noticed in Germany.[5]

[1] See *Tableau de l'Allemagne et de la littérature allemande*, 1782, where Wieland is praised as "le Lucien Allemand. . . . On peut même dire que de tous les Allemands c'est lui qui a le plus de fraîcheur dans le coloris, etc." Most of his works were translated into French at an early date.

[2] XVIII. 180; 1764.

[3] **The Trial of Abraham*, in four Cantos, Becket and Hondt, 1764. G. Herzfeld (*W. Taylor*, p. 9) doubts the existence of this translation as referred to in Goedeke (IV. ii., p. 197). But that it existed is proved by the notices in periodicals, though no copy be now found.

[4] XXX. 324; 1764.

[5] *Bibl. d. sch. W.*, XI. 331.

The first French translation did not appear until two years after this (1766).

From 1771 dates a translation of the *Nachlass des Diogenes von Sinope* (1770) under the title of *Socrates out of his Senses, or Dialogues of Diogenes of Sinope* (London, Davies).[1] It is the work of a German, Wintersted, who, judging by his knowledge of English, must have been some years in England. There are some mistranslations (*e.g.*, Cytronenmadchen = "oyster-wenches"), but on the whole it compares very favourably with the other translations made by Germans, being more accurate and more idiomatic. The *Monthly*[2] praised the work as "abounding in delicate satire, pleasant humour and excellent sentiments," and notices a likeness to Sterne. The *Critical*[3] also commented favourably, but according to W. Taylor[4] the translation was received with utter indifference by the public.

Agathon.—Two years later we come to a much more important work, a translation of *Agathon*[5] by John Richardson of York, translator of Lessing's *Fables* in 1764. The long Preface is of interest, as it shows an understanding of the development of contemporary German literature quite exceptional at that date.[6] Richardson defends German literature against the slights and attacks of French writers, and recommends it as having a special claim on English protection and encouragement, since the modern writers of Germany have largely formed themselves on English models. For a long time, he says, they have been noteworthy in the world of science and learning, but the greatest improvement made by them in the present century has been in the cultivation of their own language. Among the writers who have contributed most largely to this,

[1] First French translation, 1772.
[2] XLVI. 642; 1772.
[3] XXXIII. 216; 1772.
[4] *Hist. Surv.*, II. 314.
[5] *The History of Agathon*, by Mr. C. M. Wieland; translated from the German original, with a preface by the translator (London, Cadell. 1773).
[6] See G. Herzfeld, *W. Taylor*, pp. 9, 10.

he mentions Lessing and Weisse, Rabener[1] and—as the most important—Gellert,[1] of whom he gives a long and interesting appreciation. Wieland, he says, has distinguished himself as a satirist, a moral and a dramatic writer, and *Agathon* is acknowledged as his masterpiece. In it Richardson discovers much original genius, an extensive reading of modern as well as of ancient writers, and great skill in the delineation of the character of Agathon. "The style," he adds, "is nervous and strong, the descriptions poetical and picturesque, and in many parts we meet with that noble simplicity which is the test of true genius." But he mentions some blemishes, which he considers Wieland could easily have avoided; as for instance: three or four different strokes of satire often thrown together in the same sentence, causing confusion; immoderately long sentences (a defect which the translation aims at avoiding); the intermixing of modern subjects in a work purporting to be based on a Greek manuscript; carelessness in some expressions and indelicacy in some allusions. But from the moral point of view, Richardson judges *Agathon* much less harshly than did most English critics.

Agathon was considerably revised and altered by Wieland in later editions. This translation represents the first edition of 1766-7. It is a correct and careful piece of work, and in spite of small imperfections and a certain stiffness of style, decidedly the best early prose translation from German. Richardson gives a faithful interpretation of the text as he finds it, and yet it is no slavish imitation; long German sentences are broken up into shorter ones, their meaning well understood and made clear. The following (Book I., chapter v.) is a good example of the style of the whole:

"The rising sun, announced by the rosy-fingered morn, gilded the Ionian sea with its earliest beams, and found the whole crew, who

[1] See Chap. I. on Rabener and Gellert.

during the night had sacrificed to Bacchus and his sister Goddess, to use Virgil's phrase, buried in wine and sleep. Agathon alone, who usually arose at break of day, was first roused from sleep by the rays of the sun gilding horizontally over his forehead. As soon as he had opened his eyes, he perceived a young man before him in the habit of a slave, who viewed him with great attention. Beautiful as Agathon was, this amiable young man seemed to surpass him, both in delicacy of shape and bloom of complexion. His countenance, indeed, and his appearance, had something in it which so nearly resembled the beauties of a female form, that had he been in woman's clothes, among a company of young virgins, he would, like Horace's favourite, have easily imposed upon the most accurate observer. Agathon surveyed the young slave with equal attention, till the agreeable surprise he felt was insensibly heightened into ecstasy. The same emotions displayed themselves in the beautiful features of the young slave. Their souls acknowledged each other at the same instant, and seemed to intermix through the glances of their eyes, before they could even embrace, or their lips, trembling with rapture, could utter 'Psyche! Agathon!'"[1]

The *Monthly*,[2] in a notice of *Agathon*, which refers to its former reviews of Wieland, finds that in this work he still follows the manner of Sterne. But from the moral point of view this critic notes one very serious defect—*i.e.*, that although balance inclines in favour of morality throughout the work, there is no exemplary moral deduction at the conclusion, which should be the case, for the farewell impression is the strongest in the reader's mind. (Wieland altered this conclusion in a later edition.) The *Critical*[3] also regrets the evil moral tendency of the work, but praises the picturesque descriptions, just reasoning, and well-aimed satire, and the interesting account given of the sophists of Greece and the Republic of Athens, marred though it is by some violent anachronisms. This English *Agathon* was also noticed in Germany.[4]

From the same year dates a translation of *Don Silvio von Rosalva* (1764), it is believed from the hand

[1] "Als die aufgehende Sonne das Ionische Meer. . . . Psyche! Agathon! ausrufen konnten."

[2] LXIX. 176; 1774.

[3] XXVII. 196; 1774.

[4] *Neue Bibl. d. sch. W.*, XVI. 162.

of the same John Richardson.[1] But it appeared anonymously.[2] There is no copy of the original edition in any of the big libraries,[3] but it was reprinted in 1904 in the series *Early Novelists*, edited by E. H. Baker. In the Introduction it is stated: " The English translation of Wieland's story . . . is a very scarce duodecimo in three volumes. . . . I have come across only one copy of it, that from which this edition has been printed. The anonymous translator has done his work well, the narrative often attaining a high level of English prose."[4] There are few translations of this period which could be reprinted and read with pleasure in our own day; and that this is one of the few sufficiently testifies to its merits. The modern reprint is easily procured. The original translation was not much noticed in the reviews of 1773; but the *Monthly*[5] praises it as superior to most other novels of its class, objecting only to the indecency of some passages.

A translation of Wieland's *Sympathieen* (1756), entitled *The Sympathy of Souls*,[6] bears no date on the title-page, but the notices in periodicals assign it to

[1] *Vide* G. Herzfeld, *W. Taylor*, p. 11.

[2] *Reason triumphant over fancy; exemplified in the singular Adventures of Don Silvio von Rosalva. A History in which every marvellous event occurs naturally*. Three vols. (London, Wilkie, 1773). Goedeke (IV. ii., p. 201) only gives an edition with date 1774, and assumes it appeared in Leipzig.

[3] There is a copy in the possession of Dr. W. Kurrelmeyer, who acquired it recently. *Vide* his article, *English translations of Wieland*, *Mod. Lang. Notes*, XXXII. 225; 1917, from which some of above particulars have been taken.

[4] Baker has omitted Wieland's preface, given in the first edition (1764), though not in later ones, and included in the original version of the translation (1773). Nor does he mention the fact that the translation is an exact reproduction of the original text, with the original title of 1764, although Wieland's revised edition with much shorter title had appeared in 1772.

[5] XLVIII. 126; 1773.

[6] *The Sympathy of Souls*, by Mr. Wieland, attempted after the French and revised from the original German (printed for the Editor).

the year 1787.[1] It was made from a French version.[2] The translator was a German, named Winzer, who tells us that a mere chance having brought the French version in his way, he resolved to translate it, partly as a recreation and partly as an exercise in English. He adds that he obtained the German version with some difficulty, and too late for a minute revision, but he flatters himself that he has always preserved the sense of the original. The work is dedicated to the Queen. If the translator was—as he states in the Preface—totally unacquainted with English three years before, and had many other occupations to take up the greater part of his time, it is perhaps quite a creditable piece of work. But judged on its own merits the translation is bad. A specimen may amuse: "What felicity, O Cephise, for sympathetic souls to be able to meet! For those souls who perhaps did already love one another under the regions of another heaven, to meet again upon this globe, and after faintly remembering themselves endeavour to trace their resembling features as one recollects a dream, which left a confused, but agreeable sensation on one's ideas." Foreign idioms are frequent and mistakes in grammar occur. Comparing it with the original, there are many passages where Wieland's meaning is not given exactly; but here the fault may be partly due to the French translation,[3] which was probably imperfect. The *Critical*[4] speaks of the work as already well known in England (which seems to point to an earlier translation, of which, however, I could find no trace). This critic condemns the translation as following too servilely the French version, which he speaks of as itself very free. The *Monthly*[5] judges the translation

[1] The *Brit. Mus. Catalogue* suggests 1795, which is impossible.
[2] *La Sympathie des Âmes*, Paris, 1768. Trad. par F. P. Fresnois.
[3] Not in Brit. Mus.
[4] LXIV. 394; 1787.
[5] LXXVIII. 167; 1788.

less severely, calling it "the commendable work of a young foreigner." The work itself, which this critic knows from the English translation only, he judges to be the least good of Wieland's works, being "a mere string of sentimental and devotional rhapsodies, wanting the relief of cool reasoning and manly reflection."

From 1775 dates an anonymous translation of two dialogues of Wieland:[1] (1) *Araspes and Panthea, or the Effects of Love*, and *Socrates and Timoklea, on apparent and real Beauty*.[2] The translator has not been identified till now; but a note in the *Monthly*[3] refers for "more of this author's productions" to their notice of *Don Silvio von Rosalva*, which proves him to have been again John Richardson. The work can here be judged only from the review in the *Monthly*, referred to above. The first dialogue with its long discussions on mystical philosophy and theology presents much difficulty to a translator, and he may perhaps be pardoned some stiffness and awkwardness in style. The second dialogue is much simpler. From a short extract given in the *Monthly*, it seems well translated.

Twenty years later we come to a translation of Wieland's *Göttergespräche*,[4] taken from the *Teutsche Merkur*, in which they first appeared. The translator is W. Taylor, who in the Preface sums up Wieland's attitude towards the thought of his time in these words: "The notions of this age are moving in religion, from superstition towards infidelity: in morals, from puritanism toward libertinism; and in politics from

[1] *Dialogues from the German of Mr. Wieland. To which is prefixed an *Essay on Sentiment*, by the Author (1775). (There is no copy in the Brit. Mus. Morgan, *Biblio. of Ger. Lit.*, p. 557, gives one in the Lib. Con.)

[2] The originals date from 1758 and 1754.

[3] LII. 508; 1775.

[4] *Dialogues of the Gods*, written originally in German by C. M. Wieland (London, Johnson, 1795).

despotism toward democracy. On each walk, Wieland will be found to outstride the average progress of public opinion, but to stop short of the ne-plus-ultra men, who would substitute atheism to faith, agamy to matrimony, and anarchy to government." The volume contains Nos. IX., X., XI. and XIII. of the *Dialogues*, all of which treat of ideas suggested by the French Revolution. The Tory and Conservative press naturally did not approve of them, one reviewer remarking satirically that "doubtless the innovating party think it a great matter to have gained such an advocate as Wieland; but in reality the dialogues boast no great ingenuity of thought, nor subtlety of argument." When Taylor, over thirty years later, was choosing *Dialogues* to insert in the *Historic Survey*, he evidently considered these on the subject of the French Revolution no longer suitable to the times, and inserted instead five others on more varied subjects (Nos. I., III., V., VI., VIII.).

A translation of several other *Göttergespräche*[1] appeared in the same year (1795) in Tooke's *Varieties of Literature*; also two short pieces from Wieland: *On the liberty of reasoning in matters of belief* (I. 43) and *On the liberty and licentiousness of the press* (I. 252). The Dialogue between Jupiter and Juno on the subject of monarchy and kings served W. Taylor as a model of his Dialogue between Charles I. and Louis XVI. (mentioned below). A short speech of Jupiter's will give some idea of its character, and of the translation—a very good one.

"I am very much obliged to thee and to old Homer! But to speak honestly, what may have passed for truth in those rude ages of the early infancy of the world, is so no longer, when we are speaking of a people that has at length, by experience and civilisation, attained to that point, where, master of its reason, it is become strong enough to shake off the yoke of old prejudices and idle conceits. Nations have

[1] *Eine Lustreise ins Elysium; Göttergespräche*, V., VI., VIII., IX.; *Gespräche in Elysium*, III.

their infancy and childhood as well as individuals; and as long as they are as ignorant, as weak and as irrational as children, they must be treated as children; and be governed by blind obedience to an authority, which is not accountable to them. But as individuals do not always remain children, so neither do nations. It is a trespass against nature, to endeavour by force or fraud, or (as is commonly the case) by both, to keep them in perpetual childhood; but it is folly and wickedness at once, to continue to treat them as children when they have already grown to maturity."

More important than Taylor's translated *Dialogues* are these two original ones,[1] imitated from Wieland, and suggested directly by those in the *Varieties of Literature*. Taylor says: "The train of ideas therein contained are here often alluded to, and occasionally thwarted." In the first, Jupiter, Apollo, Numa and Socinius take part, and the general tendency is a defence of Unitarianism. We remark here the first signs of Taylor's later polemics against the Reformation.[2] The second is a dialogue between Charles I. and Louis XVI. G. Herzfeld[3] gives a full account of both these dialogues, neither of which, in his opinion, can be for a moment compared to their prototypes.

From 1796 dates a volume of **Select fairy tales from the German of Wieland*,[4] a work now not to be found, but highly praised in the *British Critic*,[5] where the translation is ascribed to the author of Weber's *Sorcerer* and *Black Valley* (*i.e.*, J. Powell). The *Monthly*[6] also praises tales as "fanciful and amusing." The *Critical*,[7] on the contrary, condemns many of them as "criminally licentious," and all as displaying little genius.

There are two translations of *Peregrinus Proteus*

[1] *Dialogues of the Gods. An imitation of Wieland. Month. Mag.*, II. 463; 1796 and V. 351; 1798.

[2] *Month. Mag.*, XXVI.; *Hist. Surv.*, I. 187.

[3] *W. Taylor*, pp. 32, 33.

[4] London, Johnson, 1795.

[5] IX. 559.

[6] XXV. 213; 1798. Mentions *the Car*, *Silvester and Rosina*, *the Druid* and *the Combat*.

[7] XXII. 357; 1797.

(1791). The first appeared anonymously, in 1796;[1] but the translator is known[2] to have been Mr. Tooke,[3] compiler of the *Varieties of Literature* and historian of Russia. Mr. Tooke gives Wieland's preface to the edition of 1791, but none of his own. It gives a better idea of Wieland's work than the later abridged version, and is on the whole an accurate translation. But it is spoiled by a too close adherence to German constructions, which gives a want of ease and fluency to the style, and makes some sentences difficult to follow without close attention. A review of *Peregrinus Proteus* in the *Analytical*[4] with a long analysis of the work and many extracts is probably from the pen of W. Taylor. It speaks of Wieland's celebrity in England as a philosopher, satirist and politician, and praises the abundance and variety of his literary production and the richness and originality of his genius. The *Critical*[5] examines the work from the moral point of view, and decides that a few trite moral sentiments clothed in charming language are poor compensation for the mischief which might follow from its direct incitement of the voluptuous passions.

Eight years later was made another translation of *Peregrinus Proteus*, but this time in an abridged form.[6]

[1] *The Private History of Peregrinus Proteus the Philosopher*, by C. M. Wieland. Translated from the German. London, Johnson, 1796.

[2] See *Month. Mag.*, IV. 19 (1797) and XLI. 124, where W. Taylor names Tooke as the translator.

[3] *Rev. William Tooke*, 1744–1820. Became English chaplain at St. Petersburg in 1774, and while there made frequent visits to Poland and Germany, and made the acquaintance of Kant at Königsberg. In 1792 he returned to England and devoted himself to literary pursuits. He contributed largely to *Month. Rev.* and *Gent.'s Mag.* In 1800 he published his *History of Russia.* He also translated from the German the sermons and devotional exercises of a Swiss divine, G. F. Zollihofer.

[4] XXV. 196; 176.

[5] XXIII. 472; 1798.

[6] *Confessions in Elysium, or The Adventures of a Platonic Philosopher*, taken from the German of C. M. Wieland, by John Battersby Elrington, Esq. (London, Sidney, 1804).

The translator declares that he has altered the original plan of the work with the aim of making his volumes rather a pastime than a study. He hopes to entertain his Readers with the "extraordinary adventures and eccentricities of a Fanatic!" In accordance with this intention Elrington has made considerable changes in plan and arrangement. The prefatory discourse between Lucian and Proteus is omitted, and what follows is not a dialogue between the two, as in Wieland, but a plain recital made by Proteus himself. Some of Lucian's remarks are put into the mouth of Proteus in the form of reflections, but most of the long discussions about Christianity, etc., are either entirely omitted or much curtailed, and only the story of the adventures of Proteus remains. At the end of the first volume Peregrine meets Agathon, who proceeds to recount the story of his life, so the greater part of the second volume is not *Proteus* but *Agathon*. Here, too, the original is much curtailed and rearranged. In the last pages Peregrine speaks again, and tells of his discovery of Psyche as his sister, and the reunion with Danaë, but the conclusion is left to conjecture.

Elrington understood German thoroughly and succeeded in making a continuous whole out of the curious amalgamation of the two works. The translation is rather free, but not inaccurate. Only his style often lacks simplicity, and he is very fond of such expressions as "superlatively dazzling charms," and "the alabaster whiteness of those beauteous orbs blushed with roseate hue," etc.

The *Critical*[1] this time condemns *Proteus* even more severely than before. The adventures are said to be scarcely probable, the descriptions neither antique, appropriate, nor quite decent; *Agathon*, here reintroduced, ought, in the opinion of this critic, to have instead been condemned to everlasting oblivion, and the English reader would have lost little had both

[1] III. 359; 1804.

it and the *Confessions* remained in their Teutonic garb. The *Confessions* were also shortly mentioned in the *Monthly Magazine*,[1] with the comment that Wieland has here tried to describe Grecian manners and Grecian systems, but without much success.

Oberon.—We must now return to the year 1798 for the most noteworthy translation from Wieland—Sotheby's *Oberon*, the work which more than any other made Wieland's reputation in England,[2] and by which—together with his translation of Virgil—Sotheby's own name is most likely to live.

But before treating of Sotheby's translation, an earlier attempt must be mentioned. Probably scarcely one in a hundred of those who know Sotheby's *Oberon* are aware that another translation had been made, fourteen years before, yet never published, mainly because of Wieland's disapproval of any translation of his works. Hence the attempt was forgotten and recalled from oblivion only within the last few years.[3] The translator was James Six[4] who, in September, 1781, went to Braunschweig as tutor to J. Stanley (one of the translators of *Lenore*). Both took lessons in German from Eschenburg. During one year in Braunschweig Six studied German literature, prose and poetry with zeal and avidity. *Oberon* gave him special delight, and in 1782 he wrote to Eschenburg

[1] XVIII. 594; 1804.

[2] It played a certain part in the English romantic movement of the time.

[3] W. A. Colwell, *The First English Translation of Wieland's Oberon. Mod. Lang. Notes*, XXII. 95; 1907.

[4] James Six, Jr., son of James Six, Sr., of Canterbury (†1796), the author of several scientific works. James Six, Jr., went abroad and died at Rome in 1786, aged twenty-nine. A notice in the *Gent.'s Mag.*, January, 1787, says: "He was a young man of great natural ability and extensive learning. He understood the Hebrew, Greek, Latin, Italian, French and German languages, and in most, if not all of them, had a well-grounded and accurate knowledge. Two beautiful Odes, translated from the German, give no mean idea of his poetical powers." These two Odes from Stolberg appeared in the *Gent.'s Mag.*, 1784.

from London that he had begun a translation of it. In January, 1784, he sent him from Montpellier a specimen from Book IX., saying he had finished ten Books.

Eschenburg judged the translation very favourably and showed the stanzas to Wieland, who, however, while commending the translation as such, expressed very strong objections to *any* translation of the work in a foreign language. His letters to Eschenburg in the subject are both curious and interesting, and some passages may be quoted from them here.[1] Having first thanked Eschenburg for the pleasure he received from the specimens of the translation of his *Oberon*, Wieland continues:

" Ganz offenherzig zu reden, erschrecke ich allemal, wenn ich von einer Übersetzung irgend eines meiner Werke in eine ausländische Sprache höre . . . ich bin wenigstens sehr überzeugt dass keines meiner Werke seines Inhalts wegen für Nationen die in jener Betrachtung so viel vor uns voraus haben, interessant sein kann. Die Form, das Colorit, die Musik, der Versification kann vielleicht einen *Oberon* für einzelne Ausländer, die ihn im Original lesen . . . als eine Art von Phänomen unterhaltend machen ; so ungefehr, wie es lustig genug wäre, einen Bären mit einer Art von Grazie tanzen zu sehen ; aber dann fühle ich nur desto stärker, wie wenig selbst von diesem, mir eben nicht sehr schmeichelhaften Interesse, das ich und meinesgleichen, Engländern, Franzosen und Italiänern, durch die überraschende Verwunderung, dass die Sprache der Musen aus Organen wie die unsrigen doch noch so menschenähnlich klingt, gewähren können, wie wenig, sage ich, von diesem geringen Verdienste selbst, in einer Übersetzung übrig bleibt, und wie mir insonderheit, der nichts zu verlieren hat, der mit seiner Sprache, mit seinen Versen, beynahe Alles verliert, selbst durch die beste Übersetzung so viel genommen wird, dass mir ganz unbegreiflich ist, was man zu London oder Paris mit dem Übrigbleibenden machen soll. Sie sehen also, dass ich meine Stimme nie dazu geben würde, noch jemals gegeben hätte, wenn ich von jedem der mir die unverdiente Ehre mich zu übersetzen erweisen will, oder schon erwiesen hat, zuvor gefragt würde und gefragt worden wäre. Kurz ein Gedicht kann sehr gut für die Nation seyn, für die es geschrieben ist, zumal in einem Zeitpunkte wo ihre Litteratur erst anfängt einige Gestalt zu gewinnen ; und sehr unbedeutend für Nationen, die schon lange im Besitz aller Arten von Werken, des Genies, des Witzes und der Laune sind, und es in allem diesem zu einer Vollkommenheit

[1] See Schorr's *A.f.L.G.*, XIII. 503.

gebracht haben, die bey uns nicht einmal möglich ist. Diese und ähnliche Betrachtungen . . . konnen und sollen mich doch nicht verhindern, dem Talent ihres Freundes Gerechtigkeit widerfahren zu lassen, und sowohl die Geistesgaben als die Geduld und Beharrlichkeit zu bewundern welche dazu gehört, ein so langes Gedicht in gleichmässige gereimte englische Stanzen überzutragen. Ich müsste sehr undankbar sein, wenn ich ohne Gefühl für die Ehre wäre die Er mir dadurch erweist; und viel mehr über die menschlichen Schwächheiten hinweggesezt als ich bin . . . um nicht auf eine sehr angenehme Art durch den Gedanken gekitzelt zu werden, dass mein *Oberon*, für den ich selbst eine Art von Vorliebe habe nicht ohne Erröthen gestehen muss, einem Engländer Liebe genug einflössen konnte, um dem Gedanken ihn in Brittannien zu naturalisiren nicht widerstehen zu können. Indessen sehe ich doch bey allem dem mit der grössten Wahrscheinlichkeit voraus, dass *Oberon* in England nur eine sehr schwache Sensation machen, ja von den Reviewers vielleicht noch schlimmer empfangen werden wird, als ehemals *Agathon*, und ich wünschte daher wohl eben so sehr um Herrn Six als um meines armen Selbsts willen, dass er diese Arbeit bloss als eine Art von gymnastischer Übung seines Geistes ansehen, der Welt und seiner Nation aber sich lieber durch eigene Ihm rühmlichere Arbeiten zeigen wollte" (March 25th, 1784).

In a further letter of May 17th, Wieland expressed agreement with Eschenburg on two points: "Nehmlich, dass die englische Sprache gerade diejenige ist worinn *Oberon* am wenigsten verlieren wird, und dass Herr Six die Mine hat mit diesem eben nicht sehr leichten Abenteuer zu seiner und meiner Ehre zu stande zu kommen," and gave his consent to a specimen of Six's work being printed in the *Deutsches Museum*. The fragment appeared in September, 1784,[1] but Six was —naturally enough—discouraged by Wieland's attitude, and though he had completed the whole poem in May, 1784, he never published it. It would be interesting if the manuscript were found. Six died in Rome only two years later, aged twenty-nine.

Six translated from the 1780 edition in fourteen books.[2] In form his translation is a closer imitation of the original than Sotheby's, keeping the eight-line

[1] II. 232-247.

[2] The stanzas given in the *Deut. Mus.*, Book IX. 52-57, are Book VIII. 14-29, in the edition in twelve Books (1790) used by Sotheby.

stanza, the same metre and almost the same rhymes. It is very literal, and the meaning is usually well brought out. But there are cases where Six quite misses the point—*e.g.*:

> "Wie hätt ihm jetzt die Hütte, wo er kaum
> Noch glücklich war, nicht schrecklich werden sollen?"

is not

> "His cot, that refuge of calamity,
> How shall he now its recollection bide?"
> (Canto LV.)

And "im Rausch des Selbstbetrugs" is not "midst the fire of youth." As far as one can judge from the few stanzas it is a less poetical rendering than Sotheby's, but it has good points, and it is a pity that Wieland's attitude prevented the publication. It would be interesting to have the two different versions of the poem.

Here is a specimen of Six's work:

> "His mien that innate excellence bespoke,
> Which under meanest weeds lies ill-conceal'd;
> His look his soul's philanthropies reveal'd;
> And, tho' his neck was bowed by age's yoke,
> Seem'd ever turned to heaven. Composure sate
> And homefelt comfort, on his brows sedate;
> And like the rock, which nether storms defies,
> His cloudless front appear'd above the world to rise."
> (IX. 52. In 1790 ed., VIII. 14.)

Sotheby,[1] probably—and one may add fortunately—quite unaware of Wieland's bann on a translation of

[1] *William Sotheby* (1757–1833). Born in London, educated at Harrow, entered the 10th Dragoons at seventeen; married and retired in 1780, and devoting himself to a literary life, became a prominent figure in London literary society, and knew Scott, Wordsworth, Coleridge, Southey, Miss Edgeworth, Byron, Moore, etc. Neither his original verse nor his historical tragedies had much success, but his skill as a translator secured for him a wide literary reputation. He printed his translation of the *Georgics* with Voss's German and other translations. He also translated Homer. In 1816 he toured in Italy and returned by Germany in 1817, and published his impressions of this tour in *Poems*. He died in London, 1833.

Oberon, published his version of the work in 1798,[1] after rapidly acquiring a knowledge of German for the purpose. The want of some kind of preface or introduction to the work is regretted by H. Crabb Robinson in a letter to the *Monthly Magazine* (February, 1800). He says: " The Legend of Huon is not very well known to English readers, and we naturally seek information about what so much delighted us." He calls *Oberon* " the most valuable present to our national literature from the German."

In his translation Sotheby has not reproduced exactly the original metre, which is the Italian " ottava rime " altered freely as Wieland thought would best suit the different character of the German language. Sotheby has transformed this into a distinctly English metre—the nine-line Spenserian stanza, which was based on a Middle English eight-line popular stanza, modelled in its turn on a well-known Old French ballad stanza.[2] This Spenserian stanza became very popular with English poets. Sotheby chose it for his *Oberon*, but made a slight change in the rhyme formula, his ninth line rhyming with the fifth and sixth, and not with the sixth and eighth as in Spenser. The English *Oberon* with its fixed rhymes, definite number of feet in each line and regular cæsura in the ninth line reads on the whole more smoothly than the original. The translation is faithful, but the sense has often to be much extended to fill out the extra line. Sometimes Sotheby expands the last two lines to three, or often adds a completely new line—*e.g.*:

> " Ei, ei, wo denkst du hin, erwidert Siegwine's Sohn,
> Wo hörtest du dass Franken je geflohen ?"

---

[1] *Oberon, a poem from the German of Wieland*, by William Sotheby, Esq. (London, 1798). Second edition, 1805, with illustrations by Fuseli ; third edition, 1826 ; another edition, 1844.

[2] See Schipper's *History of English Versification*, II. 7.

becomes:

"Ha, friend, what think'st thou then? says Sigwine's son,
Was ever known a Frank his foe to shun?
Right onward lies our path though hostile hordes infest."
(II. 2.)

This enforced amplification of the original is the necessary drawback of the nine-line stanza, and Sotheby, on this account, was a good deal criticised for his choice. W. Taylor in the *Annual Review*[1] (1800) considers that the superfluous line often gives a trailing character to the narrative. Otherwise he praises Sotheby's version for its "smoothness of versification, elegance of phrase and majesty of diction." The *Monthly*[2] also regrets the diffuseness brought about by the extension to nine lines. Later critics have judged more favourably of Sotheby's choice of stanza, thinking it the most suitable for a long English poem. The extra line gives an impressive conclusion to the stanza, and it must be admitted that the added lines are always in the spirit of the original, and fit logically into the whole.[3]

The following stanza is a very good example of Sotheby's style:

"In other worlds, in realms of fairy-land
She seems to pass; and sure, had never seen
The heaven so blue, the lap of earth so green
Or leaf so fresh on vernal bow'r expand;
For where the mountains round in guardian rows
Shelter the bosom that their heights enclose,
And fence from blasts that on their summits beat,
Grapes richly clustering swell with genial heat;
Dark hangs the ripening fig, the golden orange glows."
(VIII. 12.)

---

[1] V. 499.
[2] XXVI. 567; 1798.
[3] Sotheby omits Sherasmin's tale (VI. 35-85), considering it sufficiently known to English readers by the *January and May* of Pope.

Or the following, where the first two lines seem to me especially good:

> " In vain the night with vapour-laden wing
> Enwraps the viewless canopy above ;
> No darkness dims the all-seeing power of love—
> There eyes whence rays of light celestial spring
> Each in the other fix'd their souls behold.
> Night is not night to them—but ever roll'd
> Heaven and Elysium, round and round them flow—
> Their sunshine from within expands its glow
> And rous'd at every look, new senses sweet unfold."
>
> (V. 85.)

These extracts are sufficient to show Sotheby's manner of treatment. The translation is uneven, some parts being much better than others; but taken as a whole it is certainly the best poetical translation of the time, and one of the finest in English. It shows a thorough knowledge of German, great command of expression and mastery of verse and literary taste, though it just lacks real poetic power. The descriptive parts are the best, as for instance that of the whole court madly dancing (l. 47 *ff.*). In dialogue it often misses the force and directness of the original.

Reviews of *Oberon* appeared in all the leading periodicals. Some have been already quoted.[1] The *Analytical*[2] praises it as " a highly polished translation of a highly polished poem," and gives a long analysis with many extracts. The *British Critic*[3] says that *Oberon* will delight all those for whom poetry hath charms, and considers that Sotheby has conferred on his author a new spirit and a new grace, and in some cases even improved on his original. (In one case at least the critic seems right—*i.e.*, I. 28.) This critic is

[1] A French translation of *Oberon* by De Boaten was noticed in *Gent.'s Mag.*, LV. 387 ; 1785. It gives a short notice of Wieland and a sketch of the poem, and hopes for a good English translation of it.

[2] XXVIII. 279 ; 1798.

[3] XII. 515 ; 1798.

specially pleased that *Oberon* is free from any trace of the infidelity, democracy and general tone of modern philosophy, which abounds in the *Dialogues*. The *Critical*,[1] on the other hand, considers that the merits of *Oberon* have been greatly exaggerated, and that it contains little to elevate the mind or amend the heart. It will be popular merely because it is lively and licentious. *Oberon* was also noticed in the *Analytical*[2] and the *Monthly Magazine*.[3]

Sotheby's *Oberon* was mentioned in 1801 in the *Neue Bibliothek der schönen Wissenschaften*,[4] and criticised on the whole justly. The critic says: "Er ist mit Sorgfalt gearbeitet. Die Versification ist sanft und harmonisch; doch ist sein Ausdruck im Ganzen etwas weitschweifig und bisweilen schwach."

It may be interesting to quote here the opinion—not indeed very favourable—of two great English poets on *Oberon*. Southey says in a letter to W. Taylor, February 24th, 1799: "Judging by what I hear and feel, I do not think the *Oberon* will be popular in England, at least not in Sotheby's translation. It only diverts, it does not kindle the imagination; it does not agitate and make the heart beat like the wonders of Ariosto and Tasso. Wieland's opinion of the effect of story is contrary to all experience—witness the *Thebaid*—witness the *Henriade*."

Wordsworth[5] gives his opinion of *Oberon* in his account of the visit to Klopstock in 1790: "I told him the *Oberon* had just been translated into English. He asked if I was not delighted with the poem. I answered that I thought the story began to flag about the seventh or eighth book, and observed that it was unworthy of a man of genius to make the interest of a

[1] XXIV. 58; 1798.
[2] XXVIII. 283.
[3] X. 201; 1801.
[4] 1799, p. 311.
[5] See W. Knight's *Life of Wordsworth*, I. 175; 1889. Coleridge apparently once tried his hand at a translation of *Oberon* (*vide* Stokoe, *German Influence*, etc., p. 98).

long poem turn entirely upon animal gratification. . . . I thought the passion of Love as well suited to the purposes of poetry as any other passion, but it was a cheap way of pleasing to fix the attention of the reader through a long poem on mere animal enjoyment. . . . It is the province of a great poet to raise people up to his own level, not to descend to theirs. Klopstock agreed and confessed that on no account whatsoever would he have written a work like the *Oberon*. He spoke in raptures of Wieland's style. . . . I said I did not perceive any very striking passages in the poem, but that I made allowance for the imperfections of a translation."[1]

Sotheby sent a copy of his translation to Wieland with a sonnet; at which the author expressed great satisfaction, and, this time, no displeasure at being translated. A translation of his letter on the subject "to a gentleman resident in England" (no name is given) was sent to the *Monthly Magazine* (October, 1798). The translation is rather carelessly done. The mistakes were pointed out by a contributor "A. B." the next month, who gave the original letter and a translation of his own, much better and correct except in one point, *i.e.*, "Sie hat alle Grazie *des* Originals" he translates "of *an* original," a different meaning.

Wieland's letter (also in the *Teutsche Merkur*) runs:

"Herrn Sotheby's Übersetzung machte mir ein überraschendes und noch in keinem ähnlichen Falle gefühltes Vergnügen; denn sie ist ein aechtes Meisterstück. Sie hat alle Grazie und Zierlichkeit des Originals und kann gleichwohl für ein Modell der Treue und Übersetzlicher Genauigkeit gelten . . . was Herr Sotheby geleistet hat ist so viel, und seine

[1] Sidney Colvin in his *Life of Keats* (1917) suggests that Keats was well acquainted with *Oberon* in Sotheby's translation, and quotes one passage from *The Cap and Bells*, where he "catches a strain reminiscent of *Oberon*" (vide *John Keats* [1917], p. 87).

Übersetzung ist in so hohem Grade 'con amore e gusto' aufgearbeitet, dass ich sehr ungerecht, ungenügsam und überlaunisch sein müsste wenn ich noch mehr forderte, und diesen in Old England wahrlich seltener Freund unsrer so lange dort verkannter Germanischen Literatur nicht recht vielen Dank dafür wüsste, mich auf eine so ehrenvolle Art den Britten bekannt gemacht zu haben."

Sotheby also wrote a masque called *Oberon* (1802) in blank verse, into which he wove some of the principal incidents of Wieland's poem. He has shown a good deal of ingenuity in moulding them into a dramatic form, and his language, specially in the fairy-songs, is harmonious and poetical. A melodrama founded on Sotheby's *Oberon—Oberon's Oath, or the Paladin and the Princess*, by Thompson—was acted at Drury Lane, May 21st, 1816. It was afterwards printed. There was a disturbance the first night, but it was favourably received on four other occasions.[1]

Oberon was dramatised a third time by Planché as *Oberon, or the Elf-King's Oath*, given at Covent Garden on April 12th, 1826. This seems to have been the most successful of the dramatisations, and ran to thirty-one performances.[2]

In a review of *Oberon* in 1806[3] W. Taylor refers to another translation of the poem begun some years before, but never published. Some specimens were circulated in private correspondence, and from one of these Taylor gives a few stanzas (I. 12-26) for comparison with Sotheby's. The unknown translator used the Chaucerian stanza of seven lines, with no fixed scheme of rhymes. This shorter stanza had many advantages, as it is always easier to condense than to extend the sense, and this translation is therefore sometimes simpler and more direct in expression

[1] *Genest.*, VIII. 535. [2] *Genest.*, IX. 349.
[3] *Annual Rev.*, V. 499; also *Hist. Surv.*, II. 408.

than Sotheby's. "But," as Taylor judges, "if Sotheby loses something of the easy familiarity and picturesque precision of the original *Oberon*, he makes ample amends by smoothness of versification, elegance of phrase and majesty of diction."

The following stanza gives a good idea of both translations:

"An unknown wood, a sky so raven black,
And what for the first time invades his ear,
The lion's thundering growl, now far, now near,
Amid the deadly stillness of the hour
Deep from the distant mountains bellow'd back—
The living wight who ne'er knew fear before
All this with ease I ween, might teach to tremble sore."
(*Annual Review.*)

"The starless gloom of raven feather'd night
That wrapped the welkin round, the wood unknown,
And, for the first time heard, the thundering tone
Of lions, that th' accustomed ear affright;
Tones, from the midnight death-like silence round
Fearfully echoing, on each side rebound,
As on from rock to rock their horrors roll'd:
These might have moved the stoutest warrior bold
And hearts unus'd to fear had trembled at the sound."
(SOTHEBY, I. 15.)

Oberon was the last important work of Wieland's translated before 1830. After this there are only a couple of minor works, and some fragments in periodicals, etc., mostly from the pen of W. Taylor.

In Taylor's *Tales of Yore* (1810) there are two from Wieland. One, *The Religion of Psamnius*,[1] is a detached episode taken from *The Golden Mirror*, the other *Koxkox and Kikequetzel*,[2] a tale imitated from Sterne. The *Critical*[3] called the latter a "silly reverie, showing that not *all* Wieland's works deserve translation."

In the *Monthly Magazine* of 1819[4] Taylor inserted a *Dialogue between Hecate, Luna and Diana*, and in the

[1] Vol. I. [2] Vol. III.
[3] XVIII. 443; 1810. [4] XLVII. 308.

same periodical in the following year[1] a *Dialogue between Brutus and Charlotte Corday*.[2] This dialogue is said to have had considerable influence in stimulating the student Sandt to the murder of Kotzebue (1820), and Taylor gives this as his reason for presenting it to the public "as a literary curiosity just at this moment."

Taylor's *Geron the Courteous* (from Wieland's Arthurian poem) appeared first in the *Monthly Magazine* of 1822.[3]

Two translations were made from Wieland in 1823, one possibly and the other certainly inspired by W. Taylor.

The first is a translation of a fairly early work of Wieland's, *Die Grazien* (1770).[4] No name appears on the title-page; but the Prefatory Remarks are signed with the monogram probably standing for Sarah Taylor, afterwards Sarah Austin,[5] well known for her efforts to make the best minds of Germany familiar to English readers. The work is copiously annotated, the notes giving explanations of the mythological allusions, and also parallels from Greek, Latin and

[1] XLIX. 211.

[2] From *Brutus und Corday, eine Unterredung*, 1793.

[3] LIV. 311; LVII. 406, 509; later in *Hist. Surv.*, II. 325.

[4] *The Graces, a classical allegory, interspersed with poetry and illustrated with explanatory notes: together with a poetical fragment entitled Psyche among the Graces.* Translated from the original German of Christopher Martin Wieland (London, Whittaker, 1823).

[5] *Sarah Austin*, 1793–1867. Born in Norwich. Her father, John Taylor, had literary tastes, and she received an excellent education under her mother. In 1820 she married John Austin, the jurist, and went to live in London, where she made many literary friends, among them J. S. Mill. In 1833 she published *Characteristics of Goethe*, translated from the German of F. von Müller, with valuable original notes illustrative of German literature. In 1827 she went to Germany with her husband and settled at Bonn. They remained many years abroad, living in Germany, Malta and France. During this time she collected materials for the work by which she is best known, *Germany*, 1760–1814 (1854); it is an interesting and thoughtful survey of Germany's institutions and manners. She also translated a *Tour by a German prince in England, Ireland and France*, 1832; Ranke's *History of the Popes* (1840), and his *Reformation in Germany* (1854).

modern literatures, specially Italian—Petrarch, Sanazarro, Maffei, Metastasio, etc. In connection with Book IV. an extract is given (in English) from Gessner's pastoral *Daphnis and Phyllis*, in order that the reader may compare it with Wieland's treatment of the same subject. These notes show a very wide knowledge of general literature.

The translation is usually correct, but the style is sometimes heavy and the verse translations especially often lack the lightness and grace of the originals; while a change of metre often alters their character. Yet sometimes the choice of a new metre is happy, as in this one of the most charming of the verse translations:

" Quick, with whisper soft she cries
Lest the sleeper ope his eyes.
Sisters, hither, tripping light,
Come, and view this beauteous sprite!
Maiden none, yet still as fair
As our fairest maidens are.[1]
Mark its locks of golden hue,
Shoulders mottled, white and blue:
Like a bird, it droops its head,
Couch'd upon a flowery bed.
Sisters, did you ever see
Such matchless form and symmetry?"

(" Schwestern, rief sie, doch nur mit halber Stimme," etc.
—Buch VI.)

W. Taylor reviewed *The Graces* in the *Monthly*,[2] praising the skill of the translator. *The Graces* was not noticed in the other reviews, and does not seem to have become popular in England. Hardly anyone today could read this mixture of allegory, mythology and pastoral; and even in 1823 the time of popularity of such works was already past.[3]

[1] There are often such impure rhymes, *e.g.*, office and trice; shone and lone, etc.

[2] CII. 333; 1823.

[3] One may note here that a French imitation of *Die Grazien* was published in London in 1771. (See Goedeke, IV. ii., p. 202.)

The other work from the same year is *Crates and Hipparchia*,[1] translated by C. R. Coke, a native of Norwich, afterwards for many years an assistant at the British Museum. The book was published by private subscription; and among the subscribers besides Taylor's own name, appear the names of most of his friends: Borrow, Robberds, etc.—proving that this work owed much to Taylor's influence and encouragement.[2] The translation is very fair.

The *Monthly*[3] praises the simplicity and fidelity of the translation, and speaks of Wieland as more popular in England than any other German writer except Goethe.

After this there only remain to be noted some fragments of translations in periodicals, and some pieces in the *Historic Survey*.

There are two articles with extracts on *Aristippus*:[4] the first a letter signed " Germanicus " in the *Literary Gazette* (1821),[5] giving an analysis of the work and a description of the philosophy of Socrates, together with an extract from Chapter XIII.; the second No. XXI. of the *Horæ Germanicæ* in *Blackwood*[6] (1825), giving a short sketch of Wieland's literary career. " He wrote this work after he had renounced the Platonic Philosophy and moroseness of his early opinions. . . . The character of Aristippus, founder of the Cyreniac sect, was exactly suited to be a vehicle of his new tones. Of all his works it is perhaps the best written. The characters are drawn with consummate art, every trait is minutely marked and yet, like a highly finished engraving, the minuteness and

[1] *Crates and Hipparchia, a tale in a series of letters*. Translated from the German of Christopher M. Wieland, by Charles Richard Coke (Norwich and London, 1823).

[2] *Cf*. G. Herzfeld, *W. Taylor*, p. 47.

[3] CIV. 441.

[4] H. C. Robinson once intended translating *Aristippus*, but gave up the idea on hearing that Mellish also was planning a translation (see letter of May 11, 1801). Mellish's translation never appeared.

[5] P. 24 and foll. nos.

[6] XVII. 673.

number of the lines never obtruding, only serve to present us with a beautiful and harmonious whole." Many extracts are given in quite good translation.

A fragment from *Der goldne Spiegel* was once translated in the *Lady's Magazine*, another in the interesting article already mentioned in the *Foreign Quarterly* (1828), and the episode from Chapter IV., *The Religion of Psamnius*, by Taylor, in the *Historic Survey*.[1] Another short piece in the same is the concluding scene of the opera *Rosamond*.[2]

The only translation in the *Historic Survey* appearing there for the first time is that of the *Wintermärchen*[3] (1776). In a letter to Southey, July 6th, 1804, W. Taylor had said: "I have been trying to translate Wieland's *King of the Black Isles*, but have stuck fast in displeasure." However, he succeeded in the task at a later date, since it appears here with the four other episodes which make up the narrative. The translation keeps the same metre, and though often free gives a good idea of the original. Taylor often adds a few lines of his own. A specimen may be given from the *Fisherman and the Genius*, as there is no other example here of Wieland's Tales in Verse.

> " Once more he throws his narrow bound,
> And flings the circling net around ;
> Then lands and draws the net aground,
> Plies his alternate handiworks,
> Watches the lessening ring of corks,
> And feels, with palpitating joy,
> His is not now a vain employ ;
>
> " He pulls against some weighty burden.
> 'Thank God ! I now shall have my guerdon ;
> My luck is turned, my chance is coming.
> How my poor brats, and my good woman,
> Will jump for joy, and laugh and cry.
> That father's load is of good omen.'
> So thought he, looking thankfully
> Up to the dawn-embellish'd sky.

[1] II. 296. [2] II. 480. [3] II. 379.

> " Hope's blushes are but transient glows;
> Soon were to follow ohs and woes;
> When he has slowly dragged his treasure
> Upon the pebbly beach,
> He only finds in sad displeasure
> Within his reach,
> O'ergrown with sea-weed, slime and shells,
> An ass's skull, and nothing else."

> (" Er wirft sein Netz noch einmal aus
> * * * * *
> Vermengt mit Rippen, Schlamm und Steinen."
> —II. 19-32.)

Before leaving the *Historic Survey*, there remains a mistake of Taylor's to be corrected. He says:[1] " At Tübingen Wieland also began an epic poem in Ossianic prose, entitled *Arminius, or Germany Freed*, which has been translated into English. He sent MSS. of first cantos to Bodmer . . . soliciting critical opinion of this literary patriarch, who thought well of specimen and printed a complimentary acknowledgement to his unknown correspondent." It is true that Wieland began an epic poem in hexameters under this title (1750-1), not knowing that at the same moment in the opposite literary camp Schönaich was writing an epic poem on the same subject, which he sent to Gottsched. In spite of Bodmer's approbation, Wieland himself was not satisfied with his work, and the fragment remained in MS. until published in 1882.[2] Hence it could scarcely have been translated into English in Taylor's lifetime. He had evidently heard of the translation of Schönaich's *Arminius* and mistook it for Wieland's.

It will have been noticed that several of Wieland's most important works were not translated at all before 1830. Of the *Aristippus* there are only the few extracts. Of *Musarion* and *Die Abderiten* nothing at

[1] II., p. 311.
[2] Muncker, *Deut. Lit. Denkm. d. XVIII. Jhr.*, VI., Heft.

all. W. Taylor in 1804 expressed a hope in the *Critical* that Sotheby would add *Musarion* to his admirable *Oberon*, and that *Die Abderiten* would soon find a translator. But his hopes were not fulfilled.

SOPHIE DE LA ROCHE (1731-1807).

Her novel, *Die Geschichte des Fräuleins von Sternheim*, was edited by Wieland (1771) and for many years passed as his work. Two English translations of it were made in 1776: (1) **The Story of Lady Sophia Sternheim*, by John Collyer; (2) **The Memoirs of Miss Sophie Sternheim*, by Edward Harwood.[1] According to the *Monthly*[2] the second is a much more pleasing version of a work " which abounds in striking sentiments and variety of character and incident, but has gross faults of extravagance and improbability."

[1] I found no copy of either of these. A later edition (Jones, 1797) in the Bodleian is entered under J. Collyer. In the Preface it is announced that the author is now known to be S. de la Roche, " one of the most amiable ladies of the age."

[2] LV. 157 and 319; 1776.

CHAPTER IV

A.—HERDER. B.—MINOR WRITERS OF THE "STURM UND DRANG": KLINGER; LEISEWITZ; SCHUBART

J. G. HERDER (1744-1803).

HERDER became known in England but slowly. The time of his greatest influence in Germany—of the publication of the *Fragmente* (1766-7), of the *Kritische Wälder* (1769), of his friendship with Goethe in Strassburg (1770)—was many years before the awakening of interest for German literature in England; and Herder's importance in connection with the whole "Sturm und Drang" movement was not recognised there until years after his death. As might be expected it was Herder's historical, theological and philosophical writings which first attracted the attention of English readers. "Their spirit appealed more particularly to the advanced teachers of England, for it was stimulated alike by the whole rationalistic awakening of Germany in the eighteenth century, and by the free thought of England."[1]

Some of his works were introduced in the original, and found a few, but these few diligent, readers. The *Monthly*[2] noticed *Vom Geist der Ebräischen Poesie* (1782) in 1784, recommending it warmly to all lovers of Hebrew literature, and gave a longer and very favourable account of it in 1789.[3] In the same magazine, between 1795 and 1800, there are notices from the pen of W. Taylor of many of Herder's shorter theological and devotional treatises. The first im-

[1] See *Herder and America*, by M. D. Learned. *German American Annals*, II. 9; 1904.

[2] LXX. 240.

[3] LXXX. 642.

portant translations date from 1800 and 1801. After this, for many years, nothing new appeared, and Herder seemed forgotten. But about 1820 we note a revival of interest in him. The year 1823 gave the first important critical account of Herder in De Quincey's Essay,[1] "which remains in many respects the most original estimate of Herder in the English language."[2]

W. Taylor's remarks on and translations from Herder first appeared as part of the *German Student* papers in the *Monthly Magazine* for 1821, and were expanded in the *Historic Survey*. These critical pages on Herder are among the best in the book. G. Herzfeld[3] quotes the passage beginning "Herder may be regarded as the Plato of the Christian world" as "ein Prachtstück Taylorischen Stiles." Further noteworthy criticism of Herder appeared about the same time in Carlyle's references to him in his Essays on Jean Paul and on Goethe.[4] The first important translations after 1801 date from 1827 and 1828. An anonymous poem, *Lines to the memory of Herder, the German Philosopher*, appeared in the *Gentleman's Magazine*[5] of the following year.

The first, and also the most noteworthy of the early translations, is that of Herder's *Ideen zur Philosophie der Geschichte der Menschheit* (1784-91), translated in 1800 by T. Churchhill.[6] In the Preface the translator expresses a good deal of diffidence with regard to his own work; but this very diffidence is rather a recommendation, for it shows him to have a real appreciation of German and of the work to be translated. Mr.

[1] Vide *De Quincey's Works*, XII. 116; 1880. In it some extracts are translated from the German Memoir of Herder. Tubingen, 1820. *Memoir of Herder*.

[2] *Vide* M. D. Learned.

[3] *W. Taylor*, p. 55.

[4] Vide *Critical Essays*, 1828.

[5] XCIX. ii., 89.

[6] *Outlines of a Philosophy of the History of Man*. Translated from the German of John Godfrey Herder by T. Churchhill (London, Johnson, 1800. Second edition in 1803).

Churchhill was evidently a genuine—even a too uncritical—admirer of Herder's work; and the long task was to him a labour of love. The work was done in collaboration with a friend, whose name is not mentioned. M. D. Learned calls this translation "admirably smooth and accurate," and says it is perhaps the best which up to this had appeared from German. High praise and well deserved. The long piece of work is carried out with the greatest care and thoroughness, showing clear understanding of the original text, with power of expressing the ideas in good English.

Take the following passage, not an easy one (Herder is speaking of Bonnet's *Philosophie der Keime* in connection with man's hope of immortality):

> "This system appears to me too, to be altogether inapplicable to the subject; for we speak not here of young creatures descending from a creature of the same kind, but of a dying creature, which springs up to a new state of existence. Indeed if it were exclusively true with regard to the generation of terrestrial beings and all our hope rested upon this, it would oppose insuperable doubts to this hope."[1]

Churchhill generally keeps very closely to the German, yet knows where to translate more freely—*e.g.*, "Seine verdorrete Krone tut uns leid; wir trauern um eine verwelkende Blume. Auch das Krümmern eines zerquetschten Wurmes ist einem zarten Menschen nicht gleichgültig," he translates: "We regret its blighted top; we lament the withering of a faded flower. A feeling man views not the writhing of a bruised worm with indifference." There are, however, occasional inaccuracies. One occurs at the beginning of the preface, where "Beiträge" is twice

[1] "Ja, diese Philosophie ist, wie much dünkt, auch hieher ganz ungehörig, da wir hier nicht von Absprossung eines Geschöpfs in junge Geschöpfe seiner Art, sondern von Aufsprossung des absterbenden Geschöpfs in ein neues Dasein reden; vielmehr setzte sie, wenn sie auch nur in der irdischen Generation ausschliessend wahr wäre und alle Hoffnung auf ihr beruhte, dieser Hoffnung unüberwindliche Zweifel entgegen."

translated by "Supplements" instead of "Contributions." He always renders "Vielleicht" as "probably," not "perhaps." The difficult word "Kultur" he always gives as "cultivation," which in a few cases is the most suitable equivalent; but in others "civilisation" would have been better—*e.g.*, in "die Geschichte der Kultur" (Preface, p. 1), which he gives as "history of cultivation." One must remember the difficulties of Herder's style. Even good German scholars today find it most difficult. He has often picturesque and telling expressions, not to be translated literally; and yet much is lost by putting his idea in a form more commonplace. Churchhill as translator has kept as much as perhaps is possible of Herder's spirit. In the following he quite catches the tone of Herder:

> "The breath of our mouths is the picture of the world, the type that exhibits our thoughts and feelings to the mind of another. All that man has ever thought, willed, done, or will do, of human, upon Earth, has depended on the movement of a breath of air; for if this divine breath had not inspired us and floated like a charm on our lips, we should all have still been wanderers in the woods."[1]

The work itself did not please all reviewers, but all praised the translation. A review in the *Critical*[2] gives the outline of each book with long extracts, recommending specially Book X. as "highly valuable and original." It defends Herder against the charge of infidelity, and says that "the purest religion and warmest benevolence breathe on every page." The highly orthodox *British Critic*,[3] on the contrary, judges it harshly. The reviewer says he has "taken up the book with reluctance, gone through it with tardiness

[1] "Ein Hauch unseres Mundes wird das Gemälde der Welt; der Typus unserer Gedanken und Gefühle in des Andern Seele. Von einem bewegten Lüftchen hängt alles ab, was Menschen je auf der Erde Menschliches dachten, wollten, thaten oder thun werden; denn alle liefen wir noch in den Wäldern, umher, wenn nicht dieser göttliche Odem uns angehaucht hätte und wie ein Zauberton auf unsern Lippen schwebte."

[2] XXX. i., 169; 1800.

[3] XXI. 154; 1800.

and distaste and laid it down with feeling of despair of ever meeting with satisfaction from the fashionable philosophy or metaphysics of Germany." The sublimity which the translator ascribes to the ideas of Herder seems to him "more like extravagance," and he expresses much satisfaction that there are no signs of either Herder or the still more obscure and extravagant Kant ever becoming famous in England. The *Monthly*[1] speaks in a more moderate and friendly tone. But after allowing that many of Herder's views are striking and just, many of his declamatory pages fine and animating, and that he proves himself throughout to be "a man of great information, liberal views, and of singular impartiality," the reviewer judges that Herder has fallen into the error common to his countrymen of trying to treat of too much, and of confounding what has no necessary connection, and should be kept asunder. "Taken as a systematic work, which it affects to be, nothing more desultory, or more deficient in proportion, ever came from the hands of an able and intelligent man. . . ."

In the following year (1801) there appeared *Oriental Dialogues*,[2] an anonymous and abridged translation of Herder's *Vom Geist der Ebräischen Poesie*. We have already mentioned the two notices of the original in the *Monthly*. The translator refers to the later of these, taking it to have been written on what he thought was the first publication of the work (Leipzig, 1787), not aware that this is the second edition, the first dating 1782 (Dessau).[3] He introduces the *Dialogues* as

[1] XLI. 403-420.

[2] *Oriental Dialogues: containing the Conversations of Eugenius and Alciphron on the Spirit and Beauties of the Sacred Poetry of the Hebrews*, selected from the German dialogues and dissertations of Herder (London, Cadell and Davies, 1801). The first translation of the complete work was made in America in 1833: *The Spirit of Hebrew Poetry*, translated by J. Marsh, Burlington, Vt., 1833.

[3] Both editions are identical except for title-page. See *Herder's Sämmtliche Werke*, B. Supphan, XII.

"an interesting specimen of the piety, genius and taste of Herder, whose name has been long distinguished in the annals of theology, philosophy and literature." He gives eight Dialogues in abridged form, and does not follow exactly the order of the original. The translation is clear and accurate, though the translator treats his text rather freely, evidently with the intention of making it more comprehensible to English readers. In the passages taken from the Bible, he has used the text of the Authorised Version.

The *Monthly*[1] was the only important review which noticed the work. It expresses entire agreement with the opinion of the translator that Herder is a poetical and philosophical, rather than a theological, critic, but considers that, though much of Herder's interpretation may be wild and visionary, this should not deter us from encouraging him; all free and fearless enquiry is valuable, if it shed any ray of light on the interesting subject of the Hebrew Scriptures.

There is a gap of twenty-six years between the *Oriental Dialogues* (1801) and the next translation from Herder: *Über den Ursprung der Sprache* (1827).[2] The anonymous translator in his Preface discusses at some length the distinguishing characteristics of the English and the German mind. The Germans, he says, have effected much in the sphere of the speculative life, the English in the sphere of the practical life. His own wish is "to be instrumental to more amalgamation between the Germans and English, as between internal and external life, and to counteract the prejudicial influence of the distorted judgments given in some English critiques of German works." This reciprocal approach, he considers, can be best accomplished by the exposition of the noble gifts which God has bestowed on every nation, and for this Herder's

[1] XXXIX. 134; 1802.

[2] *Treatise upon the origin of language*. Translated from the German of J. G. von Herder (London, Longman, etc. 1827).

works are pre-eminently fitted, since they show forth so clearly "that deep, internal state of existence peculiar to the Germans."

The translation is accurate and careful, showing both a thorough knowledge of German and familiarity with Herder's thought. But it is not idiomatic English; the sentences being often long and obscure and constructed on German models. Judging from this and from the tone of the preface it seems probable that the translator was a German resident in England. This treatise on language—a subject of interest to very few—seems to have been little noticed in England. The *Monthly*[1] gives a short summary of Herder's arguments for the exclusive human invention of language, remarking that the whole subject has not yet been seriously studied in England.

The following year gives another anonymous translation of a very different work—the lyrical epopee: *Der Cid, nach spanischen Romanzen gesungen*.[2] In the introduction the translator gives a short account of the story of the Cid, and discusses Herder's manner of treatment. "The portraiture," he writes, "is throughout deeply impressive. The little separate poems, like sunny rays, diffuse a light even over the remotest background of the picture." He says translating has been easy, as the versification is so little restricted. The poem is written in trochaic rhythm, for the greatest part in four-accent, unrhymed lines grouped into stanzas of unequal length. This metre is reproduced exactly in the translation, generally even with the feminine rhymes. The simple, direct and "volkstümlich" language here lends itself easily to another language so akin as English. The metre, too, is one often used in English poems. It is wonderful how, in such a literal translation, the versification

[1] VI. 132; 1827.

[2] *The Cid*, translated from the German of J. G. von Herder (London, Graves, 1828).

can be so good. Yet one feels that a little more care could have made it still better, and avoided some metrical imperfections. The sense is sometimes too much broken by the division of the lines.

The opening verses show the translation at its best—*e.g.*,

> "Deeply brooding, Don Diego
> Sat, no mortal e'er so gloomy;
> Full of grief, he daily, nightly
> Dwelt but on his house's shame.
>
> * * * * *
>
> "Deeply wounded, weak and aged
> Towards his grave he felt declining,
> While his pow'rful foe, Don Gomez
> Unopposed maintained the field.
>
> "Sleep and food he now refuses,
> Casts his eyes upon the ground,
> Steps not forth beyond his threshold,
> Speaks not even with his friends;
>
> "Hears no more their friendly counsel,
> When they come to soothe his sorrow,
> For the breath of one dishonoured
> Must, he thinks, disgrace his friend."

In a few places Herder varies the metre to five-accent lines, reproduced in the translation—*e.g.*,

> "Rather 'neath the feet of heathen chargers
> Let us die all maimed and trod to pieces,
> Than that one amid the living Christians
> With disgrace should banish us their board."
>
> (Canto LI., v. 6.)

Again, in Canto XIV., a lyrical dialogue between Rodrigue and Ximene in free rhythm of irregular lines, the English adopts the same, only without rhyme—*e.g.*,

> XIMENE.
>
> In the gloomy midnight hour
> When my deepest grief awakes
> Who comes to me?

RODRIGUE.

Perhaps some hostile ear
May listen to us here,
So open me.

XIMENE.

To one unnamed,
To one unknown
At midnight hour no door
—Can be unclosed—
Declare thyself—
Who art thou, speak?

An example has been given of each kind of metre used, and stress laid on the translator reproducing the original metres so exactly, because in this poem so much of characteristic charm depends on the metre, and it would have been completely lost had the translator foolishly chosen a metre of his own. As it is, her version, retaining much of the poetical verve of the original, makes pleasant reading. But it was apparently little read at the time.

The only other poetical translations from Herder are those by W. Taylor in his chapter on Herder in the *Historic Survey*[1]—small pieces from Herder's *Volkslieder* (1788-9), and the different collections of the *Zerstreute Blätter* (1785-1792). Taylor gives a few distichs, "in the manner of Herder," from the *Blumen aus der griechischen Anthologie*.[2] And he quotes a large portion of the preface to this little collection. From *Bilder und Träume*[3] he gives one pretty little poem—*To a dragon-fly*. From the pieces translated from Persian poetry, *Blumen aus morgenländischen Dichtern gesammelt*,[4] and the imitations of Eastern poetry, *Gedanken einiger Brahmen*, Taylor also gives a few examples. His last specimens are two of the

[1] III. 9 *ff*.
[2] *Zerstreute Blätter*, I.
[3] *Ibid.*, III.
[4] *Ibid.*, IV.

Negro Idylls, "which show," he says, "not the smooth, painless incidents of Arcadian life, but the real miseries, which every year's slave-trade repeats on the African and American shores; they are written with the tear-dipt pen of humanity." In all these poems Taylor has translated very simply and literally, rather to give a faithful representation of Herder's manner, than a finished English poem.

Taylor also gives several of Herder's short prose sketches, three from the *Paramythien*,[1] "mythological allegories, remarkable for the gracefulness of garb under which they veil the form of instruction"; and three from the *Blätter der Vorzeit*, "parables in the style of early Oriental tradition, which display an inventive and truly poetical imagination."

Two of the Paramythien were translated in the *Literary Gazette* of 1826:[2] *The Morning Hour* and *The Choice of Flora*, signed "S. H. H." The second is also one of those given by W. Taylor; but the translations are entirely different, "S. H. H.'s" being free and the original much amplified, Taylor's literal and exact.

There is one small work of Herder's, which appeared in England earlier than any other, but is placed here at the end, because when published, and for many years after, it was attributed to Goethe. Therefore it cannot be taken as showing the development of interest in Herder in England. It is a treatise: *A Tribute to the Memory of Ulrich von Hutten*,[3] of which the original came out as *Denkmal Ulrichs von Hutten* in the *Teutsche Merkur* in 1776. The trans-

[1] The first of these, *Sleep*, had already appeared in the *Monthly Mag.*, LI. 36; 1821. In the same volume appeared also a *Fragment on Shakespeare*, from Herder, translated by W. Taylor (409).

[2] Pp. 61, 94.

[3] *A Tribute to the Memory of Ulrich von Hutten* . . . translated from the German of Goethe, the celebrated Author of the *Sorrows of Werther*, by Anthony Aufrere, Esq., illustrated with Remarks by the Translator and an Appendix (London, Dodsley, 1789).

lator, Anthony Aufrere,[1] was in Germany at the time he wrote, and a passage in his Preface (Stuttgart, June 10th, 1788) shows that the mistake of attributing the work to Goethe was already being made in Germany. He writes: " Upon the perusal of the following sketch of the life of Ulric of Hutten, I was no less struck with the interest of the subject, than with the enthusiasm and bold irregularity of the style, which betrayed the hand of a master; and upon enquiry, I found that it had been written by Goethe, one of the most ingenious, elegant and nervous writers in Germany, and author of various works, amongst which that entitled *The Sorrows of Werter* is probably the most known in England, and has established his reputation."

The translation was suggested to Aufrere by a Baron von Uexküll, of Würtemberg. Aufrere says this is his first essay in translating and his " novel acquaintance with the German language which abounds with beauties and difficulties " render him diffident of his success; his greatest endeavour has been to " keep as closely as possible to the text " and to " catch the spirit of the author." Had he sacrificed some of the " closeness " and the " spirit " to writing English, he would have succeeded better. That he *could* write English is apparent from the style of the preface, but most of the translation is execrable. The longer sentences are often so unwieldy and cumbersome that it is almost impossible to get at the meaning. He can write:

" When a young, honourable and ardent man, already in those years which others wile away like plants, becomes a man for his country and early quits the lazy mode of life of the monks (there are monks in

[1] Anthony Aufrere, born 1756. Antiquary. From early life he showed an aptitude for foreign languages. Besides the work mentioned here, he translated a book of *Travels in Naples* from the German of Salis (1789). A small work which excited much attention was a political pamphlet entitled *Warning to Britons against French perfidy and cruelty* (1798). Aufrere lived much abroad and died at Pisa, 1833.

every condition), even because perhaps his genius has whispered him that he will not be enabled long to do so, he strives to do what he can, freely prefers to suffer adversity with the good, and for the general welfare, and to sacrifice rank, fortune, repose, life, and honour, nor suffers himself to be intimidated by any fresh peril, until the close of his short and tempestuous life."

G. Herzfeld[1] says of this work: "Die Übersetzung ist recht gut, sie steht entschieden über den Durchschnitt"! He must surely have pronounced this judgment upon insufficient acquaintance! It is not quite as bad all through as the sentence quoted above; but could any translation be called good, with even *one* such sentence?

The citations from Hutten's and Sickingen's letters are left in the original. The Appendix contains extracts from some of Hutten's works, a list of them, and some other notes.

A couple of reviews noticed the *Tribute*. The *Analytical*[2] finds that "even through the mist of this translation written in very uncouth English, we discover the fire of the Author of *Werther*." But the *Monthly Review*[3] disapproves of the work as being an exaggerated and injudicious panegyric, unworthy of any real man of letters.

B. Minor Writers of the "Sturm und Drang"

Only the principal works of the "Sturm und Drang" literature—*e.g.*, *Lenore*, *Götz*, and *Die Räuber*[4]—were translated into English towards the end of the century. Of the lesser writers representing the movement, little or nothing was known.

[1] *W. Taylor*, p. 11. [2] IV. 163; 1789.
[3] II. 88; 1790.
[4] See under Bürger, Goethe and Schiller.

Minor Writers

F. M. VON KLINGER (1752-1831).

Klinger was the only one whose works appeared a couple of times in translation, but these apparently did not make his name much known in England. Gillies in an article on the *Modern German Drama*,[1] in the *Foreign Quarterly* (1827), speaks of Klinger as "hitherto unnoticed in this country, though well known in his own as a bold dramatist and philosophic novelist." Gillies calls him "the greatest of Goethe's youthful contemporaries," and attributes to him—without much justification—a great influence on the author of *Faust*.

Of Klinger's youthful dramas only one of the least noteworthy, *Die neue Arria* (1776), was translated into English; it was never acted. The first scene first appeared in a periodical, the *Philosophical Herald*, and according to the anonymous translator was so well received that it induced him to present the whole as *The Modern Arria*.[2] He expresses in the Preface the most extravagant admiration for Klinger, and surprise that his extraordinary abilities should have attracted so little attention in his own country, where Schiller is actually held in higher estimation [*sic*]. The translator hopes that England will have the exclusive honour "of doing that justice to Klinger's merit which has hitherto been denied him by his own country and the rest of Europe." The reception of *The Modern Arria* by the reviews showed that few were found to endorse the translator's opinion of Klinger. The *Analytical*[3] points out as the play's principal characteristics: unnatural characters, improbable incidents, extravagant passion, ranting language and an

[1] I. 565 *ff.* Part of the Preface to *Konradin* is translated in this article.

[2] *The Modern Arria.* A Tragedy in Five Acts, translated from the German of F. M. Klinger (London, Boosey and Escher, 1795).

[3] XXII. 520; 1795.

absurd plot which violently outrages all nature; and the reviewer can nowhere discover "that degree of excellence which would uphold the translator's opinion." The *Monthly*[1] exclaims: "What of a critic who invites us to prefer Klinger to Goethe and Schiller!" The translation as such is mediocre. Klinger's style is full of fire and passion—the very essence of the "Sturm und Drang," and it would need a poet of the same fiery genius to translate it adequately. The translation often seems flat and prosaic beside the original. One must not forget, however, that the whole work is the product of a past age, and that what seems to us exaggerated or obscure in the English version is not all the fault of the translator.

In the following year (1796) came a translation of Klinger's *Reisen vor der Sündfluth* (1794), a fantastic description of the Oriental world, purporting to be taken from Oriental sources. The translation was given without Klinger's name, as genuinely taken from the Arabic.[2] Only many years later was it traced to its German source.

About thirty years elapse before we come to the next translation from Klinger—his Faust novel: *Faustus: Leben, Thaten und Höllenfahrt* (1791);[3] chiefly interesting as being the first work by George Borrow.[4] According to Borrow's biographer, Dr.

[1] XX. 472; 1796.

[2] *Travels before the Flood. An Interesting Oriental Record of men and manners in the Antediluvian World; interpreted in fourteen Evening Conversations between the Caliph of Bagdad and his Court.* Translated from the Arabic (London, Robinson, 1796).

[3] *Faustus: his Life, Death and Descent into Hell.* Translated from the German (London, Simpkin and Marshall, 1825).

[4] *George Borrow* (1803–1881), the author of *Lavengro* and the *Romany Rye*. The acquisition of languages was his favourite pursuit. At seventeen he had already studied seven—Latin, Greek, Irish, French, Italian and Gipsy, and soon began seven more, including German. While he was in a solicitor's office in Norwich (1819–24) he was a frequent guest at the house of W. Taylor, who instructed him in German and encouraged him in philological and literary studies.

Knapp,[1] the translation was made at Norwich—whence the Preface is dated—during the years 1823-24. But Mr. Clement Shorter in *George Borrow and his Circle* (1913)[2] holds the work to have been done in London, 1824. This is a small point; but Mr. Shorter suggests, which is much more important, that Borrow translated not from the German, but from the French version, *Les Aventures du Dr. Faust*, Amsterdam, 1798. He thinks that Borrow may have come across this in his wanderings after old volumes on crime, for his collection of Celebrated Trials, and may have made his translation from this without having seen the German original, and without knowing who was the author. The fact that Borrow refers specially in his preface to the engravings of the French version, one of which he reproduced, whereas the engravings are in the German version *as well*, appears to Mr. Shorter strong evidence for his case. It is true that the name of Klinger is nowhere mentioned by Borrow; and Mr. Shorter may be right. But, on the other hand, the title-page says "translated from the German"; and in speaking of the French translation, Borrow says: "It is as bad as French translations from the German usually are." It seems unlikely that Borrow would have said this without knowing the German original, and still more unlikely that, as a basis for his own, he would

Borrow read *Wilhelm Tell* with Taylor with a view to translating it, but never did so. Made many translations of German lyrics about this time; they are of no literary merit and most were never printed. Sent a version of Schiller's *Taucher* to *New Month. Mag.*, VII. 540; and of Bürger's *Lenore* to *Month. Mag.*, November, 1823. (Knapp calls the latter "probably the worst attempt ever perpetrated on the benevolent reader.") Also to *Month. Mag.*, LVI; 1823, a *Mountain-Song* from Schiller and Goethe's *Erl King*. The *Faustus* was his only big piece of translation from German. In later years he occupied himself less with German than with Danish and other languages. He admired Goethe, but often referred to him as being over-estimated.

[1] *Life, Writings and Correspondence of George Borrow*, two vols., 1899.

[2] Pp. 103-5.

have used a version of which he had such a poor opinion. Possibly he may have seen a copy of the original, which had no engravings. Further, in these years at Norwich under W. Taylor's influence, Borrow was much more occupied with German than French, and all his translating was done from German or Danish. Proof is impossible, but the probability is that Borrow translated from the German original.

In his preface Borrow labours to prove the "strict morality" of the work, pointing out that the scenes of vice and crime depicted in it are exhibited merely as "beacons to guide the innocent and unwary," and that it really contains many useful and highly valuable lessons. He does, however, omit or modify some expressions as being too strong for English ears. The translation is on the whole both faithful and correct, clear in style, and reproduces much of the spirit of the original. It is a pity Borrow did not give his labour to some work of more lasting interest.

Some of the reviews of *Faustus* were rather favourable, specially that in the *Monthly*,[1] where it is contrasted with the "feeble and mutilated version" of Goethe's *Faust*, by Lord Gower. This *Faust*, the reviewer says, comes to us entire; it is full of boldness, vigour and audacity, and in point of plan and execution, shows decisive merit of a very high order. He recommends the subject as a good one to the ballet-master of the opera-house. The *Gentleman's Magazine*[2] praises the tale as being vigorous in conception, rich in invention and glowing in description, and reflecting credit on the translator for the spirited manner of the translation, but regrets its publication as being likely to lead youth into the vortex of crime. It objects to not being informed of the name of the original German author. But there are other notices of a very different style; for instance, this in the *Literary Gazette*:[3] "This is another

[1] LX. 153; 1825.
[2] XCV. i., 615.
[3] July, 1825, 461.

work to which no respectable publisher ought to have allowed his name to be put. The political allusions and metaphysics which may have made it popular among a low class in Germany, do not sufficiently season its lewd scenes and coarse descriptions for British palates. We have occasionally publications for the fireside—these are fit only for the fire."

A letter of Borrow's to his publisher reports that the book actually was burnt in two libraries in Norwich.

It was reprinted in 1840 and again (without acknowledgment) in 1864.

J. VON LEISEWITZ (1752-1806).

Leisewitz, though a member of the Göttinger Hain, stands somewhat apart from the other Göttinger poets, both in his spirit and in the form of his work. He was the only dramatist among them. His dramas represent the essence of the "Sturm und Drang." His name appears to have been little known in England; yet his only drama of interest, *Julius von Tarent*, found a translator, while its successful rival, Klinger's *Zwillinge*, did not. *Julius of Tarent* (1800) was not, however, published separately, but appeared only in parts in the *German Museum*,[1] a monthly periodical of 1800 and 1801.[2] Of the few plays here given in full, *Julius of Tarent* is the best-known and most important.

The translator, who signs P. W. (*i.e.*, the Rev. Peter Will), seems to understand his text, though he translates rather freely, making many little additions of his own. His English, however, is poor.

It is hard to judge impartially of these "Sturm und Drang" plays; there is so much in them that any translation would appear ridiculous to us today. But something better would be possible than language so pompous and strained as this:

[1] II. 114*ff*.

[2] See Chap. IX.

"The heavens are convolved like a sheet and the feathered tribe anxiously seeks a place of security. Chaotic night erects a black banner in the centre of the combust sun."

"P. W." has all through failed to catch the characteristic tone and spirit of the play, and his translation gives little real idea of Leisewitz's work.

Julius von Tarent and *Die neue Arria* were the only specimens of the minor "Sturm und Drang" dramas which found their way to England.

We meet one allusion to Maler Müller (1749-1825) in a review of Goethe's *Werke* by Carlyle in the *Foreign Review*[1] (1828): "As far as the writer knows he is here named for the first time to English readers . . . though in any solid study of German literature, this author must take precedence of many hundreds whose reputation has travelled faster."

C. F. D. SCHUBART (1739-1791).

There is only one bit of actual translation from Schubart, but it is of special interest owing to its connection with Shelley.[2] One of Shelley's earliest poems (1810) was on Ahasuerus, the Wandering Jew; and the subject seems to have been partly suggested to him by a translated fragment of a German poem, which he printed afterwards as a note to a mention of Ahasuerus in *Queen Mab* (VII. 67),[3] adding the statement: "This fragment is part of some German work whose title I have vainly endeavoured to discover. I picked it up dirty and torn some years ago in Lincoln's Inn Fields." Medwin's account of the incident is slightly different.[4] According to this it was Medwin himself who found the fragment and brought it to Shelley,

[1] I. 426.

[2] For Shelley's connection with German Literature see Stokoe, *German Influence*, etc., chap. vi., and Appendix, p. 178.

[3] See Mrs. Shelley's *Notes* to *Queen Mab*. *Shelley*, Oxford (1912), p. 828.

[4] *Life of Shelley*, I. 54 *ff*.

but not until after some cantos of *The Wandering Jew*, of which he asserts they were joint authors, had been already written. The friends differed somewhat as to the treatment of the poem, Medwin wishing to follow the German writer, and put an end to the Jew—a consummation Shelley would by no means consent to.[1]

The manuscript of *The Wandering Jew* was refused by the publishers in 1810. It was printed for the first time in 1831, in *Fraser's Magazine*. In the edition with notes by B. Dobell (1887) no mention is made of the German fragment; but (p. 36) there is a long note by Shelley to l. 764, quoting a prose passage, saying: "I have endeavoured to deviate as little as possible from the extreme sublimity of idea, which the style of the German author, of which this is a translation, so forcibly impresses."

The passage here quoted is not the same as that in the notes to *Queen Mab*, which is a literal translation of Schubart's *Ewige Jude*. The passage quoted in *The Wandering Jew* reads like a free paraphrase and amplification of the same piece. Could it be the version alluded to by Mrs. Shelley: "This (the fragment) afterwards fell into other hands, and was considerably altered before it was printed"?[2]

Shelley's interest in the figure of the Wandering Jew continued all through life.[3] Medwin tells of how on Shelley's first visit to the Bodleian, his first request to the Librarian was for *The Wandering Jew*. The Librarian told him he knew of no work in Germany of that name, and Shelley, who had imagined that the great Oxford Library contained all books in all languages, was much disappointed. Shelley never knew the authorship of the fragment which so much

[1] *Ibid.*, p. 809.

[2] *Shelley*, Oxford (1912), p. 828.

[3] *Vide* a *Soliloquy of the Wandering Jew*, taken from the Esdale MS., and two short poems on the subject, from Medwin's *Life of Shelley*, Oxford (1912), pp. 871-2. There are reminiscences of the figure of Ahasuerus in *Hellas*.

interested him. It was not identified as a translation of Schubart's *Ewige Jude* until many years later.[1] It is to be found in the third volume (p. 424) of the *German Museum* (1801), signed with the initials "P. W." (*i.e.*, the Rev. Peter Will, the translator of numerous pieces in this paper). The text as copied by Shelley in the Notes to *Queen Mab* is not absolutely identical with that given in the *German Museum*. But this can easily be accounted for. The paper Shelley found was "copied from some old magazine," and "dirty and torn"; part of the text was probably illegible, and Shelley here supplied the missing parts himself. The last sentence given in P. W.'s translation, telling of the Jew's ultimate salvation, is not given by Shelley, who, as Medwin tells us, strongly objected to this conclusion. It reads:

> "And Ahasuerus dropped down. Night covered his bristly eyelids; an angel carried him back to the cavern. 'Sleep here,' said the angel to Ahasuerus; 'sleep in peace, the wrath of thy judge is appeased. When thou shalt awake, He will be arrived, He whose blood thou sawest flow upon Golgotha, and whose mercy is also extended to thee."

The translation as such is much better than most of P. Will's work.

It is said that Byron[2] was also well acquainted with this fragment from Schubart, and owed to it the lines in *Manfred* beginning:

> "I have affronted Death, but in the storm
> Of elements the waters shrunk from me," etc.

---

[1] An impossible suggestion is made by A. Droop in *die Belesenheit P. B. Shelley's* (Weimar, 1905), p. 124: "Es war vermutlich eine Übersetzung von Clarance Mangan im *Dublin University Magazine*, 1809." Mangan was six in 1809, and the Magazine did not begin till 1833.

[2] For Byron's connection with German Literature see Stokoe, *German Influence*, etc., chap. vii (and bibliography to this). Also J. G. Robertson, *The Relations of Goethe and Byron*, *Pub. Eng. Goethe Society*, New Series, II.

Minor Writers

Besides *The Wandering Jew*, there is in the *German Museum* (III. 426) one other short piece translated from Schubart—*Jupiter*.

We come across Schubart once in connection with Scott, whose *War-Song*—"To horse, to horse, the standard flies," is said to have been inspired by Schubart's Song *Der Abschiedstag ist da*, beginning "Auf, auf ihr Brüder."

CHAPTER V

J. W. VON GOETHE (1749-1832).

THIS chapter on Goethe must of necessity be somewhat fragmentary. To treat of all his works as they were known in England before 1830 would take not one, but many chapters. Also much of the subject has been already dealt with, and to go over it again would be needlessly to repeat the work of others.[1] In these cases I have confined myself to referring to the book or article treating of the work in question, adding any new comments of importance. The space thus saved is given to those works not discussed before—*e.g.*, *Hermann und Dorothea*, *Dichtung und Wahrheit*, etc.

DRAMAS.

The widespread popularity of *Werther* led to interest in Goethe's personality, and a certain amount of this interest was extended to his early dramas. But they

[1] (*a*) J. M. Carré, *Goethe en Angleterre* (Paris, Plon-Nourrit, 1921), and *Bibliographie critique et analytique de Goethe en Angleterre idem*. This interesting and well-ordered study by Professor Carré, who, as "chargé de cours de Littératures Modernes Comparées à l'Université de Lyon," has given years of work to these subjects, appeared after this chapter was written. I have thought it best to leave it as it stands, while recommending the reader for a complete treatment of the whole question of Goethe in England to Carré's book. The Bibliography is very full (if not always quite exact) and the whole work most valuable, in particular the study of the influence of Goethe on Carlyle and others through him. (*b*) *Vide* Eugene Oswald, *Goethe in England and America*. Bibliography (London, 1909). (*c*) Alois Brandl, *Die Aufnahme von Goethes Jugendwerken in England*. G.J., III., 27-76; 1882. (*d*) G. R. Alford, *Goethe's Earliest Critics in England*. Pub. E.G.S., VII., 8-31 (1893). (*e*) W. Heinemann, *Goethe on the English Stage*. Pub. E.G.S., IV. (1888). Articles on particular works given later.

were not as well known as those of Schiller. Schiller's and Lessing's plays occasionally appeared on the English stage; Goethe's never. His later classic dramas were translated—*Iphigenia* in 1793, *Tasso* not until 1827—and known as reading pieces to a few, but did not become in any sense popular.

Götz von Berlichingen.—Scott's translation of *Götz* is now famous. Another, which appeared at Liverpool a few weeks later, is almost unknown.[1] It is the work of a lady, Rose d'Aguilar, afterwards Rose Lawrence,[2] translator also of Gessner's *Works* (1802). This *Götz* is exceedingly free, often inaccurate, and includes several additions to the original text; the most noteworthy, a detailed description of the meeting-place of the "Vehmgericht," borrowed probably from some German romance. Miss d'Aguilar sent a copy of the book to the author with a letter dated September 20th, 1799, and another letter on March 5th, 1800. Goethe's opinion of the translation is not recorded; nor does he appear to have answered the letters. But he preserved them and they are now in the Goethe-Schiller Archiv in Weimar. F. Baldensperger gives both letters in full.[3]

The only review mentioned by Brandl is one in *The Lady's Monthly Museum*.[4] There is another in the *Monthly*,[5] not very favourable, but with rather good critical remarks on the contrast between the treatment of history in *Götz* and in Shakespeare's plays. Otherwise *Gortz von Berlingen* [*sic*] was little noticed, over-

[1] *Gortz of Berlingen with the Iron Hand. An historical Drama of the XV. century*, translated from the German of Goethe, author of Werter (Liverpool, 1799).

[2] The two names sometimes lead to the mistake that there were *two* translations. Goedeke (IV. iii., p. 145) only gives "Rose d'Aquilar." Brandl and other references only "Rose Lawrence."

[3] See Brandl, pp. 60-62; and Baldensberger, *Two unpublished letters to Goethe from an English translator of Goetz* in *Mod. Lang. Rev.*, IV. 515; 1909.

[4] III. 71; 1799.

[5] XXIX. 223; 1799.

shadowed as it was by Scott's more powerful rendering.[1] In spite of the extraordinary mistakes made through haphazard guesses at the meaning of words he did not know, Scott's work as a whole conveys the spirit and general effect of *Götz*, and with Tytler's *Robbers* it introduced the style of the "Sturm und Drang" into England.[2] The *Critical*[3] gives a most favourable review of *Götz*, saying that the author has not only imitated Shakespeare's irregularity and medley of character, but also shows the same distinguishing and powerful genius. "No Englishman capable of understanding dramatic excellence can peruse it without delight." But just at this moment the *Anti-Jacobin Review*[4] was levelling its first attacks on German literature; and Scott's *Götz* fell a victim to the general consequent reaction. It was never acted, and Scott is said to have been much disappointed at its want of success. For a long time it was almost forgotten. Gillies, in a review of *Götz*[5] with extracts from Scott's translation (1824), expresses surprise that it had never been reprinted. Since that date its worth has been generally recognised. It was carefully revised and reprinted in Bohn's Library in 1846.

Clavigo.—In Drake's *Speculator* No. XIII. for May 8th, 1790, there is an article by Ash on Goethe with some account of his early dramas, and in particular of *Clavigo*.[6] The last scene is given in a free translation, done with a good deal of spirit; and it seems a pity

[1] *Goetz von Berlichingen with the Iron Hand*, translated from the German of Goethé [*sic*], Author of the *Sorrows of Werter*, etc., by Walter Scott, Advocate, Edinburgh (London, 1799).

[2] See Brandl, pp. 60-71; and A. R. Hohlfeld, *Scott als Übersetzer*. Koch's *Studien zur vergleichenden Litteraturgeschichte*, 1903. Brandl refers Scott's *House of Aspen* directly to the influence of Götz, but in Hohlfeld's opinion Brandl's theories on this point need much modification.

[3] XXVI. 429; 1799.

[4] For its criticism of *Götz* (III. 210), see Brandl, p. 67.

[5] *Black. Mag.*, XV. 369-85.

[6] *Vide* Brandl, p. 40.

that Ash (if it is he) did not translate some of Goethe's dramas in full.

From 1798—a year before *Götz*—dates an anonymous translation of *Clavigo*.[1] It is only in Goedeke [IV. iii., p. 159] that this is assigned to B. Thompson.[2] But if it were by him it would surely have been included in his *German Theatre*. The *Analytical*[3] speaks of it as anonymous but "executed with considerable ability." Goethe is praised for the judgment he displays in the choice of subject by selecting, instead of some intricate plot, a simple and affecting story of home life, to which his powers are so admirably suited. The *Critical*[4] thinks there is something ridiculous in representing a living character on the stage, and finds the beginning of the play feeble, but the conclusion admirable and worthy of the author of *Werther*. The *Monthly*[5] in a very short notice says the play is worthy of the German Euripides and the translation unexceptionable. These reviews are all favourable, but it would be rash to conclude from this that *Clavigo* was widely popular. It was never acted, and this translation was never reprinted.[6] It is now a very rare book, none of the big libraries in Great Britain possessing a copy.[7] Carré notes a copy in the possession of a Mr. Priebsch; he says that the translator, who seemed to have a wide knowledge of literature,

[1] **Clavigo, a tragedy in five Acts*, translated from the German of Goethe, the author of the *Sorrows of Werter* (Johnstone, 1798).

[2] Brandl (p. 49), E. Oswald (p. 30), and all the contemporary reviews give it as anonymous, and it is not included in the list of B. Thompson's works in the D.N.B. Carré, *Bibliographie*, p. 38, attributes it to a Charles Leftley, † 1814; but he offers no proof.

[3] XXVIII. 175; 1798.

[4] XXV. 469; 1799.

[5] XXIII. 105; 1799.

[6] The translator of *Clavigo*—"A. T."—in the *Month. Mag.*, XVIII., 1824, was not aware of any earlier translation. For criticism of this translation see Herbert Smith, *An English translation of Goethe's Clavigo, Mod. Lang. Rev.*, VIII. 204; 1913.

[7] Morgan, *Bibl. of Ger. Lit.*, p. 152, notes a copy in the N. Y Pub. Lib.

was more competent than many at that time. The last Act is given without acknowledgment of the source by W. Taylor in the *Historic Survey*;[1] the translation seems very fair, much better than the anonymous *Stella* of the same year. There are one or two bad slips; and the style is sometimes stiff. The same scene in the *Speculator* is translated with a good deal more spirit.

The *Clavigo* and *Stella* translations of 1798 were noticed in the *Neue Bibliothek der schönen Wissenschaften*,[2] and said to be "wohlgeraten."

Stella.—In the Preface to *Stella*[3] the anonymous translator lays stress on the translation being done from the original German, and not through French. This is, of course, the earlier version of *Stella*, ending with Cecilia's "We are both thine"; and in spite of all the translator's efforts at apology for this conclusion, it sufficed to damn the work in England.[4] The *British Critic*[5] condemned its immorality in the strongest terms, as did also the *Critical*[6] and the *Monthly Mirror* (quoted by Brandl). The *Analytical*[7] judged it less harshly, quoting without criticism the translator's note as to the "curious and accomodating catastrophe." The *Monthly*[8] also gave it a rather more favourable notice. The *Anti-Jacobin* led the campaign against the "Sturm und Drang" dramas in general, and against *Stella* in particular. *The Rovers, or the Double Entertainment* (1798), though also directed against Schiller's *Robbers*, *Cabal and Love*, and a couple of Kotzebue's dramas, is more than anything else a direct, and it must be admitted, often a very witty, parody of *Stella*.[9]

[1] *Hist. Surv.*, III. 305. Extracts from same Act in *Crit.* and *Anal. Revs.* [2] 1799, p. 316.

[3] *Stella*, translated from the German of M. Goethe, author of the *Sorrows of Werter*, etc. (London, Hookham and Carpenter, 1798).

[4] See Brandl, pp. 42-3. [5] XII. 424. [6] XXXI. 350; 1798.

[7] XXVIII. 170. [8] XXVI. 59; 1798.

[9] See Brandl, pp. 51-54, who gives a synopsis of the plot, clearly showing the connection with *Stella*.

This anonymous translation of *Stella*, as such, is mediocre. Many passages are omitted or altered, and the style of the whole has nothing of the simplicity and directness of the original.

The later translation, in the sixth volume of B. Thompson's *German Theatre*, is not mentioned by Brandl.[1] It has the same faults of style, but Thompson takes fewer liberties with the text. Still there are many inaccuracies—*e.g.*, "meine Augen lagen sorglos auf dir" = "I gazed intently at you"; and badly-chosen expressions—*e.g.*, "die Weiber haben mich verstimmt" = "the women have disordered me"—(1798 translation = "distracted me"); or "Schmerzen" = "complicated agony." The whole style is heavy.

Egmont.—*Egmont* did not enjoy in England even the comparative popularity of Goethe's other early dramas. It remained altogether unnoticed. A reviewer in the *Monthly* in 1825 calls it "a good tragedy," and expresses surprise at its never having been translated. But no translation appeared till 1841.

Taylor in the *Historic Survey*[2] translated the scene between Margaret of Parma and Macchiavel (III. 7).

Die Geschwister.—A translation of *Die Geschwister* appeared at Edinburgh in 1792 in a volume entitled *Dramatic Pieces from the German*, which included also *The Conversation of a Father with his Children* from Gessner (really a translation by Gessner from Diderot, which appeared before the French original and was thus mistaken for Gessner's own), and *The Set of Horses*, by Emdorff. This last piece has been identified as *Der Postzug oder die nobeln Passionen*, by C. A. von Ayrenhoff, a comedy very popular in

[1] Carré (*Goethe en Angleterre*, p. 39), as also Goedeke, ascribe also the earlier translation to B. Thompson. But a comparison of the two translations proves them utterly different.

[2] III. 3.

Germany about 1769. There is no such writer as Emdorff.[1]

It is probable, but not certain, that the translator was Henry Mackenzie (1745-1831). In the *Dictionary of National Biography*[2] there is the following note (quoted from Allibone's *Dictionary*):[3] "It is said that after studying German, Mackenzie published in 1791 translations of the *Set of Horses* by Lessing [*sic*] and two or three other Dramatic Pieces, but there is no trace of the work in the catalogue of the British Museum or that of the Edinburgh Advocate's Library." There is, however, a copy in the British Museum; but not under Mackenzie's name—nor, of course, under Lessing's ! The translations are not attributed to Mackenzie in Edinburgh; neither do they appear among his collected works. Yet they probably are by him. Mackenzie's interest in German literature is well known ; and the preface refers the reader for an account of the German drama to his own famous paper read before the Royal Society of Edinburgh (April 21st, 1788). At the time of this paper, Mackenzie knew no German; so in these translations—if they are his—he was translating from a language newly learnt. As such they have much merit, being almost entirely free from mistranslations and inaccuracies, though his expressions are not always well chosen. In style the translator has been more successful in the other two pieces than in this of Goethe's, where the language is sometimes stiff and the dialogue unnatural. *The Sister* is not at all a bad translation of the title; though not literally correct, it gives the main idea of the piece. One reviewer[4] objected to "scotticisms" in the translation,

[1] See Review of the book in the *Bibl. d. sch. Wissensch.*, LI. 183; 1793. It says the work shows growing interest in German literature in England, but thinks that the choice of pieces could be better.

[2] XXXV. 151.

[3] P. 1177 ; also Todt, *Lessing in England*, p. 30.

[4] *Anal. Rev.*, XV. 172 ; 1793.

but otherwise commended it. The play itself he praises very highly: "The plot is simple, yet produces a wonderful effect . . . its delicate touches of sentiment and passion, supply the want of plot and incident." The *Critical* also speaks of it with praise, but considers that this lack of plot and incident would make its representation impossible on the English stage. The *Monthly* finds the incident on which the plot hangs too improbable, the simplicity aimed at by the author too artificial, and the tenderness not sufficiently natural. It commends the dialogue.

It is interesting to note that this remained the only English translation of *Die Geschwister*[1] until 1885.

Iphigenia.—In Taylor's *Iphigenia*[2] we have the first translation of a drama of Goethe, which may be said to be really worthy of its original; not reproducing, indeed, all the harmony of Goethe's verse, but in form and general effect a very faithful reproduction. An interesting and detailed study of it was made in a paper read before the Manchester Goethe Society on March 26, 1890—*W. Taylor as a translator; with special reference to his version of Goethe's Iphigenia.* Taylor's work is justly appreciated, and compared with the later translation by Miss Swanwick. We refer readers to this paper;[3] also to G. Herzfeld,[4] who treats in some detail of the translation, and to Robberd's *Memoir of W. Taylor,*[5] where a long account of it is given.

Taylor sent a copy of his *Iphigenia* to Goethe, but did not receive the acknowledgment Goethe had been

[1] A reference in Goedeke (IV. iii., p. 229) to a second translation of *Die Geschwister* in 1792 by W. Taylor is a mistake. No other authority mentions more than one translation, nor is there any evidence that Taylor ever even projected such a work (*cf.* E. Oswald, p. 30).

[2] *Iphigenia in Tauris.* A Tragedy written originally in German by J. W. von Goethe (London, Johnson, 1793). Printed by Unger in Berlin, 1794. Reprinted in *Hist. Surv.*, III. 249.

[3] An abstract will be found in the Trans. M. G. Soc., p. 160 (1790).

[4] *W. Taylor*, pp. 24-26.

[5] I., pp. 113-119.

known to give to poorer translations. An oversight, perhaps, but one can understand that Taylor felt it as a slight. Goethe makes casual mention of the receipt of the translation in a letter to Jacobi, August 11th, 1793. Schiller knew of it too. At home Taylor's work did not get the praise it deserved. It appeared just at the moment when the literary market was flooded with German translations of all kinds, and the few works of real merit were swamped by the mass of the poor or worthless. Nor yet was it likely that the classic beauty of *Iphigenia* would appeal to those who knew Goethe only through the feeble translations and still feebler imitations of *Werther*, or who were thrilled by the horrors of the "*Schauer-romane.*" It was reprinted in Berlin (J. Unger) in 1794, but not again in England. A few reviews, however, show some understanding of the work. A critic in the *Monthly*[1] discusses it at length, comparing Goethe's treatment of the story with that of Euripides. Goethe's alterations, in his opinion, contribute much to the improvement of the characters, specially to that of Iphigenia, and also to the moral effect of the catastrophe. He adds the very pertinent remark that Goethe seems to have made Sophocles rather than Euripides his model, and that perhaps no modern has more successfully imitated that great master. Much praise is given to the then anonymous translator.

C. des Vœux inserted a translation of the opening scene of *Iphigenia* with the poems at the end of his *Tasso* (1827). It is not as good as Taylor's.

Tasso.—The first complete translation of *Tasso*[2] is that by Charles des Vœux;[3] made at Weimar, inspired

[1] XI. 51; 1793.

[2] *Torquato Tasso*, translated by Charles des Vœux (1827), (London, Longmans). Second edition, revised and corrected with additions (Weimar, 1831).

[3] Charles des Vœux (1802–1833) was descended from an Irish family. He graduated from Oriel College, Oxford, 1824, entered the diplomatic service and went to Weimar in 1826. He stayed some time

by the presence and with the active encouragement of the author himself; and thus of special interest. On it was based an article by L. A. Willoughby in the *Modern Language Review* (1914);[1] giving a history of the growth of the work; also the correspondence of Goethe and Carlyle as well as other letters bearing on it; further a careful criticism of the translation. Not more is necessary than to refer the reader to this interesting article.[2]

---

and was intimate with Goethe, Ottilie von Goethe and their circle. Goethe, and specially Ottilie, took a great interest in the *Tasso* translation. (See V. Oettingen's introduction in the vol. on Ottilie's letters by the German Goethe Society.) There is a portrait of " de Vœux, Englishman " among the portraits of fourteen English visitors painted by Schmeller for Goethe (1815–1830). *Vide* R. G. Alford, *Englishmen at Weimar*. Pub. Eng. G. Soc., V. 191.

[1] *An Early Translation of Goethe's Tasso, Mod. Lang. Rev.*, IX. 223-234.

[2] A couple of examples of mistranslation to add to those given by Mr. Willoughby:

" Thou hast a poet sketched, refin'd and mild,
Who in the realms of sweetest dreams doth float "

for:

" Du hast den Dichter fein und zart geschildert
Der in den Reichen süsser Träume wohnt "

(I. 173-4),

where " fein und zart " are taken as adjectives referring to the poet, whereas they are really adverbs referring to the manner of the " Schilderung." Or:

" His whole deportment and his words have touch'd
Me so, that more than ever I do feel
Myself as multiplied "

for:

" Sein Wesen, seine Worte haben mich
So wunderbar getroffen, dass ich mehr
Als je mich doppelt fühle "

(II. 763-5),

where the whole point of the speech is lost by the rendering of " doppelt." It refers obviously to the strife in *Tasso* between the ideals of " Held und Dichter " mentioned after by the Princess. " Multiplied " means nothing at all. (1) See E. Oswald, p. 31 *ff.*; and (2) see *Hist. Surv.*, III. 311.

Faust.—The valuable American study by W. F. Hauhart, *The Reception of Goethe's Faust in England and America in the first half of the Nineteenth Century* (New York, 1909), gives a complete bibliography and discusses the various translations and fragments of translations, as well as many other points of interest. And Carré gives an interesting chapter to "L'auteur du *Faust* et les poetes romantiques."[1] There is no need to add anything further here.

PROSE WORKS.

Werther.—No German work—except perhaps Gessner's *Death of Abel* at an earlier date—was as popular in England as *Werther.* The first translation was made from a French version in 1779 and frequently reprinted. Other translations from the original German followed in 1786, 1799, 1801, 1802, and another from the French in 1789.[2] But none were as popular nor became as widely known as the first translation. It was evidently the only one generally known when Carlyle wrote of *Werther.* All of them are poor and garbled versions of the original. The *Sorrows of Werter* appeared in popular chap-books and is said to have had a place in all pedlars' baskets beside the *Pilgrim's Progress* and Klopstock's *Messiah.* An Italian version of *Werther* (*Gli affanni del giovane Verter*) was published in London in 1788 and a French version in 1792. English *Wertheriaden* appeared in the form of stories (continuations or imitations of the original), dramas, poems, letters; and were almost as popular as the original work. Several were translated into German and French. For many years Goethe was known in England only as "the author of *Werter.*"

[1] J. M. Carré, *Goethe en Angleterre*, chap. v.; *Bibliographie*, pp. 179-86.

[2] Two of the translators—probably as an advertising device—claimed personal acquaintance with Werther and his family.

Goethe

The question of *Werther* in England has been already treated very fully. J. W. Appell in *Werther und seine Zeit* (1896), Chapter I., deals with English *Werthers*, *Wertheriaden* and *Werther* on the English stage. In the *Journal of English and Germanic Philology*, XIV. (1915), there is a most interesting article by O. W. Long on *English Translations of Goethe's Werther*, with excellent critical remarks on all the early translations, and long extracts. He also discusses the English attitude towards *Werther*, specially with reference to the subject of suicide—the " moral " bearing of the work being the question that roused most interest in England. Finally, we have now J. M. Carré's exhaustive study in Chapter I. of his *Goethe en Angleterre*, and full bibliography in the companion *Bibliographie*, pp. 7-35.[1] He gives not only the translations, adaptations and imitations of *Werther*, but testimonies as to its popularity from poems, pictures, fashions, etc.

It seems unnecessary to try to summarise here what has been already written. So we shall only refer the reader to the above studies.

Dichtung und Wahrheit.—Dichtung und Wahrheit was introduced to English readers by the bitter and sneering attack made on it in the *Edinburgh Review*[2] (1816). One is reminded of Carlyle's plea for Goethe in the Preface to his *Wilhelm Meister* : " All I ask in the name of this illustrious foreigner is: that the court that tries him be pure, the jury instructed in the cause; that the work be not condemned for what it was not meant to have by persons no wise called to pass sentence on it." Here certainly not one of these conditions is fulfilled. The anonymous critic does not

[1] See Review by A. E. Turner in *Mod. Lang. Rev.*, XVI., p. 364 *ff.*; 1921. There are special notes on the *Werther* section of the *Bibliographie*, and some corrections and additions. For *Werther* in England see also A. Brandl in Vol. III. of *Goethe Jahrbuch* and E. Oswald, pp. 53-57.

[2] XXVI. 304-27.

seem to have considered that the works of a writer of Goethe's eminence and reputation deserved at least careful consideration before being condemned offhand with flippant sneers. His analysis of the work is a mere travesty of the original. The worth of his critical remarks may be judged from the following specimens: "The work is not unentertaining though disfigured by the most puerile vanity and affectation . . . the author digresses into a frequent and pompous display of reflection—sometimes ingenious, but never to the purpose. . . . He appears to us to be always deficient in literary good-breeding, in literary decorum; in short he does not display a real aristocratic feeling in his mind and habits." This article aroused much indignation in Germany, where it was translated and printed with the comment: "das heisst in England recensieren !"[1] It did not escape censure in England either. In *Blackwood's Magazine* (1818)[1]—founded as a rival to the *Edinburgh Review*—there is an article by one of the two contributors with a real knowledge of German literature, J. G. Lockhart or John Wilson, entitled *Observations on the Critique of Goethe's Life in the "Edinburgh Review."* The writer puts before his readers the position held by Goethe in the literary world not only of Germany but of all Europe, and expresses surprise as to how the editor of the *Review* could have "permitted the life of such a man to be travestied in his pages, with such empty arrogance and offensive irreverence for the sake of gratifying with a few paltry jokes the ignorant and malicious dullness of a few readers." The *Literary Gazette*[2] also attacked the Edinburgh Reviewers for their "awkward attempt at smartness." The writer alludes to the "just indignation" of the Germans at this piece of "impertinent criticism," and refutes in detail many statements of "this contemptible critic." In order to enable readers

[1] See *Goethe Jahrbuch*, VII. 309.
[2] 1817, p. 341.

to judge for themselves, he adds some extracts from the beginning of the work in a good translation.

Goethe suffered as much at the hands of the first English translator of *Dichtung und Wahrheit* as he had done at the hands of its first English critic. This translation[1] of the first fifteen Books (all that had appeared so far in Germany) though purporting to be taken from the German original, is in reality based on a French translation by M. Aubert de Vitry (1823)—a mutilated version with many mistakes.[2] Some of these mistakes were corrected by Vitry at the end; yet all were left uncorrected by the careless English translator, whose ignorance of German is proved by many bits of internal evidence:

(*a*) Proper names spelt as Goëthe and Goetz Von Berlischingen; (*b*) translation of names: "Volksbücher" as "Contes Bleus"; "die vier Haimonskinder" as "les quatre Fils d'Aimon," etc.; the translator is simply retaining the French terms. That he was ignorant not only of the German language, but also of German history, customs, and institutions—a knowledge absolutely necessary in translating a work of this kind—is proved by many blunders, *e.g.*, the hero of Zachariæ's *Der Renommist* is called a "robber"; "die Roheit" (der Studenten) becomes "savage ferocity"; the "Meistersinger" the translator had never even heard of. In many passages absolute nonsense is made of Goethe's meaning—*e.g.*, in the description of Goethe's childish attempt at sacrifice, the danger of approaching the Divinity "auf dergleichen Wegen" becomes "in any way whatsoever." At the end of Book III., after Goethe has told how he and his friends read and acted Klopstock, he says: "So pflegen Kinder und Volk

[1] *Memoirs of Goëthe* [*sic*] *written by himself.* With biographical notices by the translator of the principal persons mentioned in the Memoirs (London, Colburn, 1824).

[2] *Vide* Fernand Baldensperger, *Bibliographie critique de Goethe en France*. Paris, 1907, p. 216.

das Grosse, das Erhabene in ein Spiel, in eine Posse zu verwandeln; und wie sollten sie auch sonst im Stande sein, es auszuhalten und zu ertragen?" Of this the English translator makes: "Thus do children, like the populace, often turn the grand and sublime into subjects of ridicule and buffoonery. How was it possible for us at our age to keep up with the elevation of the author we were reading?" In the following sentence taken from the description of Charlotte Buff (Book XII.) nonsense is made by the mistranslation of the pronouns. The mistake again betrays the French, where "sa mère" could be either his or her mother. But it shows how little the English translator understood about the whole situation. "Nach dem Tode *ihrer* Mutter hatte sie sich als Haupt einer zahlreichen jüngen Familie höchst thätig erwiesen, und *den* Vater in seinem Witwenstand allein aufrecht erhalten . . ." = "After *his* mother's death, this lady had undertaken the management of the family and had consoled *his* father by the zeal and intelligence she had displayed in her care of his numerous infant children . . ." As Kästner was the last name mentioned, it appeared from this that Charlotte looked after Kästner's children after their grandmother's death, and consoled their grandfather for his loss!

In an article in the *Westminster Review*[1]—written with exceptional insight and understanding—the writer defends Goethe against the misrepresentations of such a translation, pointing out many of the worst mistakes and proving the French basis of the work. "Such a publication as this translation," he says, "is really a disgrace to our literature, and it is much to be regretted that such a pseudo-version should shut out knowledge of the original from England." He alludes to the article in the *Edinburgh Review* (1816) and says that if this translation ever reached Germany they could justly add "und das heisst in England

[1] I. 370; 1824.

übersetzen!" *Blackwood*[1] at the end of a review of *Wilhelm Meister* warns readers against "this most audacious and impudent quackery, a miserably mutilated edition of a bad French version," and refers to the article in the *Westminster*. Other reviews are of less interest. The *British Critic*[2] objects (as usual) to the moral and religious principles of the new German school, of which it takes Goethe's *Memoirs* as an example; it gives extracts from Goethe's description of his early religious experiences, of his love-affair with Gretchen, and of the writing of *Werther*, and asks if such principles and such examples can be safely circulated among the women of England. The *Monthly*[3] condemns the "diffuseness and servile garrulity of the narrative." The *Gentleman's Magazine*[4] takes quite a different view, recommending the work as "a captivating one . . . replete with instruction and amusement, while the tendencies of the author's opinions are favourable to religion and virtue." A review in the *Literary Gazette*[5]—calling the work "well translated"!—is short and superficial.

Carlyle in his *Essay on Goethe*[6] gives some account of the general reception of *Dichtung und Wahrheit* in England. He considers it to have been censured without any insight into its proper meaning, and gives his criticism of the *Memoirs* (1824) as follows: "It is our duty also to remark, if anyone be still unaware of it, that the *Memoirs of Goethe*, published some years ago in London, can have no real concern with this Autobiography. The rage of hunger is an excuse for much: otherwise that German translator, whom indignant Reviewers have proved to know *no* German, were a highly reprehensible man. This work, it appears, is done from the French, and shows subtractions, and, what is worse, additions."

1 XV. 631; 1824.
2 XXII. 559; 1824.
3 CVI. 534; 1825.
4 XCIV. 139; 1824.
5 P. 211; 1824.
6 *For. Rev.*, II., 1828; *Critical Essays*, I.

Die Italienische Reise.—Some extracts from the second volume of *Die Italienische Reise*, then under the press, were given in fairly good translation in the *Literary Gazette*[1] of December, 1817. The passages chosen are the description of the passage from Messina to Naples, May 14th, 1787; and the Letters from Palermo of April 9th and 12th.

The *Edinburgh Review*[2] in a second article reviews *Aus meinem Leben, Zweiter Teil*, 1816, in the same tone as before. The writer apprehends "that this volume will be judged, by most readers, to be almost as doting as the preceding ones, without being equally entertaining."

Wilhelm Meisters Lehrjahre.—The *Monthly*[3] noticed the original *Wilhelm Meister* in 1798, with favourable comments, calling it a "remarkable production in classic style . . . with nothing of the extravagant and monstrous so common to German literature." Well-translated extracts are given from the chapters on Shakespeare and *Hamlet*, as of most interest to English readers. This was the first serious attempt in England to estimate a work of Goethe's.

From this time until Carlyle's famous translation in 1824,[4] *Wilhelm Meister* was forgotten. Carlyle revived interest in it, and at the same time laid the foundations of a real knowledge of Goethe in England. He says in the Preface: "Minds like Goethe's are the common property of all nations; and for many reasons all should have correct impressions of them." It is with the purpose of giving English readers this opportunity of judging for themselves that Carlyle undertook this translation. Some passages in his letters written at this time are interesting, and throw a curious light on his contradictory feelings towards *Wilhelm Meister*

[1] Pp. 353 and 388.
[2] XXVIII. 83-105; 1827.
[3] XXVII. 543.
[4] *Wilhelm Meister's Apprenticeship*. A Novel translated by T. Carlyle (Edinburgh, 1824; 2nd ed., 1839).

as he worked at it. A letter to his future wife, Miss Welsh, September 18th, 1823, speaks of it as "a book which I love not, which I am sure will never sell, but which I am determined to print and finish. There are touches of the very highest, most ethereal genius in it; but diluted with floods of insipidity, which even I would not have written for the world." Three days later, in a letter to James Johnstone, he says: "Goethe is the greatest genius that has lived for a century, and the greatest ass that has lived for three. I could sometimes fall down and worship him; at other times I could kick him out of the room." There are frequent references to it in other letters to Miss Welsh. On March 7th, 1824, he sent her the last pages of the translation, saying: "I fear, however, you will never read it; the romance you see is as dull as ever. . . . I am going to write a fierce preface, disclaiming all concern with the literary or moral merit of the work, grounding my claims to recompense or toleration on the fact that I have accurately copied a striking portrait of Goethe's mind, the strangest, and in many points, the greatest now extant. What a work! Bushels of dust and straws and feathers with here and there a diamond of the purest water." The Preface was hardly so fierce as all this promised; though he does call the hero "a milk-sop, whom with all his gifts it is difficult to avoid despising."

De Quincey's virulent attack[1] on *Wilhelm Meister* andits author is almost too well known to need summing up here. His ultimate point is, he says, not a quarrel with this particular book—"a bad book more or less is of no great importance"—but his mark is Goethe himself and his "coterie of admirers." His expressions are strong: "Not the baseness of Egyptian superstition, nor Titania under enchantment, nor Caliban in drunkenness, ever shaped to themselves an idol more weak and hollow than the modern German has set up

[1] *Edin. Rev.*, X. 189 *ff.*, and 291 *ff.*; 1824.

for his worship in the person of Goethe." *Wilhelm Meister* is, he considers, the best work with which to destroy the beginning of Goethe's prestige in England, for "no other is so likely to be revolting to English good sense." Not only the work itself, but also the translation is attacked. De Quincey objects to Scotticisms, barbarisms, exotic phrases, lawless innovations and archaisms. Most of his criticisms are far-fetched, and touch only unimportant points. Of the general merits of the translation he says nothing. His personal remarks are in bad taste—as when he attributes the alleged coarseness of diction to the translator's "insufficient acquaintance with good society." In a reprint of his works (1859) De Quincey suppressed these personal allusions to Carlyle, and the more violent expressions against Goethe. The analysis of *Wilhelm Meister* is written in a harsh, sneering tone, but part is undeniably witty and amusing—*e.g.*, *The Gallery of Female Portraits*—and, though exaggerated, has some grains of truth.[1]

In a letter to his brother John, January 22nd, 1825, Carlyle speaks of De Quincey's article as "a vulgar and brutish review," adding: "I know it and believe it and feel it to be a book containing traces of a higher, far higher spirit, altogether more genius than any book published in my day: and yet to see the Cockney animalcules rendering an account of it! praising it or blaming it! sitting in judgment on Goethe, with the light tolerance of a country justice towards a suspected poacher!"

Jeffrey in the *Edinburgh Review*[2] followed De Quincey, but in a rather less violent strain. At the beginning he says: "We cannot understand how it could ever appear an admirable or even a commendable performance. To us it appears, after most deliberate

[1] A reviewer in the *European Magazine*, LXXXVI. 442; 1824, agreed in the main with de Quincey.

[2] XLII. 408-49.

consultation, eminently absurd, puerile, incongruous, vulgar and affected; and though redeemed by considerable powers of invention and some traits of vivacity, to be so far from perfection, as to be almost from beginning to end a flagrant offence against every principle of taste and just composition." But after giving an analysis of the work with many quotations, Jeffrey says he feels inclined to abate some of the censure bestowed. It is, in his opinion, a "striking instance of diversity of national taste"; but rather an object of wonder than of contempt, showing that if taste be local and variable, genius is permanent and universal. Jeffrey does not, he says, wish to join in the general censure of the "alleged grossness and immorality" of *Wilhelm Meister*. But the *British Critic*[1] lays special stress on the immoral tendencies of the work. It admits Goethe's poetry and eloquence, but hopes that "the canting infidelity of his *Memoirs* and the gross indecencies of *Meister* and the horrid blasphemies of *Faust* will exclude him from English drawing-rooms!" A short review in the *Literary Gazette*[2] praises the author as showing a great knowledge of men and things, but characterises the novel as "a tale of perverted mysticism and unprincipled obscenity." The *Monthly*[3] gives great praise to the translator, but cannot quite join in his admiration of Goethe. *Werther* is mentioned as Goethe's masterpiece. A writer in *Blackwood*[4] also considers *Werther* superior to *Wilhelm Meister*, and wishes Carlyle would translate it. But this article contains much more reasoned criticism than the others, and presents Goethe in a fair light and just proportion, noting (1) that he has exerted a greater influence on the literature of his age than any other; (2) that he has almost created the literature of his own country; (3) that he has exerted a prodigious influence on the

[1] XXII. 559-72.
[2] 1824, p. 504.
[3] CVI. 528; 1825.
[4] XV. 619-32; 1824.

literature of others. "*Wilhelm Meister* is one of those lumber-rooms which could be found nowhere but in the palace of a Crœsus."

Of the translation as such there is scarcely any necessity to speak; it is so well known. Fidelity, Carlyle says, is the only merit he has aimed at; and he succeeds in this aim. He retains even some idiomatic peculiarities of the German—*e.g.*, "a well-readied meal" for "ein wohlbereitetes Essen," "help-needing" for "hülfsbedurftig." Some of Carlyle's later mannerisms of style appear already in this early work, and were objected to by some reviewers.

Carlyle's verse translations are not always so happy; but were praised by several contemporary critics. In Mignon's Song the change to the jumpy anapæstic measure from Goethe's quiet iambics absolutely destroys the poem. One verse will show this:

> "Know'st thou the land where the lemon-trees bloom?
> Where the gold orange glows in the deep thicket's gloom?
> Where a wind ever soft from the blue heaven blows
> And the groves are of laurel and myrtle and rose?
> Know'st thou it?
> Thither, O thither,
> My dearest and kindest with thee would I go."

Then hear:

> "Kennst du das Land, wo die Citronen blühn?"

Wilhelm Meister's Wanderjahre.—In 1827 Carlyle brought out his translation of the *Wanderjahre*,[1] taken from the Cotta edition of 1821. It concludes with the verses at the end of Chapter IX., Book III. In the second edition of 1839, Carlyle did not change anything, though a new and much-expanded version of the original had appeared in the meantime. The

[1] *Wilhelm Meister's Travels, or the Renunciants.* A Novel by Goethe. In *German Romance*, IV.; 1827. The date, 1828, given by Morgan, *Bibl. of Ger. Lit. in Eng.*, p. 179, for a translation by A. Gunloyson, is a misprint. The date should be 1882.

long Preface was reproduced afterwards in his *Critical Essays*. Of the *Wanderjahre* he says: "Its immediate reception is doubtful, or rather not doubtful, for it is too likely that these *Travels* will surprise and disappoint the reader—and the reader of the *Apprenticeship* more than any other. Nevertheless, though they may be caviare to the general, there are not wanting tastes among us to discern worth and worthlessness, even under the disadvantage of a translation, and to pronounce on both." Speaking a year later in the *Foreign Review* (1828) of the reception of the *Wanderjahre*, he says: "The book has been translated into English, and underwent the usual judgment from our reviews and magazines; it was to some a stone of stumbling, to others foolishness, to most an object of wonder."

The original *Wanderjahre* had been noticed in the *Monthly*[1] of 1822 by W. Taylor. He finds the incoherence of the book its greatest fault; its originality its greatest merit. But the greater part of the article is taken up with a good translation of the episode of the "Flight into Egypt" from the first four chapters—"an adventure more characteristic of the author, and more singular in structure than any which follow."

Die Wahlverwandtschaften.—No complete translation of *Die Wahlverwandtschaften* was made till 1854,[2] but it was reviewed—with some translated extracts from Ottilie's *Book of Aphorisms* (*Tagebuch*)—in the *Monthly* of 1812.[3] The writer considers this novel much inferior to *Werther*, but superior to *Meister*; "The pathetic powers of Goethe seem to have diminished with old age, but his knowledge of human nature has increased." He praises the beauties of style, intimate knowledge of feminine nature, and the dramatic distinctiveness of the characters; but

[1] XCVIII. 532.
[2] Trans. R. D. Boylan for Bohn's Library, Vol. IV.
[3] LXVIII. 540; 1812.

objects to the want of incident, the neglect of climax in the interest, some indifference to moral purity, and a tendency to sentimentality.

Byron mentions reading a translation of *Die Wahlverwandtschaften* (see K. Elze, *Byron*, p. 480), but it was apparently a French translation.[1]

In the *Monthly* of 1829[2] appeared a review of the first two volumes of *Goethes und Schillers Briefwechsel*, with some interesting remarks, and many extracts, mostly taken from the correspondence about *Wilhelm Meister*. The extracts from the Letters are well-chosen and very fairly translated. The *Foreign Review* also noticed the *Briefwechsel* with favourable comments and extracts.

There remain a few minor pieces of translation from Goethe.

In 1799 the *Observations on the Laokoön* were translated anonymously from "M. Goethe, author of the Sorrows of Werter," in the *Monthly Magazine* (VII.). The article is accompanied by a plate of the Laokoön.

In 1821 another little treatise of Goethe's was translated by G. H. Noehden—*Observations on Leonardo da Vinci's celebrated picture of the Last Supper.*[3] This translator[4] knew Goethe in Weimar, 1818-19; and as he was interested in the fine arts, the talk with Goethe often turned on sculpture and painting. On January 11th, 1819, Goethe sent Noehden this Essay, and the plan of translating met with his fullest approbation. Later in the year Noehden visited Milan; and

[1] See J. G. Robertson, *Goethe and Byron*. Pub. of Eng. Goethe Soc., New Series, II., p. 43, 1925.

[2] X. 525-33.

[3] First printed in *Über Kunst und Altertum*, III. (1817).

[4] G. H. Noehden (1770–1826). Born in Göttingen; came to England in 1793; 1818 became tutor to Crown Princess of Saxe-Weimar; afterwards held an appointment at the British Museum, and died in London. Translated Schiller's *Fiesco* and *Don Carlos* (see Rea, *Schiller's Dramas*). Published *Elements of German Grammar*, 1807.

in the introduction to the *Observations* he gives a description of the picture from his own visits and tells its history.

Some spurious works were also translated into English under Goethe's name. *Ulric von Hutten* has been already mentioned under its real author—Herder.

In 1804 a novel in three volumes, *Heliodora, or the Grecian Minstrel*, was translated as "from the German of Baron Goethe."[1] The real author was W. A. Lindau.

POETICAL WORKS.

Hermann und Dorothea.—The first translation of *Hermann und Dorothea* was made in verse by Thomas Holcroft, 1801.[2] But it gives a very distorted picture of the original, and has no real merit. In the Preface, Holcroft speaks of the high esteem in which the poem is held in Germany, quoting in proof Schlegel's criticism of it in the *Jenaische Allgemeine Zeitung*. He then goes on to a discussion of German and English versification; it has no particular interest. His own translation is made in blank verse with frequent interruptions and variations, and frequent introduction of the trochaic foot—changes he considers may be happily made in English blank verse. Holcroft's versification and general style deserve little praise. He seems to forget that merely to invert the word-order of a prose sentence does not necessarily make it poetry—*e.g.*,

> "Having housed the hay, our fruits to store
> And the loaded fields to reap
> To-morrow early we begin;"

or:

> "In either hand a jug she took and went,
> Anxious the burden Hermann asked to bear."

---

[1] Vide *Monthly Mag.*, XVIII. 660; 1805.

[2] *Hermann und Dorothea*, a poem from the German of Goethe, by Thomas Holcroft (London, 1801).

One could quote many more examples of such awkward constructions, and some of his expressions are not English at all—*e.g.*, "an endeavoured smile." Holcroft amplifies considerably, and consequently his version fails to reproduce simplicity and directness of the original. Often his additions are just what one feels that Goethe, with his artistic sense, purposely omitted. There are many such examples in the passage quoted below. It is a good example of Holcroft's versification, and also shows how much his changes and amplifications weaken and distort the original. The whole spirit of Goethe's poem and his delicate shades of meaning are quite lost, as is also the simplicity, which is the special charm of a passage such as this, and which shows Goethe's highest art. Holcroft's version reads more like a cheap novelette:

> "The steps they both descended; down they sat
> Upon the wall; but sat the maid not long.
> She stooped to lave and Hermann stooped to aid
> And, by the firmament reflected, play'd
> Their forms within the waters; trembling yet
> Approaching; to smile too timid, yet seemed
> As though they much desired to meet and kiss.
> Oh! of this soul-creating fountain let
> Me drink! the youth exclaimed and gave the maid.
> And deep the draught—it was the draught of love!
> Silent they sat, each leaning on a jug,
> Eloquent silence! not to be endured
> By virgin sensibility—and Dorothea spoke:
> Why came you here,
> So soon, so distant, so alone and how?
> Downcast was Hermann's eye; but then so soft
> Her voice embolden'd, he look'd up and saw
> O Gods! a face how guileless and how sweet.
> Yet naught of love he could there read, but clear
> Intelligence, demanding sound discourse.
> Therefore of love he had no pow'r to speak.
> He thus began . . ."
>
> (VII. 37-53.)

Altogether, the best one can say for Holcroft's translation is that it brought *Hermann und Dorothea* before the notice of English readers. Whether it would have been better left unknown, than known in such a form, is another question.

The principal reviews gave it faint praise. The *British Critic*,[1] as usual, attacks Goethe as an upholder of revolutionary principles and an enemy of all social order, but acknowledges that this tale shows great abilities, and praises it as an interesting story of humble and simple life. The translation is justly appraised as proving a total want of poetic taste and feeling. The *Monthly*[2] analysed the poem at length with many extracts, commenting on it very unfavourably: "This performance is purely and characteristically German, and cannot be possibly admired by those who have not a true German taste. . . . We consider it unique in its own species of composition, and despair of ever meeting any parallel to it in our future researches. . . . If it be poetry, M. de Pourceaugnac [*sic*] was very much misinformed when he was assured that he had spoken prose all his life. . . . It deserves, however, to be commemorated as a very remarkable instance of perverted taste both in nations and individuals since the poem is much read in Germany." In the analysis the reviewer has frequently missed the point of the original. The reader who knew *Hermann und Dorothea* only from this analysis and extracts from Holcroft, would probably not feel inclined to know more of it. Of Goethe's poem he would have no idea at all.

H. Crabb Robinson writes as follows to his brother (June 2nd, 1803) of Holcroft's translation: "That Holcroft should be capable of making such verses and have given us instead of the living original a putrid carcase, is quite a riddle to me . . . the

[1] XVIII. 591. [2] XXXIX. 383; 1802.

Reviewers are almost pardonable for not suspecting the admirable beauties of Goethe's poem."[1]

Holcroft sent his translation to Goethe, and received from him the acknowledgment, denied to Taylor's *Iphigenia*, in a letter dated May 29th, 1801. As a free adaptation of his poem to English taste, Goethe expressed approval of the work and gave it higher praise than it deserved, mentioning only one point in which he objected to Holcroft's deviation from the original. Goethe adds that he hopes to receive later further notes promised by Holcroft, and then to take the opportunity of expressing his opinion of four translations of *Hermann und Dorothea*, lying before him. No record, however, remains in his letters of his having done this.

A note in Stein's edition of Goethe's Letters (V. 21; 1904) gives these four translations as one Danish, one French, and two English, by James Mellish.[2] These last never appeared in print. One was announced in *Der Neue Deutsche Merkur*,[3] as to be published by the London firm of Constantin Geisweiler (the publishers of Mellish's *Maria Stuart*) with introductory remarks by Goethe on the English, French and Italian translations of the poem. Schiller, in a letter to Noehden, August 24th, 1799, mentions that Mellish had sent his translations of the poem to Bell, and that it was about to be published. Apparently the negotiations with both publishers broke down, for nothing further is known of its fate.[4] Goethe knew of the translation and spoke of it to Schiller in a letter dated May 2nd, 1798: "Die englische Übersetzung meiner *Dorothea*, welche Herr Mellish unternommen hat, ist, wie er mir gestern sagte, fertig;

[1] An unedited letter, "Letters from Germany" MS., p. 248. Passage quoted by J. M. Carré. A.S.N.S., Bd. 128, Heft 1, p. 185.

[2] See Chap. X.

[3] III. 65; 1801.

[4] *Cf.* J. L. Haney, *Goethe in England and America*, *Mod. Lang. Notes*, XVI. 255; 1901. E. Oswald, p. 24, does not mention Mellish's translation. Nor does Carré.

er will mir die vier ersten Gesänge zeigen, die er mit hat. Ich selbst kann so was gar nicht beurteilen, ich will veranlassen, dass Schlegel sie zu sehen kriegt, der das Verständniss beyder Sprachen mehr studiert hat."

There does not seem to be even an extract from Mellish's translation in print by which to judge it. But from the quality of his other work, one can safely say that his *Hermann* must have been far superior to Holcroft's; and it is a pity it was never published.[1]

Mellish also translated Goethe's masque *Palæophron und Neoterpe*, written for the festival of the Duchess Amalia's birthday, October 24th, 1800. Mellish's translation was printed at Weimar[2] and again in the *Monthly Magazine*.[3] The masque is preceded by a short introduction by W. Taylor, telling of the festival at Weimar, where it was first represented. Goethe referred to it in a letter to Cotta, January 29th, 1801.

The poem is in rhymeless iambic trimeters and is translated in the same.

To return to *Hermann und Dorothea*.

A prose translation appeared anonymously in 1805.[4] The translator says that in the original poem the great simplicity of manners and incident is a defect in the eyes of many and he has aimed at adapting it to English readers. He says he does not intend to "deviate in essentials from Goethe; but he has allowed himself so many alterations in incident and character that by the end little of the spirit of the original poems remains. The inn "zum goldenen Löwen" becomes a large and fashionable hotel. Canto II. begins with a de-

[1] Could the manuscript be in the Goethe-Schiller Archiv at Weimar?

[2] *Masque for the festival of 24th October*, 1800. From the German of Goethe by the translator of Goethe's *Hermann und Dorothea* and Schiller's *Maria Stuart* (Weimar, Gadicke, 1801).

[3] *A Masque*, by Goethe; translated from the original manuscript by Mr. Mellish of Weimar, XI. 232; 1801.

[4] *Hermann und Dorothea*. A Tale. Translated from the German of Goethe (London, 1805).

scription of Hermann, with "his manly graceful figure, and handsome, prepossessing countenance"; it closes with a long description of the character of the host and of his relations with his son. Moral reflections and explanations are constantly added. *E.g.*, at the end of Canto VI. after: "So stand er ohne Gedanken" is added: "Let us hope that his pure and ardent love will be requited with holy affection." And at the end of Canto VIII.: "Amiable and excellent pair, we must leave you awhile and return to the good host and hostess. Do not apprehend, dear reader, lest Dorothea should meet with any new accidents; she is safely guided by tender and watchful love." After Dorothea's slip on the stone towards the end of Canto VIII. it explains how: "Hermann felt a manly sensibility in bearing one of the most estimable and beautiful of her sex in his arms." The translator found the conclusion of the tale too abrupt and extended it a little, adding a speech of Hermann's father and a few words about the union of the young couple and their subsequent happiness. The translation—where it follows the original closely—is correct and the style very fair. It makes quite a readable prose tale, but a tale very different from Goethe's poem. Here is the same passage as the one quoted from Holcroft:

"Thus speaking, she descended the broad steps with Hermann, and they sat on the low wall of the fountain. She stooped to fill one of her pitchers, and Hermann took the other. As they inclined, they saw their forms at the bottom of the clear stream, and their eyes met with expressive sweetness in the azure mirror. The young man, penetrated with the most pleasing emotion, expressed a wish to drink; his companion offered him her pitcher, and they sat on the wall with the sweet confidence of ingenuous friendship. Dorothea, however, desirous to learn by what accident her friend was there, said: 'Our meeting is as unexpected as it is agreeable. May I ask what brings you here so far from the high road, and without your horse and carriage?' At this question, which so nearly touched his heart, the youth pensively cast his eyes to the ground; but soon raising them, he met the gentle and encouraging looks of Dorothea and his fears were calmed; yet he durst not venture to mention his passion. The manners of the virgin were friendly and open, but they implied good sense, and betrayed no marks of love. Her inquiry was reasonable, and demanded a rational reply. He therefore collected himself, and answered in the confidential tone of friendship. . . ."

Yet this translation is superior to Holcroft's, and in spite of the intentional differences in style and manner, would give a somewhat better idea of the original. The *Annual Review*,[1] in noticing this translation, gave the original poem high praise, calling it "A Vicar of Wakefield in verse," "a poem which if a man does not like, he should learn to like." But he considers that Goethe has a competitor and even a surpasser in this species of composition in Voss, author of *Luise*. He has not much praise for either translation. Holcroft's, he says, is not close enough, nor elegant enough to render a new style of writing attractive. In the prose version he notes how the descriptive introduction spoils the original, which from the first line excites curiosity. He wishes that "an artist-translator had undertaken this work and given a faithful copy of the original in all its peculiarities." One heartily concurs with his wish. No further translations appeared before 1830. Two undated ones by Whewell and Cochrane date from 1840 and 1850.

W. Taylor thought the poem would translate best in the original metre (*vide* Letter to Southey, March, 1821). He translated the beginning of Canto II. in the *Historic Survey*. Here are the opening lines:

"Soon as the well-made son had re-enter'd the tavern, the preacher
Look'd at him, sharply examining mien and behaviour acutely,
With the inquisitive eye of a person accustomed to judgment,
Smil'd then, and thus addressed him in words of friendliest accent:"

Goethe's other long poem in hexameters, *Reineke Fuchs*, was not translated until 1845; the *Achilleïs* fragment not until it appeared in Vol. XIV. of Bohn's *Collected Works*, 1848-90.

[1] III. 346.

To close this survey of Goethe's works in England up to 1830, we quote from a letter of H. Crabb Robinson to Goethe on this subject, dated January 31st, 1829:[1] "The slow progress your works have till lately been making among my countrymen has been a source of unavailing regret. Taylor's *Iphigenia in Tauris*, as it was the first, so it remains the best version of any of your longer poems. Recently des Vœux and Carlyle have brought other of your greater works before our public—and with love and zeal and industry combined, I trust they will yet succeed in redeeming *our* literature rather than your name from the disgrace of such publications as Holcroft's *Hermann und Dorothea*, Lord Leveson Gower's *Faustus*, and a catch-penny book from the French, ludicrous in every page, not excepting the title—the *Life of Goethe*."

[1] *Diary*, etc., II. 389-90.

CHAPTER VI

SCHILLER

This study is confined to Schiller's prose-works, since his plays and poems (three being taken as typical specimens: *Das Lied von der glocke*, *Der Spaziergang*, and *Der Taucher*) have been already treated by Mr. Rea in his book *Schiller in England*.[1] Mr. Rea has not quite exhausted the subject. Many translations are dismissed very shortly, where a more detailed study would be interesting; and he treats very cursorily of the various adaptations of Schiller for the English stage. But his work has since been supplemented by articles on separate plays, and to these the reader is referred; as also to the reviews of Mr. Rea's book which give corrections and additions.[2]

Schiller's Robbers in England, by Margaret Cooke,[3] is an interesting study, tracing the influence of the play on Wordsworth, Coleridge and Shelley. Dr. Willoughby in his article on *The Robbers*[4] gives a careful and detailed account of the various translations, adding much interesting information as to adaptations

[1] *Schiller's Dramas and Poems in England*, Thomas Rea, M.A. (London, 1906).

[2] *Vide* Dr. Karl Kipka, *Studien zur vergl. Litgesch*, Bd. VIII., Heft I., p. 140; 1908. F. W. Lieder, *Jour. of Eng. and Ger. Phil.*, VIII., p. 269; 1909. For other German reviews see L. A. Willoughby's article, *English Translations and Adaptations of Schiller's Robbers*, *Mod. Lang. Rev.*, XVI., pp. 297; 1921.

[3] *Mod. Lang. Rev.*, XI., pp. 156-175; 1916.

[4] *Vide* Dr. Karl Kipka, *Studien zur vergl. Litgesch*, Bd. VIII., Heft I., p. 140; 1908. F. W. Lieder, *Jour. of Eng. and Ger. Phil.*, VIII., p. 269; 1909. For other German reviews see L. A. Willoughby's article, *English Translations and Adaptations of Schiller's Robbers*, *Mod. Lang. Rev.*, XVI., pp. 297; 1921.

for the stage. Dr. Willoughby gave an equally valuable account of "*Kabale und Liebe*" *in English Translation* in a paper read before the English Goethe Society on March 28th, 1924.[1] There is still room for a detailed study of early translations of some other plays.

Die Jungfrau von Orleans.—On p. 82 Mr. Rea mentions a translation by the Rev. T. Salvin in 1824, published with the same translator's version of *Maria Stuart*, which Mr. Rea discusses. But in the chapter on *The Maid of Orleans* he makes no further mention of Mr. Salvin's translation. Hence a few words may be said about it here.

Salvin's[2] translation is a careful and conscientious piece of work. He shows a good knowledge of German, even difficult passages being well understood. There are, however, a few examples of incorrect or loose translation—*e.g.*:

1. "Der fürchterliche Salisbury, der *Mauernzertrummerer*"
   = ". . . the destroyer of the *Moors*"!
2. "In rankes Erz sollst du die Glieder schüren"
   = "A shining casque shall deck thy crested head."
3. "Denn wenn im Kampf die Mutigsten versagen,
   Wenn Frankreichs letztes Schicksal nun sich naht."
   = "And when in fight the stoutest hearts grow tame,
   And France strives feebly 'gainst the foeman's power."

But the general level of translation is good, as will be seen from the following passage (Prolog., 3er Auftritt. Raimond: "Lasst ihr den Willen . . ."):

[1] Pub. of the Eng. Goethe Society, New Series, I., pp. 43-66.

[2] *Rev. Hugh Salvin*, a naval chaplain. He does not appear to have published any other translations from German. He published one from Latin in 1828.

> "Oh! give it her.
> Well does this warlike ornament become her,
> For in her breast lodges a manly heart.
> Ye wist how she subdued the tiger-wolf,
> That fierce and ravenous monster, which had thinned
> Our sheepfolds. While the shepherds stood aloof,
> She all alone, the lion-hearted maid,
> Strove with the wolf and tore the lamb from him,
> Which he was bearing in his bloody jaws.
> However valiant be the head that wears this helm
> None can beseem it better."

And this, the opening lines of Johanna's lyrical monologue (Prolog., 4er Auftritt):

> "Farewell, ye mountains, ye beloved groves,
> Ye dear and peaceful vallies [*sic*], fare ye well!
> No more Johanna roves your haunts among.
> She bids you all a long and last farewell.
> Ye meads, which I have watered oft, ye trees
> Which I have planted, bloom in freshest green
> As ever, and thou echo, which so oft
> Hast in this vale made answer to my songs,
> Ne'er wilt thou list Johanna's voice again."

The verse is very fair though sometimes rather heavy. It is not that of a poet.

A translation of 1835 by J. Drinkwater-Bethune is certainly more successful than Salvin's, reading almost like an original. On the other hand, Salvin's is much superior to G. Egestorff's translation of 1836, which is often unnecessarily diffuse and in poor verse. Egestorff apparently did not know of any earlier translation, as he mentions only seeing "some extracts from a very unsuccessful attempt." This can hardly have been either of those already mentioned—unless Egestorff's judgment is much at fault.

A review of Salvin's *Mary Stuart* and *Maid of Orleans* appeared in the *Monthly Magazine*.[1] The review gives much more space to *Mary Stuart*, transcribing in full the interview between Mary and Elizabeth in

[1] CV. 370; 1824.

both Mellish's and Salvin's versions. Of the *Maid of Orleans* he only says: "This is not a drama of equal value. Indeed, the total dissonance of the catastrophe from all historical testimony and the improbability of many subordinate incidents—such as Johanna falling in love with a young Englishman—place this among the least fortunate of Schiller's exertions." The concluding scene is then given. The reviewer praises the translator and hopes for more translations from his pen.

HISTORICAL WORKS.

Schiller became known as an historian for the first time in England in 1799 by a *History of the Thirty Years' War.*[1] The translator, a young officer named Blaquiere, in a Preface dated from Dublin, pleads for the indulgence of the public for the performance of a young and inexperienced writer. But he hopes, nevertheless, that the work will be acceptable to English readers, since the transactions described in it, though more particularly interesting to Germans, are still not altogether foreign to English history. As an introduction Blaquiere gives a translation of Wieland's preface (1791).

This translation is made from the first edition of the *Geschichte des dreissigjährigen Kriegs* as it appeared in the *Historischer Kalendar für Damen* (1793), and thus differs in many respects from the two later ones, made from Schiller's revised edition of 1802.

Blaquiere had only too much cause to plead for the indulgence of the public towards his work; for he neither knew enough German, nor could he write good enough English, to attempt such a task. He often misconstrues—*e.g.*, "Der Friede, welcher den

[1] *The History of the Thirty Years' War in Germany.* Translated from the original German of Frederic Schiller, Aulic Counsellor and Professor of Philosophy at Jena, by Captain Blaquiere of the Royal Irish Artillery, two vols. (London, 1799).

Ständen des Reichs die vollkommene Religionsfreiheit einräumte, hatte doch einigermassen für den Untertan gesorgt, indem er ihm das Recht ausbedung, das Land, in welchem seine Religion unterdrückt war, zu verlassen," he translates as: "The peace, which yielded religious toleration, had provided for the subject, by leaving him in quiet possession of the country in which he professed his religion"—which is exactly what it did *not*. "When they were not excited by a prospect of indemnity at the expense of the enemy" is not at all the sense of: "wo ihn nicht gar die Nationaleifersucht zu einer feindseligen Schadenfreude reizte." "Die Theilnehmung der Staaten an einander" Blaquiere translates as "the balance of power among states," and hence draws quite different conclusions from those intended by Schiller, who was speaking of the interdependence between states. There are many obscure passages—*e.g.*: "and according as citizens among themselves, and princes among their peoples, began to assume an appearance of opposition, entire kingdoms were opposed to each other in situations hitherto unknown to them." Whatever that may mean, it certainly does not give the sense of the German: "So wie Bürger gegen Bürger, Herrscher gegen ihre Untertanen, durch die Reformation in andere Verhältnisse kamen, rückten ganze Staaten in neue Stellungen gegen einander." Curiously enough, other equally difficult passages are rendered correctly. Besides actual mistranslation, there are many mistakes in English. Words are wrongly used—*e.g.*, "conjunction" for "conjuncture," "the entire" for "the entirety," "benign" for "beneficial," etc. "Einzig und ohne Nebenbuhler" he translates as "single and without a competitor," where "single" cannot be used in this sense. As one critic remarked: "Whatever be Mr. Blaquiere's knowledge of German, he has certainly still to learn English."

The following passage from the conclusion of the

work gives a good idea of the general style. He always condenses the original, sometimes rather successfully, but other times much confounding the sense of the German. The style is laboured.

"The colossal labour of concluding this famous ever memorable and holy treaty, which had to combat with the greatest apparent obstacles, which was to unite the most opposite interests; the concatenation of circumstances which must have combined to terminate this laborious effort of policy; what it cost to open the negotiations amid the alternate vicissitudes of a bloody war, and conclude them under every disadvantage; what the conditions were of a peace which terminated a bloody war of thirty years, and the influence which it had upon the general system of European policy: these must be left to another hand and a more convenient opportunity. The limits are already surpassed which the author of the present sketch had originally proposed and however great the undertaking was to relate the history of the war, that of the peace of Westphalia is one of no less importance. The abridgement of such an event could not here be given with the necessary brevity, without reducing to a skeleton the most interesting and characteristic monument of human wisdom and passions, and thereby depriving it of the attention of the public for which I write, and of which I now respectfully take my leave."

("Was für ein Riesenwerk es war . . . und von dem ich hier Abschied nehme.")

The shortcomings of the translation prejudiced most reviewers against the work itself. The *British Critic*,[1] indeed, sets out by admitting that it would be a gross injustice to the author to try to form any idea of the original through this translation, yet concludes that, seen even through the mist of translation, the work by no means comes up to expectations. With regard to its popularity in Germany, this critic judges that this can afford but a doubtful criterion of its worth since *there* literature and history are so new. He makes a personal attack on the translator, reminding him that "*men* should write, but *youth* should study." The *Critical*[2] judges more favourably, praising specially the manner of writing and the drawing of the characters;

[1] XV. 478.

[2] XXIX. 43; 1800.

but it regrets the sudden conclusion and the want of references. It also notes the incorrectness of the translation. The *Monthly*[1] expresses on the whole disappointment with Schiller's work, but thinks, nevertheless, that a well-executed translation would be favourably received by the public. It apologises to Schiller for showing him to readers in extracts from such a poor translation; but it regrets having to speak so harshly of the "young and modest translator." Only the *Monthly Magazine* gives Schiller's work whole-hearted praise, as showing "the rich versatility of his talents." It welcomes this translation of an instructive work from the German, having been recently alarmed at the great influx of dramas and novels. But this critic is also alone in praising Blaquiere's translation.

The next translation of the *Thirty Years' War* was made nearly thirty years later, in 1828 (from the edition of 1802), by James Marriott Duncan.[2] He refers to Blaquiere's version as being very difficult to procure. His own translation was, he says, begun by way of passing leisure hours; the publishing of it came from the desire of friends, and from the general attention being given at the time to German literature. Of the work itself he merely mentions the importance of the events it describes, and its high reputation throughout Europe.

Duncan's translation is done with great care; though he does not always choose the best English. Keeping so closely to the original, he has awkward English constructions, and his version sometimes lacks ease and fluency. But it is in every way a great improvement on Blaquiere's. The following passage shows it at its best. It does not all read so well:

[1] XXXIII. 395; 1800.

[2] *The History of the Thirty Years' War in Germany*. Translated from the last edition in German of Frederic Schiller by James Marriott Duncan (London, 1828).

"The glorious victory of Gustavus Adolphus at Leipzig caused a great change in all the subsequent conduct of this monarch, as also in the opinion both of his enemies and friends. He had now vied with the greatest general of his age; he had tried the power of his tactics and the courage of his Swedes against the choicest of the Imperial troops, reckoned the best in Europe, and he was superior in this contest. From this moment he felt a greater confidence in himself, and confidence is the mother of great actions. From henceforth a bolder and a firmer step is to be remarked in all the military operations of the Swedish King, more resolution also in critical circumstances, a more imperious language towards his enemies, more self-importance towards his allies, and even his liberality itself showed rather the condescension of the master. His natural courage was seconded by the religious elevation of his mind; he readily confounded his cause with that of heaven; he beheld in Tilly's defeat a decisive judgment of God against his adversary and considered himself merely as the instrument of divine vengeance."

("Die glorreiche Schlacht Gustav Adolfs bei Leipzig . . . in sich selbst aber ein Werkzeug der göttlichen Rache."—Bk. III., chap. i.)

In the same year as Duncan's (1828) a third translation[1] of the *Thirty Years' War* appeared in Edinburgh, as Volumes XVIII. and XIX. of *Constable's Miscellany*. No. XVIII. contained the *Thirty Years' War*; No. XIX. two short pieces: *The Trial and Execution of the Counts Egmont and Horn* and *The Siege of Antwerp*,[2] originally intended to form portions of a second volume of *The Revolt of the Netherlands*, never completed. The translator was a George Moir;[3] an advocate in Edinburgh, and later a friend of Carlyle's. He published in the same year a translation of *Wallenstein*.[4]

[1] *The Historical Works of Frederic Schiller*, from the German, by George Moir, Esq. Translator of Wallenstein (Edinburgh, 1828).

[2] The first appeared in the *Neue Thalia*, VIII; the second in the *Horen*, 1795.

[3] *George Moir* (1800–1870). Born in Aberdeen, educated in Edinburgh. Made Carlyle's acquaintance about 1830, and in 1831 was one of "fifteen English friends" who joined with him in sending a present and an address to Goethe; was professor of rhetoric and belles lettres at Edinburgh, 1835-1840; was collaborator and adviser in the *For. Quar. Rev.*, 1827.

[4] See Rea, p. 57 *ff*.

The *Historical Works* are preceded by an interesting sketch of Schiller's literary career. It shows that by this time the real Schiller was known in Great Britain, chiefly through Carlyle's work, to which Moir proclaims himself greatly indebted. He calls it "the ablest piece of biographical criticism which this century has produced." At the end he gives a few extracts from Schiller's correspondence, and an account of Schiller's introduction to Goethe.

This is the first really adequate translation of the *Thirty Years' War*. It is as careful a piecc of work as Duncan's, but much better in execution. Moir almost always gets the best English equivalent for the German: *e.g.*, "Staatsraison" = "considerations of state policy"; "Unvermerkt" = "insensibly"; "in drei stürmischen Regierungen" = "in three tempestuous reigns" (Blaquiere has = "boisterous"). For "Milde" in "in seiner Milde selbst war mehr die Herablassung des Gebieters," Duncan has "liberality"; Blaquiere "mildness," Moir the best word, "clemency." The passages wrong or half-wrong in Blaquiere are right in Moir. How much better his work is will be easily seen by comparing the following passage with the same as given from Blaquiere. (They are taken from different editions, hence a few sentences omitted in Moir's.)

"The colossal labour attending the completion of this solemn and ever memorable treaty, which is known by the name of the peace of Westphalia; the endless obstacles which were to be surmounted; the contending interests which it was necessary to reconcile; the chain of circumstances which necessarily concurred in order to terminate this tedious, but precious and permanent work of state policy; the difficulties which attended the very opening of the negotiations, maintaining them when opened amidst the ever varying vicissitudes of the war; finally concluding the conditions of peace, and still more the carrying them into execution; what were the conditions of this peace; what each contending power gained or lost by the toils and sufferings of a Thirty Years' War, what influence it exerted upon the general system of European policy: these considerations must be left to another pen. The history of the peace of Westphalia constitutes a whole as important as the history of the war itself. A mere abridgment of it would reduce to a mere skeleton one of the most interesting and characteristic movements of human policy and passions, and deprive it of every feature calculated to fix the attention of the public, for which I write, and of which I now respectfully take my leave."[1]

Schiller's *Abfall der Niederlande* was shortly, but very unfavourably, noticed in 1789, in *The Gentleman's Magazine*,[2] and the *Analytical*.[3] In 1807 it was translated by Thomas Horne,[4] who intended it to serve as an introduction to a history of Philip II., by a Dr. Watson. Schiller's historical essay, Horne says, has long been justly admired by critics as a classical performance, and he hopes that a long and complete acquaintance with the German language has enabled him to translate it with correctness and taste. He compares Schiller's genius to that of Burke.

Horne's translation includes only part of the original. It is divided into four sections; the first giving Schiller's "Einleitung," the other three Schiller's "Erstes Buch"—the earlier history of the Netherlands, and character studies of William of Orange, Egmont, and Margaret of Parma—up to the second last paragraph. Here the translation ends.

As far as it goes, it follows the original closely and correctly enough. Yet there are inaccuracies—*e.g.*, "the exorbitant power of Charles inflamed the jealousy of the Belgians, a passion that is the ordinary symptom of imbecility" does not translate: "das Übergewicht Karls weckte zu gleicher Zeit das Misstrauen bei den Niederländern auf, das stets die Ohnmacht begleitet."

[1] Carlyle is said to have made a partial translation of the work in 1827, and presented it to Longmans, who refused it. The appearance of Moir's version may have prevented him from making further attempts to publish his own.

[2] LIX. 639. [3] III. 605.

[4] *History of the rise and progress of the Belgian Republic until the Revolution under Philip II., including a detail of the primary causes of that memorable event.* From the German original of Frederic Schiller, by Thomas Horne (London, 1807).

The original is often amplified—*e.g.*, "und die zertretenen Felder nährten ihre Pflüger nicht mehr" becomes: "the fertile plains being converted into a wilderness did no longer suffice for the support and sustenance of the husbandman." Amplification may sometimes be necessary to make the sense clear, but Horne uses it too much, and often makes quite arbitrary additions to the text. On the whole, however, the translation is good, though greater simplicity and clearness would make it much better. The *Critical*[1] found fault with a certain floweriness of diction (to be attributed rather to Horne than to Schiller).

The reviewers now praised Schiller much more highly than in 1789. The *Critical*—except for the blame given above—thinks the translation well done, and commends the original as abounding in a rich harvest of reflections, even if wanting in clearness of narration. The *Monthly*[2] in a long article with many extracts speaks of it as "a production of no imposing form, but of pre-eminent merit." It praises "the vivid and nervous style, happy arrangement, and artful and impressive narrative," and expresses surprise that the translator should assign to such a work so inferior a station as merely an introduction to Dr. Watson's History. The *British Critic*[3] also praised both the work and the translation.

To conclude, a short passage may be given as a specimen of the latter:

"Nothing can be more easy and natural, than a transition from civil to religious liberty. An individual or a community, who, under the mild influence of a happy constitution, are become acquainted with the dignity of human nature, having thoroughly imbibed the spirit of those laws, which are the supreme oracles of distributive justice, and which they have perhaps framed themselves; their intellectual faculties being more vigorous from constant exercise and their organs of sense more acute and distinguishing, from a delicious and voluptuous life; whose natural spirit has been exalted and sublimated

[1] X. 426; 1807.
[2] LIV. 242; 1807.
[3] XXXI. 457.

by internal security and affluence : such an individual and such a community, I say, are of all others the most averse to bend under the galling yoke of an oppressive hierarchy, and the most eager to vindicate their liberty."

(" Die Niederlande unter Karl. V. 'Nichts ist natürlicher als der Übergang . . . und sich früher als andere wieder davon emporrichten.")

A passage such as the above would naturally appeal to English people; and Horne's translation seems to have been pretty widely read. The *Thirty Years' War* dealt with events more exclusively German; *The Belgian Republic* had a more direct connection with English traditions. In past centuries, the English too had been the enemies of Spain, and both their religion and their relationship with the house of Orange roused their feelings on the side of the revolted provinces.

Of Schiller's philosophical and æsthetic prose writings practically nothing was translated into English before 1830. The *German Museum* (1801) included translations of two Essays from Schiller: (1) *Essay on the effects of a well regulated theatre* (II. 382); (2) *The Legislation of Lycurgus* (III. 283).[1]

FICTION.

Schiller has lived as a dramatist and a poet. His novel and tales are almost forgotten. Yet some of these were very popular in his own day, especially *Der Geisterseher*, a tale intended by its author to have deep philosophical significance. The public regarded it merely as an amusing and thrilling tale of mystification and intrigue: and so Schiller, disgusted, never gave it a real conclusion. It had several spurious continuations and a host of imitators.

[1] *Was kann eine gute stehende Schaubühne eigentlich werden?* *Thalia*, Heft I., 1787. *Die Gesetzgebung des Lycurgus und Solon.* *Thalia*, Heft XI.

The *Ghost-Seer* also became popular in England for the same reasons as in Germany—helped probably by being partly an attack on the Jesuits—and became the model of many tales of mystery and horror. Byron mentions in a letter from Venice, April 2nd, 1817, the great impression which the *Ghost-Seer* made on him as a boy.[1]

The first translation was made in 1795[2] by one D. Boileau (according to a pencil note in the copy in the British Museum). The translation was suggested by the favourable notice of the Fragment in the *Monthly*.[3] It is taken from the first edition of the German, published separately.[4] The conclusion, which did not appear in this separate edition, was given in the *Neue Thalia*[5] in the form of a long correspondence. The contents of these letters is given by our present translator in a considerably abridged form and from memory. In a notice of this in the *Monthly*[6] Schiller is referred to as already a popular writer in England. The critic considers that the applause given to the *Ghost-Seer* in Germany rather overrates its merits, but that it is, nevertheless, a novel of great originality.[7]

A prefatory notice to the second translation by William Render[8] (1800) alludes to the imperfect and unsatisfactory conclusion of the tale in the earlier version. Render hopes that a faithful translation of the whole work will be acceptable to all admirers of Schiller. Only the first volume of the two is in the

[1] See Stokoe, *German Influence*, etc., pp. 160, 161.

[2] *The Ghost-Seer or Apparitionist, an interesting fragment*, found among the papers of Count O——, from the German of Schiller (London, Vernor and Hood, 1795).

[3] September, 1794.

[4] Leipzig, Göschen, 1789.

[5] 1787. Heft IV. 68-94.

[6] XVIII. 346.

[7] For resemblances with Coleridge's *Remorse*, see Stokoe, *German Influence*, etc., p. 127.

[8] *The Armenian, or the Ghost-Seer. A History founded on fact.* Translated from the German of Schiller, author of *The Robbers*, *Don Carlos*, etc., by the Rev. W. Render (London, Symonds, 1800).

British Museum; but the two volumes are to be had in a reprint of 1831. The first volume contains a few letters not given in the earlier edition. Most of the second volume is a spurious continuation, not really by Schiller. It tells of the further career of the Armenian and his horrible death; also of the Prince's last years, his profession of the Catholic faith, and his death by lightning.

The third translation[1] was made many years later by Thomas Roscoe in the third volume of his *German Novelists* (1826). Roscoe's remarks in his introduction show the significant change which had taken place in the English attitude towards Schiller, largely due to Coleridge, and then to Carlyle, whose *Life of Schiller* Roscoe calls "a work in every way worthy of the great character it commemorates." With regard to the *Geisterseher*, Roscoe justly points out that (as already mentioned) Schiller did not write it to indulge the prevalent taste for romantic terrors, but rather to exemplify certain opinions of his own. "He was too serious in all he said and did to write merely for his own amusement or that of others."

Roscoe makes no allusions to the two earlier translations. In the first of these, as has been seen, the conclusion is imperfect; while the second admits a long spurious continuation. So Roscoe's version has at least the merit of being the only one to give *Der Geisterseher* as Schiller really left it. As to the actual translations, Boileau's and Render's both follow the original faithfully, and on the whole correctly. But inaccuracies can be found in both. Sometimes Boileau is more exact; sometimes Render. Render translates "temperament" by "temperance," where Boileau comes nearer to the sense with "inclination." Roscoe translates altogether more freely, and his version sometimes makes pleasanter reading; but it is full of

[1] *The Apparitionist. A Fragment. Extracted from the Memoirs of the Count von O——.*

inaccuracies and careless mistakes. He would have done well to have studied the earlier translations, correct in all the passages where he is wrong.

Here are a few of his worst mistakes:

1. "Niemand war mehr dazu geboren, sich beherrschen zu lassen, ohne schwach zu sein"; "No one perhaps was more exposed than he was to suffer himself to be influenced and commanded by the opinion of others, *more liable to mental weakness*."

2. "Selbst aus seinen Spielen war die Freude verbannt" = "even pleasure was banished from his sports," where the position of "even" completely changes the meaning.

3. "Ich bilde mir ein, man verkennt uns" = "I suspect we are known"—just the opposite.

4. "Und gewiss wäre er eine Zierde des Thrones geworden, den er durch ein Verbrechen ersteigen zu wollen sich bethören liess" = "And he would most assuredly have proved himself an ornament to a throne which threw a strange glamour round him from a desire of ascending it by a crime"—where the English is anything but clear, but if it expresses any idea, it is not that of the German.

Apart from such obvious mistakes, many expressions are very feebly rendered—*e.g.*, "die heftigen Gemütsbewegungen des handelnden Menschen" becomes: "the mental exercise of the man of business." Of the three translations Boileau's is decidedly the best.

One of the imitations of *Der Geisterseher*, Cajetan Tshink's *Geschichte eines Geistersehers* (1791), appeared in English in 1795, translated by the Rev. Peter Will.[1] It was a work popular in Germany at the time; but these long tales of wonder and magic are scarcely readable today. The English of the translation is

[1] *The Victim of Magical Delusion, or the Mystery of the Revolution of P——l. A Magico-Political Tale, founded on historical facts.* Translated from the German of Cajetan Tschinck by P. Will (London, Robinson, 1795).

fair, but foreign idioms occur. The reviewer in the *British Critic* recommends it to all who delight in the marvellous, while admitting that it afforded him personally little amusement. He prefers it, nevertheless, to the *Ghost-Seer*, " a production of the same school as above, but less consistent and more dull."

There were no less than four translations of *Der Verbrecher aus verlorenen Ehre* before 1830. The earliest (probably that alluded to by Holcroft in the preface to his tales) appeared in the *German Museum* (II. 144 *ff.*) in 1801 signed " F." In point of exactness it compares very favourably with the much later translations of Roscoe and Holcroft. It is free from Roscoe's careless mistakes, and often is more exact than Holcroft. *E.g.:*

" als einen losen Buben " { = " as a wild youth " (" F ")
= " as a waggish boy" (Holcroft).

" ertrotzen " { = " obtain by defiance " (" F ")
= " obtain " (Holcroft).

On the other hand,

" Wilddieb " { = " deer-stealer " (" F ")
= " poacher " (Holcroft).

In the style there is a good deal of stiffness.

The other three translations all date from twenty-five years later.

The second, by a German named Wapler,[1] was printed at Augsburg, and is full of the grossest misprints—punischment, looded, cudge (for cudgel), etc. Many odd mistakes betray the translator's ignorance of English, and even when he is correct he keeps one conscious of dictionary and grammar. Here is a specimen:

[1] *The Criminal become so from lost* [*sic*] *of honour*, translated from the original German of Frederic Schiller by Lewis Wapler (Augsburgh, 1825).

"An oppressive consciousness of indigence, joined to offended pride, penury and jealousy, assaults in crowds his sensibility; hunger impels him to roam at large in the wide world; vengeance and passion retain him to his native country. He becomes a poacher a second time; but Robert's redoubled vigilance frustrates his prospects a second time. Now he suffers the whole severity of the law, for he has nothing more to give, and in a few weeks he is delivered over to the house of correction in the capital."

The third translation in the *German Novelists*[1] is, of course, much better English, and much more readable; but has Roscoe's usual careless mistakes. Wapler has at least the merit of having understood the text—*e.g.*, "denn ich hatte ihm Gutes getan und konnte ihn keines persönlichen Hasses beschuldigen"="For I had done him a favour and was guilty of no personal hatred, at least against him" (Roscoe). "For I had rendered him a service, and could not suspect him of any personal hatred against me" (Wapler).

The fourth translation, by Holcroft, in his *German Tales*[2] (1826) is much the best of the three. The style is better than Roscoe's, all whose mistakes are avoided. Yet Holcroft makes a few slips of his own. In translating "er war sinnlich" as "he grew thoughtful" he makes two mistakes. Again here Wapler is right with "he was sensual."

Roscoe also gave three shorter tales from Schiller—the *Sport of Destiny*, *Fraternal Magnanimity*, and a *Walk among the Linden Trees*.[3] The first had been already twice translated: by W. Tooke in the *Varieties of Literature*[4] (1795); and again anonymously in 1820 in *Blackwood's Magazine*.[5] This translation in *Blackwood* is more correct than Roscoe's, and altogether a more faithful copy. This is specially evident in the concluding paragraphs, where Roscoe

1 *The Criminal or Martyr to lost honour.*

2 *The Dishonoured Irreclaimable.*

3 *Das Spiel des Schicksals; Eine grossmütige Handlung aus der neuesten Geschichte; Der Spaziergang unter den Linden.*

4 II. 508.

5 VIII. 375; 1820.

allows himself many liberties, as one example will show:

> "Aber konnte er ihm auch das Herz dazu wiedergeben, das er auf immer für den Genuss des Lebens verstümmpelte."

> "But could he also restore to him that heart which he had forever untuned for the enjoyment of life?"—(*Blackwood*).

Roscoe here invents freely:

> "Never, however, could he win back the sincere good-will and attachment which had once distinguished him; his heart was closed to all the enjoyments of life."

CHAPTER VII

DRAMATIC WORKS

This chapter includes all dramatic works not treated of elsewhere, as are Goethe's and Schiller's. Its two divisions correspond to the two periods in which German dramas became known in England: the first to *c.* 1810, including the years when the rage for German drama was at its height—1798-1802, with Kotzebue as the central figure; the second *c.* 1815-1830, when the new school of German drama (Grillparzer, Müllner, Werner, etc.) became known in England, not, indeed, as affording popular amusement, as in the earlier period, but by more careful study and much better translations.

Chronological arrangement has been found most convenient for Part I.; a personal division under the names of the most important dramatists for Part II.

PART I. (*c.* 1785-*c.* 1810).

In 1766 a work entitled *Harlequin, or a defence of the grotesque*, appeared in English, translated from the German of Justus Möser by J. A. F. Warnecke. The translator remarks that the present bad condition of the German stage is due not to the fault of the performers, nor to the want of genius and taste in German dramatic authors, but rather to the want of favour of princes and the absence of a central resort of taste, as is Paris to the French, or London to the English. Among German dramatists he mentions in particular Lessing—"whose *Sara Sampson* is a masterpiece of tragic performance"—as "one of those who, with proper encouragement, might have added lustre to the

German stage." But *Harlequin* was an isolated effort, and probably little read. No general interest was taken in England in German drama for twenty years after this date. In 1786 the *Edinburgh Magazine* published an article entitled *Sketch of the origin and progress of Dramatic Poetry in Germany* which may have been known to Henry MacKenzie, whose famous paper, *An Account of the German Theatre*, was read before the Royal Society of Edinburgh on April 21st, 1788.[1] Mackenzie was at that time ignorant of German, and based his remarks chiefly on Friedel and De Bonneville's *Nouveau Théâtre Allemand* (1782-85). He gave the most conspicuous place to Schiller's *Robbers*.[2]

Mackenzie's lead was soon followed in England in N. Drake's *Speculator*, a series of daily papers appearing between March and June, 1790.[3] Stokoe gives an interesting account both of Mackenzie's paper and the *Speculator* articles. A translated fragment of *Clavigo*, which appeared in the *Speculator*, is discussed here in Chapter V.

On November 11th, 1790, *The German Hotel*, a translation, or rather adaptation of J. C. Brandes' (1735-1799) *Der Gasthof* was given at Covent Garden, being probably the first representation of a German play on the English stage. The translation is attributed by some authorities to Marshall, by others, with more probability, to T. Holcroft.[4] Holcroft speaks of it in his *Memoirs*.[5] At the first performance

[1] Vide *Transactions of the Royal Society of Edinburgh*, II. 152 *ff.* (1790). Reprinted *Edinburgh Magazine*, 1790, and in the *Sentimental and Masonic Magazine* (Dublin), 1792. See Stokoe, *German Influence*, etc., pp. 27-32 and pp. 34, and Hans Schwarz, *Henry Mackenzie*, Inaugural Dissertation, Wintertür, 1911.

[2] *Vide* Rea, pp. 7, 8.

[3] These Essays are attributed by some to E. Ash. But they were reprinted with some additions and alterations in N. Drake's *Literary Hours*, 1798.

[4] *Biog. Dram.* (II. 263) gives Marshall. Genest. (VII. 22) says: "attributed to Marshall but probably written by Holcroft."

[5] II. 68.

of *The German Hotel*[1] the predominantly serious turn and style of a play performed under the title of a comedy rather surprised the English audience; but they soon got used to the singularity, and applauded heartily. In the advertisement to the printed edition, the Author says that the applause exceeded not only his own hopes but the play's intrinsic merits. It ran successfully for thirteen nights. The translation is literal in some parts; in others pretty free. The scene is laid in the hall of a large hotel and the plot is quick and lively, probably making a better acting than reading play. *The German Hotel* was noticed by several reviews, and on the whole favourably.[2]

Neither *Götz* (1799), nor *The Sister*, nor Ayrenhoff's *Set of Horses* in the *Dramatic Pieces from the German*[3] (1792) appeared on the stage.

The next German play to be acted was *Emilia Galotti*, given at Drury Lane in 1794. It was an utter failure, running only three nights.

The only other play of Lessing's acted in England was *Minna von Barnhelm* given as *The Disbanded Officer* at the Haymarket in 1796.

In 1795 the *Secret Tribunal*, a play by J. Boaden based on Kramer's *Hermann von Unna*, was given at Covent Garden with a good deal of success.

Reynolds' tragedy of *Werter*[4]—based on Goethe's novel—was given in the same year in the same theatre.

Klinger's *Die neue Arria* was translated as *The Modern Arria* in 1795. Leisewitz' *Julius von Tarent* appeared in parts in the *German Museum*, 1800-1801 (see Chapter II.). These were the only specimens of

[1] *The German Hotel.* A Comedy, as performed at the Theatre Royal, Covent Garden (Robinson, 1790).

[2] *Analytical*, IX. 217; 1791. *Monthly*, V. 345; 1791. *Critical*, LXIX. 698; 1790. *Lady's Magazine*, XXI. 567 *ff*. and 657, which devoted several pages to a synopsis of the plot with extracts.

[3] *Vide* Chap. V.

[4] *Vide* Brandl, G. J., III., and Appell, *Werther und seine Zeit.*, chap. i.

the minor "Sturm und Drang" dramas which found their way to England. Neither appeared on the stage.

In 1796 A. Thompson gave a translation of some scenes of A. Meissner's (1753-1807) *Bianca Capello* and of his *German Theatre at Venice*—more properly a narrative of a drama than a real drama—in his *German Miscellany* (Perth, 1796).[1] But neither of these appeared on the stage. A comedy of Kotzebue's in the same collection will be mentioned later.

From 1798 date translations of two now forgotten historical dramas by Franz Kratter—*Natalia and Menzikoff, or the Conspiracy against Peter the Great* and *The Maid of Marienburg*. The translation of the first is very poor and full of unEnglish idioms. The second is not procurable.[2] They received several and somewhat contradictory reviews.[3] Neither of these dramas appeared on the stage.

In 1798 a farce by Mowbray, *The Devil of a Lover*, based on Veit Weber's *The Sorcerer*, was acted at Covent Garden, but without success.[4]

A tragedy called *The Inquisitor*, translated freely by Holcroft from a German play, *Diego und Leonore*,[5] was acted at the Haymarket at about the same time. According to Baker,[6] "this marvellous, mysterious, terrific production was laughed down." And the *European Magazine*[7] says: "The play was of a gloomy nature, abounding in the marvellous, mysterious, and terrific; but the audience were hilarious." Baker[8] gives another play of the same name in the same year, from the German by J. P. Andrews and H. J. Pye, which was never acted.

1 *Vide* Chap. IX.

2 Extracts given in *Crit. Rev.*, *Month. Rev.*, and *Anal. Rev.*

3 *British Critic*, XII. 668; 1798. *Critical*, XXIII. 230. *Analytical*, XXVII. 615. *Monthly*, XXVI. 340.

4 *Biog. Dram.*, I. 160.

5 German author's name not given. It is by J. C. Unger, 1775.

6 II. 326. 7 XXXIV. 41. 8 II. 326.

August Kotzebue.—Of the short but brilliant "Glanzperiode" of the German stage in England (1798-1802), when it dominated all dramatic interests, Kotzebue is the central figure and prime factor. It would be necessary here to devote a chapter to him alone, had not the ground been already covered by Walter Sellier's *Kotzebue in England* (Berlin, 1901). This valuable study gives a full account of all the dramas of Kotzebue as they were acted in England, with the minutest details as to their representations, etc., find careful references. We therefore give here only the briefest survey of Kotzebue's plays in England. A list of translations will be found in the Appendix.

After Kotzebue's name had been, by the *Indians in England* in A. Thompson's *German Miscellany* (1796), first introduced to English readers, and his fame first founded by *The Negro-Slaves* of the same year, he conquered the English stage by *The Stranger* (1798), an adaptation by Sheridan[1] of an English translation of *Menschenhass und Reue*. It was an immediate success, and soon outdid even Shakespeare's plays—much acted at the moment—in popularity. Covent Garden produced in the same season *Lover's Vows*—represented forty-two nights—and four of Kotzebue's comedies in the following winter.

The extraordinary success of Sheridan's *Pizarro* (1799)—adapted from a translation by M. Geisweiler of *Die Spanier in Peru*—is well known. It went through twenty editions in one year. On the stage it drew crowded houses for sixty-seven nights at Drury Lane in the first season, afterwards in the other London theatres as well, and soon in the provinces. Sellier notes a representation as far off as Athlone (Ireland) in 1837 as "Shakespeare's celebrated play of *Pizarro*"!

Other Kotzebue plays—too numerous to mention here—appeared on the London stage in these years.

[1] *Vide* Leopold Bahlsen, *Kotzebue and Sheridan* (Berlin, 1889).

The public soon tired of his sentimental "Rührstücke"—*The Wise Man of the East*, adapted by Mrs. Inchbald (1799), was the last of these to be given (1800)—but the vogue of his spectacular pieces and farces lasted much longer. *The Stranger* was acted every year up to 1842, and was the last of Kotzebue's plays to be given in London (1872). *Pizarro* was acted in London till 1840 and revived in 1855.

A new "Schaustück"—*Kamshatka* (from *Graf Benjowsky*)—was given at Covent Garden in 1812. It was not very successful. But *The Virgin of the Sun* (*Die Sonnenjungfrau*) in the same year was very popular, as was also a farce, *How to die for love* (*Blind geladen*). In the following years there were no new plays staged, though several translations were made. The next and the last is *The Poachers*, adapted from *Der Rehbock* ("ein durchaus frivoles Stück" in the opinion of one German critic), given at Covent Garden in 1824. It was well received both by the public and the newspaper critics, and was still running in 1830.

Interest in Kotzebue led to interest in other less-known German dramatists. We must now return to mention some of these, whose plays were translated—though for the most part not acted—during these years.

The most important is—

A. W. Iffland (1759-1814), several of whose plays were translated in 1799 and 1800, though none found worthy of the stage. He is praised in general by the English critics as being less extravagant and more moral than Kotzebue, but as having less force and stage effect. The translations are mainly poor.

The earliest is an anonymous and inaccurate translation (1799) of *Die Hagestolzen* as *The Bachelors*. It was noticed in the *Critical*,[1] which thinks the heroine country-girl will appear forward and foolish in England, though she may be simple and natural to Germans.

[1] XXVI. 474.

The Nephews (1799) is a free translation by Hannibal Evans Lloyd[1] of *Die Mündel.* The translation is good, but the dialogue sometimes lacks naturalness. The *Monthly*[2] comments on it very harshly: "We could hardly believe that such trash pleased in foreign theatres, if even greater nonsense of foreign origin did not attract plaudits and tears in our own."

The Foresters, translated by Miss Plumptre, from *Die Jäger* (1799), is noticed by Baker[3] as a play containing much good writing, but as not suitable for English theatres. The *Monthly*[4] thinks the moral excellent, but the whole play languid and drowsy. The *Critical*[5] also finds it dull, but an interesting picture of rural life.

The Lawyers (1799), translated by a German, C. Ludger, from *Die Advokaten*, is accompanied by a few remarks on Iffland, "The Garrick of the German stage," the "dramatic rival of Kotzebue in the closet." The translation decidedly betrays the hand of a foreigner. One meets such expressions as: "You open to me the prospect of paradisic futurity," or "The man of my heart must act in full." The *Monthly*[6] praises Iffland as exhibiting in this play discrimination of character and delicacy of sentiment, but condemns all his plays as "being encumbered with the vapid commonplace of the German theatre."

[1] *H. E. Lloyd* (1771–1847). Philologist and translator. Lived in Hamburg 1800–1813. He suffered much during the occupation of Hamburg by the French and joined the inhabitants in taking up arms against them. On his return to England he received a post in the Foreign Office. Had an extensive acquaintance with Continental languages, and is said to have dictated in three at once. His friendship with Klopstock and unpublished translation of the *Messiah* have been mentioned in chap. ii. He published translations of German works of travel, archæology, etc., and several books on German and English language.

[2] XXXII. 323; 1800.

[3] *Biog. Dram.*, II. 245.

[4] XXX. 213.

[5] XXVII. 59.

[6] XXX. 211. Also *Crit. Rev.*

Crime from Ambition (*Verbrechen aus Ehrsucht*) (1800), by Maria Geisweiler, is, as a translation, so poor that it is merely German in English words. It reads badly, and on the stage would be impossible. It received an uncomplimentary review in the *Critical*.

The last play translated from Iffland was *Conscience*, by B. Thompson, in the fourth volume of his *German Theatre* (1801).

An interlude in one act, *The good Neighbour*, is given by Morgan (*Bibl. of Ger. Lit.*, p. 274) as altered from Iffland by W. Dunlop in 1814 and published in New York.

Besides actual translations, Iffland gave matter for several English plays—*e.g.*, part of the plot of *Beggar my Neighbour, or a Rogue's a Fool*, a comedy ascribed to Mr. Morton, is borrowed from *The Nephews*.[1]

The German Theatre (1801), by Benjamin Thompson.[2] These six volumes contain ten plays of Kotzebue, besides *Emilia Galotti*, *The Robbers*, *Don Carlos*, *Stella*, and several plays of now forgotten authors: *Otto von Wittelsbach* and *Dagobert, King of the Franks*,[3] by J. M. Babo; *The Ensign*, by Schroeder; and *Count Koenigsmark*, by Karl Reitzenstein. Some had appeared separately between 1798-1800. The *European Magazine*[4] says: "The volumes will afford a complete satisfaction to all who are desirous of becoming acquainted with the beauties and defects of the German stage; the Dramas are selected with judgment and the talents of the translator appear in a most favourable light." Here

[1] *Biog. Dram.*, II. 52.

[2] *Benjamin Thompson* (1776 ?–1816). Went to Hamburg as agent for his father, who was a merchant, and there learned German. Occupied his spare time in translating plays by Kotzebue and other German dramatists, which he collected in the *German Theatre* (1801). Sheridan adapted *The Stranger* from Thompson's translation of *Menschebhass und Reue* (1798).

[3] "An interesting piece," *Biog. Dram.*, II. 151.

[4] XL. 114; 1801.

one cannot quite agree. The translations are not worth very much. Thompson takes great liberties with his text and is often careless and inaccurate. Still, his work is superior to that of most of the translators of the time; and his versions of Kotzebue's plays—specially that of *The Stranger*[1]—are better than most contemporary translations. The selection of dramas is interesting, showing the rank given in England to the various German dramatists of the day. To Kotzebue are given three of the six volumes. From Goethe and Schiller are translated only one or two of the plays then published in Germany. None of the plays in *The German Theatre* were acted. A second edition was published in 1806.

Another play of Babo's — *The Strehlitzes* (*Die Strelitzen*)—came out in *The German Museum* (1800-1), also Leisewitz' *Julius von Tarent*;[2] and *The Mystery*, by Vulpius, famous in England as the author of *Rinaldo Rinaldini*. None of these were acted, nor are they even mentioned by Baker.[3]

A collection of plays taken from the *Schauspiele für Kinder*, very popular about this time in Germany, was published at Hamburg in 1801 under the title of *The Juvenile Dramatist*.[4] The plays are intended to be educative, rather than entertaining. The three volumes include several plays by C. F. Weisse;[5] two by J. J. Engel,[6] and several not ascribed to any author.[7] The translation is a curious mixture of involved, pompous language in the longer speeches,

[1] *Vide* Sellier, p. 21. [2] *Vide* Chap. IV. [3] *Biog. Dram.*

[4] *The Juvenile Dramatist*, or a selection of plays from the most celebrated German writers upon education. Translated from the originals (Hamburg, 1801).

[5] *The modish young lady; The Birthday; Filial Piety; The Ill-Bred Boy; The Greyhound; Nature's Magic or A bad conscience.* The originals first appeared in *Der Kinderfreund*, and afterwards separately.

[6] *The Page; The grateful Son.*

[7] *The Young Gamesters; The Generous Offender; The Little Family Dispute; The Young Archers.*

and efforts at vivid colloquialisms in other parts. It is often too literal to be good English. *The Juvenile Dramatist* seems to have had but few readers in England, where less interest was then taken in educational questions than in Germany. These didactic plays, all pointing an obvious moral, were not noticed in any of the English reviews.

In 1804 M. G. Lewis's *Rugantino*[1] (taken from Zschokke's *Abällino*) was given with great success at Covent Garden.[2] Another version entitled *Abellino, The Venetian Outlaw*, translated by R. W. Elliston from a French translation, *L'Homme a trois Masques*, was given with equal success at Drury Lane, 1805.[3] There were also other dramatisations, one at the Royal Circus.

The Theatrical Recorder—a series of plays published in periodical form by Thomas Holcroft, 1805-6—included several translations from the German, done by himself and by his sister, Fanny Holcroft. In the second volume there is a translation of J. J. Engel's *Der dankbare Sohn* as *The Affectionate Son*. It is made from a French version in *Le Nouveau Théâtre Allemand*, Holcroft having had no copy of the original at hand. Comparing the translation with the original we find it not always correct. The mistakes may come from the French translation,[4] but Holcroft himself is often careless in his translating. "Herr Pfarrer" is always called the "curate," that common mistranslation of the French "curé." The earlier translation of the same play in *The Juvenile Dramatist*, being taken from the original, is often more correct in particular points than Holcroft's, but Holcroft's English reads much better.

C. F. Weisse.—In the same volume of *The Theatrical Recorder* there is a translation, by Fanny Holcroft, of C. F. Weisse's tragedy of *Rosamunde*—the only drama of Weisse's translated into English before 1830,

[1] *Vide* Chap. VIII.
[2] *Biog. Dram.*, III. 131.
[3] *Genest.*, VII. 649.
[4] Not in Brit. Mus.

if we except the children's pieces in *The Juvenile Dramatist*.[1] Miss Holcroft does not appear to have known of these. In the *Remarks* she speaks of Weisse as "perhaps disputing the palm of excellence with Lessing." The original is in alexandrines; the translation in blank verse, with occasional alexandrines, perhaps unintentional, for Miss Holcroft's versification is not very good, and there is little harmony in her verse. Other German plays in the *Theatrical Recorder* are *Minna von Barnhelm* and *Emilia Galotti*. None were put on the stage. After this, few German plays, except occasionally Kotzebue's, were either translated or staged.

The popularity of German drama in England did not last long; but its influence was long felt. A review of Harriet Lee's *The Three Strangers* in 1826[2] traces this play to that influence, and goes on to discuss in an interesting article the reasons for the enthusiasm with which German drama was greeted when first imported, about thirty years before. (1) It was received as the near, though late kindred, of the English Elizabethan dramas, the qualities in which they differed being forgotten in those where the resemblance was most striking. (2) Public taste at that moment was satiated with productions of frigid and regular beauty of the pseudo-classic dramatists, who wrote by rule. In the reaction against this excessive tameness, nothing was better suited to the new taste than the German dramas, whose chief characteristic was exaggeration in everything—excessive horrors, impossible extremes of happiness and misery, and characters half angels, half demons. (3) The absence of any real genius among native dramatic writers of the time. With the possible

[1] In 1789 a little collection of *Moral Songs for Children* was translated from Weisse's *Kleine Lieder für Kinder zur Beförderung der Tugend*. They are absolutely without literary interest.

[2] *Europ. Mag.*, I. 138; 1826.

exception of Sheridan, Kotzebue may be fairly said to rank as high as any of them. He soon became the general favourite, and the actors—many of whom found their best " show-rôles " in his plays—were often at the same time directors of the theatres, and were only too ready to give the public what they wanted, the theatres being absolutely dependent on public favour.

German drama had both its enthusiastic admirers and its bitter opponents. The *Critical* was, at least at first, on the side of its admirers. In a review of *Götz* (1799) it says: " There are those who despise the German dramas, but except for the best plays of our unrivalled Shakespeare, we know of none comparable to them . . . French and Italian plays are praised and neglected. German plays are continually read, and though faulty and incorrect, daily become more popular." Among the dramatic critics Dutton fairly consistently opposed the introduction of the German drama, though he defended it against the exaggerated diatribes of Hannah Moore and others.[1] Miss Moore, together with the *British Critic*,[2] voiced most loudly the opposition to German drama on the ground of its immorality. But its bitterest enemy was the *Anti-Jacobin Review*. Herford[3] says that the *Anti-Jacobin's* Parody of *The Rovers*[4] in 1798 killed German drama in England for many years. This may be an exaggeration. But this and other parodies helped to hasten a reaction which was bound to come. Another Conservative periodical, *The Meteors* (1799-1800),[5] gave a humorous burlesque, specially intended to ridicule *The Robbers*, entitled " *The Benevolent Cutthroat*, translated from an original German drama written by the celebrated Klotzboggenhagen, by Fabius Pictor." Only part of one Act was written. " The parody is a

[1] *Vide* his *Dramatic Censor*, and Sellier, p. 51.
[2] *E.g.*, review of *Stella*, XII. 424.
[3] *Age of Wordsworth*, p. 138.
[4] Vide *Stella*, chap. v. [5] No. III., 1799.

series of wild, outrageous exaggerations and absurdities, and has no resemblance whatever to *The Robbers*."[1]

In another number there is a satirical piece entitled *Prologue for any German Play*. We find more poetic outbursts against German drama in other periodicals. In the *European Magazine*[2] (1799) there is an *Ode to German drama*, addressed as:

> " Daughter of Night, Chaotic Queen !
> * * * * *
> Bound in thy necromantic spell
> The audience taste the joys of hell."

(Suggested by " The proud only taste of pain " in Gray's *Hymn to Adversity*: " Daughter of Jove, relentless Queen.") Schiller, " the sublimely mad," and Kotzebue are called " the gigantic pair," who overshadow all others. In *The Gentleman's Magazine*[3] of the following year there is an *Ode on the Prevalence of the German Drama*, beginning:

> " Say, from what cause proceeds the modern rage
> Of German dramas on the English stage ?
> Must British tears for ever cease to flow
> Save through the fount which streams from German woe ?
> And Laughter lose its empire o'er the pit
> Except when forced from heavy German wit ?"

The writer goes on to ask how Shakespeare can be appeased at being thrust aside to make way for these German dramatists:

> " Immortal Shakespeare ! How shall we appease
> Thy shade, indignant now at wrongs like these ?"

He then addresses Sheridan, and asks him how he can " banish Avon's bard for Kotzebue ?"

These verses are of interest merely as giving some idea of the popular rage for German drama when the

[1] Rea, *Schiller in England*, p. 14. [2] XXXV. 260.
[3] LXX. 1084 ; 1800.

"Pizarro-fever" was at its height. But in spite of the critics, and of the reaction led by the *Anti-Jacobin*, that rage did not, as we have seen, die down quite so completely or so suddenly as has sometimes been supposed. Kotzebue's plays were popular long after 1801, and some new translations were made from him and others through the first decade of the nineteenth century. Not only German dramas but also German novels gave freely used stuff to many English dramatists—*e.g.*, Dibdin's comedy, *Guilty or not Guilty* (1804), was founded on a novel translated from August Lafontaine—*The Reprobate*.[1]

As late as 1811, a burlesque on German drama, in which the satire of the *Anti-Jacobin* was revived, was given at the Haymarket on July 26th with great success. Its title runs: "The Quadrupeds of Quedlingburgh; or the Rovers of Weimar. Tragico-Comico - Anglo - Germanico - Hippo - Ono-Dramatico-Romance." There was also a verse prologue.[2] *The Biographia Dramatica*,[3] after noticing the applause with which it was greeted, says: "But the laugh was at a thing of other days; the German drama is past and gone—it is beyond the reach of ridicule—its absurdities cannot be revived—and they cannot now furnish matter for even the slight ridicule of a passing burlesque." But, as Sellier points out, to speak of the German drama as absolutely dead in 1811 is an exaggeration. We have noted new translations from Kotzebue in this very year; and some of his plays held their own in London and the provinces for many years after. Nevertheless, it is true to say that as a matter of general interest and enthusiasm, German drama in 1811 *was* a thing of the past, and this burlesque thereon suitably closes the first part of this chapter. It will have been seen that this German drama, so popular in England in the last decade of the eighteenth

[1] Translated by M. Charlton, 1802.

[2] *Vide* Sellier, *Kotzebue in England*, p. 77.

[3] III. 465.

century, included few pieces of real merit, and was in the main an outpouring of worthless stuff. The mature masterpieces of Goethe and Schiller, on the other hand, became known but slowly and then only to a few.

PART II. (*c.* 1815-1830).

In this second period, interest in German drama showed itself in a very different way. German plays did not become in any sense popular. They were not acted;[1] few were even translated or published entire. But in all the literary journals having at all to do with foreign literature, many articles appeared on "the New School of German Tragedy"; and through the efforts of such German scholars as W. Taylor, Gillies, Lockhart, Sarah Austin and Carlyle, careful studies were made and good translations. In both accuracy and style these later translations are immeasurably superior to the earlier productions of B. Thompson, A. Plumptre, M. Geisweiler, etc.

In 1817 *Blackwood's Magazine*, just started under the editorship of Lockhart, began the series of "Horæ Germanicæ" which aimed at presenting to English readers fragments of works of less-known German authors with a careful analysis of their plays. With a few exceptions (*e.g.*, *Faust*) the greatest German classics were omitted. Most of these articles were by R. P. Gillies; a few by Lockhart, De Quincey, Sarah Austin, etc.[2] The "Horæ Germanicæ" came to an end in 1828, but other articles of the same kind appeared

[1] Among the few German plays given in these years is an adaptation of Schiller's *Cabale und Liebe* as *Ravenna, or Italian Love* at Covent Garden, December 3rd, 1824. It was not very successful, and only ran three nights (vide *Genest.*, IX. 302). Among plays based on German models were several adaptations of *Der Freischütz* in 1824 and after; and adaptations of *Oberon* (*vide* chap. iii). Kotzebue's most popular plays still continued to be represented.

[2] Poole's *Index* is incorrect in attributing them all (except the *Laokoon*, No. XVIII.) to Gillies. *Vide* Chap. X., Gillies.

both before and after this date. In 1825 there is an article by S. A(ustin) on "The New German School of Tragedy."[1] She briefly traces the evolution of the German drama from the "domestic prose tragedy" of Lessing, through Goethe and Schiller, to Müllner and Grillparzer (quoting from *Die Albaneserin* and *Die Ahnfrau*). She concludes by defending the German stage from three accusations commonly levelled against it: (1) its propagation of French philosophy; (2) its immorality; (3) its fatalism. In the following year, in the *European Magazine*,[2] an article on the German drama treats particularly of Werner's *Twenty-fourth of February*. It purports to be the first of a series of notices of the German drama, but before 1830 no further notices appeared.

The *Foreign Quarterly Review* was begun in 1827 with the special purpose of dealing with foreign literature. Cochrane was editor, but Gillies took a large part in the direction, and G. Moir (translator of *Wallenstein*) was an active collaborator. An article in the first volume (pp. 565-95) on "The Modern German Drama" is probably by Gillies. He speaks shortly of earlier plays, mentioning, curiously enough, Holcroft's *Nathan* and not W. Taylor's, whose *Iphigenia* also he passes over. Moir's *Wallenstein* is much praised; also Coleridge's as "very beautiful, but now unobtainable." Kotzebue is spoken of as once overrated, but now underrated in Germany and elsewhere. Coming to the newer dramatists, Gillies says that since 1810 a host of dramatists have acquired well-deserved celebrity, and blames those English critics who condemn them all as ill-adapted to English taste, merely because they belong to the "German school."

Finally, in 1829, we have Carlyle's article on "German Playwrights"[3] (Grillparzer, Klingemann and Müllner—all classed as "Poetasters"), which he calls

[1] XVIII. 286. [2] II. 605. [3] *For. Rev.*, III. 94-125.

"an enquiry into the dramatic trade of Germany." It is cleverly and amusingly written (in particular a passage on the popularity of Kotzebue), and pours justifiable ridicule on the "Schicksalsdramen." But with what is really worthless, Carlyle condemns as "not German literature, but the scum of German literature" much that is of real value; and these early judgments of his can certainly not be taken as final.

To come now to particular dramatists:

ZACHARIAS WERNER (1768-1828).

Werner received a large share of attention in articles dealing with German drama, and was regarded by some critics as indisputably the greatest German dramatist after Goethe and Schiller.[1] This seems ridiculous to us; but not only in England but also in Germany Werner was thus overestimated by his contemporaries. His *Martin Luther, oder Die Weihe der Kraft*, was reviewed in the *Monthly*[2] as early as 1810, by W. Taylor, who gives a synopsis of the piece, discusses its merits and defects and compares the author in many points to Schiller.

In 1821 there appeared an analysis with extracts of *The Mother of the Maccabei* (*Die Mutter der Macchabaer*). The writer, in a general survey of German literature, attempts to explain its special characteristics (1) by its youth, (2) by its want of a national character. He then examines Werner's play, giving an outline of the plot, and many extracts in English blank verse. He considers that Werner excels in description, particularly when connected with religious feeling, no writer since Milton having shown himself so thoroughly imbued with the spirit of the Scriptures. He regards Werner as superior to Müllner, Korner or Grillparzer, all of whom he consigns "to rot in well-merited oblivion."

[1] Vide *Europ. Mag.*, II. 605; 1826.

[2] LXII. 497.

The *European Magazine*[1] (1826) gave an analysis with extracts of the *Twenty-fourth of February*: (*Der vierundzwanzigste Februar*) . . . remarking the resemblance to Lillo's[2] *Fatal Curiosity* (1736). The reviewer judged the tragedy to be "fantastic and extravagant, but full of power, passion and poetry and enough to stamp Werner as a great dramatic poet." The *Twenty-fourth of February* was described again in the following year by Gillies in *Blackwood*.[3] He alludes also to Lillo's tragedy, but says that Werner has made of a story common in old romances a work of tremendous and overpowering interest; and that, though some may call it too horrible and repulsive, true genius shines through it all. These estimates of the play are absurdly exaggerated. The extracts in both articles are well translated—Gillies's a good deal the better, keeping more faithfully to the original, and better in expression and versification.

In 1828 we have an article on Werner by Carlyle[4] in which he treats of Werner's *Lebensabriss* by Hitzig (Berlin, 1823) and of several of his dramas. He gives several extracts[5] in translation from *Die Söhne des Thals*, and a bit of the preface to *Das Kreuz an der Ostsee*—"in some respects the best of Werner's dramas." *Martin Luther* he thinks is undeservedly popular. He gives no extracts, but discusses it with regard to characters, etc., at some length. *Die Mutter der Macchabaer* he considers the worst of all Werner's pieces—"a pale, bloodless, ghost-like affair." Carlyle concludes by a summing up of Werner's character; he insists on the sincerity of his conversion to Catholicism.

1 II. 605.

2 George Lillo (1693–1739), author, too, of *George Barnwell*.

3 XXI. 464; 1827.

4 *For. Rev.*, I. 95-141.

5 Part I., Act IV., i.; Act V., i., 2. Part II., Act V., fragments. He also translated a letter from Werner to Hitzig on the occasion of his mother's death.

Blackwood in 1829 gave an analysis—probably by Gillies—with long extracts of *Attila, King of the Huns*. The continually varying metres of the original are imitated to a certain extent in the translation, which thus gives a good idea of the general effect of the piece. *Attila* is now quite forgotten.

ADOLF MÜLLNER (1774-1829).

Müllner was known in England principally as the author of *Die Schuld*, fairly popular about 1820. According to Gillies: " Müllner did then unconsciously excite admiration among the enlightened circles of London and Edinburgh as much as Goethe by *Werther* forty-five years before."[1] Gillies's translation of Müllner's *Schuld*[2] was his first attempt at a work from the German. *Guilt* was only printed privately and circulated among friends. Gillies says that it had at once an unexampled success, and that he received many letters on the subject, among others from the managers of Covent Garden and Drury Lane to ask if he would adapt the tragedy for the English stage. At the time Gillies replied that he had no time to meet their wishes, but later he did prepare an amended version of *Die Schuld* for Harris (of Covent Garden). There is no evidence, however, that it ever reached representation.[3]

But according to his Advertisement, Gillies did originally intend his translation to be adapted for the stage and for this reason he used blank verse. By this change from the light trochaic rhymed lines of Müllner to the much statelier blank verse of the translation, the entire character of the piece is changed and

[1] *Memoirs of a literary veteran*, II. 246-50.

[2] *Guilt, or the Anniversary*: a tragedy in four Acts. From the German of Adolphus Müllner, by R. P. Gillies (Edinburgh, Ballantyne, 1819).

[3] Not given, *Genest.*, IX.

much of its peculiar charm is lost. Otherwise Gillies's translation is good and very faithful.

At the same time another and independent translation[1] was being made in London by a Captain W. E. Frye.[2] Gillies saw it announced only after he had begun his own:

> " But had I known of Captain Frye's new version,
> It would have damped my spirit of exertion."

Frye had seen *Die Schuld* acted in Germany in the preceding year, and his admiration for it, as well as "an ardent zeal and enthusiasm for the German language and literature," led him to attempt the translation. Frye also did his work with a view to adaptation to the English stage; like Gillies changing the metre to blank verse and making many further alterations, rearranging the scenes, reducing the five acts to four, cutting down several speeches, and altogether translating much more freely than Gillies. Yet though free, his version is not incorrect, and he evidently knew German well. But his verse is less good than Gillies's, and does not always read smoothly. Part of Hugo's monologue (Act IV., sc. v.)—with an obvious reminiscence of *Hamlet*—will exemplify both:

> " This life is so contracted
> And so—*so* long that other !—If we knew
> That other state—who knows ?—haply it were
> Not quite so terrible. Perchance no more
> Than earth presents—anger and punishment,
> And then forgiveness. Only the dark veil
> That shadows it—*this* overpowers our senses,
> And turns into an hell of ceaseless pain
> The present and the future :—and we feel

---

[1] *Guilt, or the Gipsy's Prophecy*. A tragedy by Adolphus Müllner. Followed by Schiller's *Ideals* and the *Cranes of Ibycus*. Translated from the original German. By W. E. Frye, Captain of Infantry (London, 1819).

[2] Frye also translated some German poems into Italian. Vide *Monthly Review*, XC. 437 ; 1820.

An impulse, even from the terror of the darkness
To plunge at once into its awful bosom;
For oftentimes 'tis nothing to encounter
What thought and fancy rendered horrible!—
If it were *Nothing!*—Oh, but this word only
Is frightful unto men!—*Eternity*.
Raises the sinner's hair on end—And *Nothing!*—
Who can explain it?"

(Gillies.)

"This life so short—'tis but a day—an hour—
And the least error—then the other life
So long—Could one decide? Who knows? Perhaps
The state beyond the grave is not so awful
As we imagine? 'Tis, perhaps, little otherwise
Than here on earth—anger—then punishment
And then forgiveness—'tis th' impenetrable night
That veils it o'er, so much affrights our fancy;
'Tis this depicts eternity an hell;
So that from innate horror of the scene,
We fain would spring into eternal night,
And there an end on't: 'tis our wayward fancy
Doth oft frame wild surmise and visions strange,
Which fill the bosom with unusual terror;
But view them close, they vanish into nothing!
Annihilation! At that sound, the soul
Doth shrink—Eternity! At that dread word
The sinner's locks do stand on end—alike
They both appal us—both present a picture
We dare not look upon—O state of doubt,
Thou greatest, direst, torture to the mind!"

(Frye.)

("Und dies Leben ist so kurz,
Und so lang, so lang das and're!
* * * * *
Nichts—und—wer—wer fasst das?")

Guilt was judged, in the *Monthly*,[1] very unfavourably as more like a sentimental German novel than a tragedy, though "as in all these anomalous productions, there are some passages of considerable force and beauty; truly *German* in its moral effect and in its horrors."[2]

[1] XCII. 331; 1820.

[2] In the *Ideale* this critic finds "some striking commonplaces," but from his remarks it is clear that he did not understand the "Grundgedanke" of the poem at all.

Lockhart, on the contrary, in a review of *Guilt* in *Blackwood*[1] (1819), judged Müllner to be "the rising genius of German drama."

In 1819 Gillies in *Blackwood*[2] gave a complete translation in blank verse of Müllner's short dramatic sketch, *The twenty-ninth of February*, taken from the second version of the play where the conclusion is a happy one—a change of catastrophe approved by Gillies, though he admits that the moral effect of the first version of darkest horror might be stronger.

In 1820 Gillies gave a short account and partial translation of *König Jugurd*[3]—"the greatest and most affecting of all the works of Müllner." The original is in iambic lines of five feet, but rhymed. The translation is in blank verse throughout.

He followed it in 1822 by *Die Albaneserin*,[4] another "Schicksalsdrama." Gillies gives here the whole of Act I., scene iii., and several shorter extracts, translated in blank verse from the mixed blank verse and rhymed iambics of the original. Sarah Austin in 1825[5] translated a couple of short extracts from *Die Albaneserin*, keeping more exactly to the original metre. She discussed also Müllner's other dramas, but without giving extracts. Carlyle also criticised *Die Albaneserin*.[6] His comments are all unfavourable, and he denies to Müllner as to Grillparzer all dramatic or poetic talent. It must be admitted that Carlyle's analysis of these "Fate-tragedies" is both clever and amusing; they lend themselves easily to his sarcasm. But he failed to see where real merit was hidden, as in Grillparzer.

1 VI. 124-36. Hor. Ger., I.
2 VI. 397-409; 1819. Hor. Ger., III.
3 *Black Mag.*, VII. 408-18 and 545-61; 1820.
4 *Black Mag.*, XII. 218-25; 1822.
5 *Black. Mag.*, XVIII. 291-2; 1825.
6 *For. Rev.*, III. 113 *f.*; 1829.

Dramatic Works

HEINRICH VON KLEIST (1777-1811).

Even in Germany Kleist did not receive during his lifetime due recognition. In England he was still scarcely known many years after his untimely death, and he has remained to our own day little understood or appreciated.[1] In the "Horæ Germanicæ," where appear many plays of inferior merit to the best of Kleist's, he is not even mentioned. Nor is he in S. Austin's article on the "New School of German Tragedy" (1825). His name occurs for the first time in the article on "Modern German Drama" by Gillies in the *Foreign Quarterly*[2] (1827), where he is spoken of as "one of the most extraordinary of the new German dramatists, who remains unknown even by name in England." He was introduced for the first time to English readers by a review of his works in the same periodical in the following year.[3] Gillies dwells at length on the life and character of Kleist, giving a translation of a letter written during his imprisonment at Châlons—"a characteristic passage *re* Death and suicide," and of some of his last letters written at Berlin—"which (enigmatical as they are) illustrate his peculiarities better than any criticism." As to Kleist's merits as a dramatist, Gillies totally disagrees with the opinion expressed by Tieck in his *Dramaturgische Blätter*, that Kleist is superior to Müllner, Houwald, and other living authors, and the only German dramatist worthy to be named after Goethe and Schiller; yet admits that Kleist has many merits and truly extraordinary talents; only his impatience and irritability prevented him ever gaining a thorough mastery over them.

There follows an analysis of *Der Prinz vom Homburg*, with a careful and exact translation of parts of Acts III. (beginning and end), IV. (end) and V.

[1] *Vide* F. Lloyd and W. Newton, *Prussia's Representative Man* (1875), p. 14.

[2] I. 565.

[3] II. 671-696.

August von Klingemann (1777-1831).

Klingemann—more noteworthy as a successful theatre director (he was stage manager of the Court Theatre at Brunswick) than as a dramatist—was not much known in England. A few of his numerous dramatic productions were noticed in the reviews. Gillies admired him greatly, saying that he came nearer than any other writer to the spirit and power of Schiller.

The first notice of Klingemann is in No. XV. of the "Horæ Germanicæ" (1823),[1] where Gillies analyses his tragedy of *Faust*—the first two acts minutely, with long extracts. Gillies thinks Klingemann's *Faust* worthy of notice, because "it is in many respects more truly *German*, and therefore to English readers more novel in character, than that of Goethe."

Klingemann is one of the "German Playwrights" treated by Carlyle in the *Foreign Review*[2] (1829). Carlyle discusses, or to be more exact ridicules, the two dramas of *Ahasver* and *Faust*. From *Faust* he translates part of the vii. and xiii. scenes of the last Act—characterising them very aptly as "scenes of the most bewildering supernatural transactions." Here is the conclusion of this *Faust*, as translated by Carlyle:

> "Stranger (*in highest fury*). Down, thou accursed! (*He drags* Faust *by the hair towards the background; at this moment amid violent thunder and lightning the scene changes into a horrid wilderness; in the background of which a yawning chasm; into this the* Devil *hurls* Faust; *on all sides Fire rains down, so that the whole interior of the Cavern seems burning; a black veil descends over both, so soon as* Faust *is got under.*)
>
> "Faust (*huzzaing in wild defiance*). Ha, down! down! (*Thunder, lightning and fire. Both sink. The curtain falls.*)"

Ahasver was reviewed in the *Foreign Quarterly*[3] by Gillies with an outline of the plot and several extracts from Acts I., II., IV., and V. He gives it as "a

[1] *Black. Mag.*, XIII. 649. [2] III. 105-113. [3] I. 590.

psychological curiosity, rather than a fair specimen of the German drama."

Carlyle's depreciation of Klingemann did not pass without comment. In a review (with partial translation) of his historical tragedy of *Henry the Lion*[1] in *Blackwood*[2] (1830), the writer hopes "that this fine play will become popular in England, and that its sober majesty will redeem the fame of one of the most celebrated dramatists of Germany from so sweeping a condemnation." This is evidently directed against Carlyle's critique.

C. T. KÖRNER (1791-1814).

Rosamunde.—Körner did not become known in England till several years after his death. Two of his poems were translated in *Blackwood* in 1818 and 1819, and one in the *Monthly Magazine*, 1818. But the first mention of any importance is the analysis with extracts by Gillies in 1820,[3] of his tragedy of *Rosamunde*,[4] which he calls a "most affecting tragedy, admirably adapted to scenic representation . . . and entirely free from those attributes vulgarly ascribed to the 'German school.'" Gillies tells in his *Memoirs*[5] how one day in October, 1819, Mrs. Siddons came and listened to the reading of his translation of *Rosamunde*, and expressed an opinion that it might be easily adapted for the English stage.

Ten years later (1830) appeared an anonymous translation of the whole of *Rosamunde*. The translator apparently did not know of Gillies's extracts. His principal object was, he says, scenic representation, and with this end in view he has omitted a few short

[1] Heinrich der Löwe is the national hero of Brunswick.

[2] XXVI. 316-340. Writer makes mistake of attributing *Martin Luther* (really by Werner) to Klingemann.

[3] *Black. Mag.*, VIII. 47-58; 1820.

[4] *Rosamond: A Tragedy from the German of Theodore Körner* (London, Simpkin and Marshall, 1830).

[5] II., chap. xi.

scenes (*e.g.*, i., 3) and cut down some long speeches; but none of his alterations are of much importance. The translation rather freer than Gillies's, but never incorrect, and the verse is smooth and harmonious.

As a specimen of both translations here are a couple of speeches from the touching scene at the end (v., 11) where Eleanor, Henry II.'s Queen, tears Rosamond's children from her, and compels her to take poison:

Rosamond. " Heaven protect me !
Here at thy feet, O cruel queen, I lie.
Have mercy ! Leave me but these little ones !
If thou hast feelings in thy heart, of woman—
If thou wert not in some wild desert born
Of savage beasts—by fierce hyænas nurs'd,
Have mercy ! Yet, if once, as we are told,
The lamentations of a mother pierc'd
The lion's heart, so that he did renounce
His precious booty, can'st thou be *more* cruel,
And art thyself a mother ?
Queen. Nay, the brood
Of youngling vipers I do fear no less
Than I do hate the serpent. One quick pressure
Shall make me free from both !
Rosamond. Oh, tell me then
What is their crime ? Not even in dreams
Could they have injur'd thee. Oh, grant to them the boon
Of their poor little lives—this is not much—
Oh, leave it to them ! Name to me some lone
And desert scene, where I for evermore,
May from the king remain concealed, and there
Drag on mine hours in humblest poverty.
But spare my life, and leave to me my children—
And every morn I for thy soul will pray,
And with my last words bless thee !"

(Gillies.)

Rosamond (*throwing herself at* Queen's *feet*). See me at thy feet !
And spare, oh, spare my unoffending babes !
If yet a touch of pity still remains—
If not in deserts born of savage beasts—
If not by monsters suckled, yet have mercy.
A time has been, when, for a mother's tears,
The raging lion has renounced his prey
And can'st thou be more ruthless—and—a mother ?

QUEEN. The adder-brood is to be feared no less
Than is the parent dam. One pressure makes
Secure of both.
ROSAMOND. Oh, say, what is their crime?
Not even in dreams could they have injured you.
Then spare their little lives—it is not much!
Let them but live and name some desert spot
Where from the king I may conceal my head!
Leave me to pine in wretchedness and want,
Let me but live—and spare, oh, spare my children,
And every morn together we will kneel,
Uplift our hands in prayer for thee and thine,
And bless thee with our latest breath."

(1830.)

(" Gott! zu deinen Füssen
Lieg'ich! Erbarme dich! Lass mir die Kinder!
* * * * *
Und segne dich im letzten Augenblick.")

One might have thought that *Rosamond*, treating the well-known English story of the "Fair Rosamond," would have pleased in England; yet it apparently did not, nor was it ever staged. As a play it rather lacks dramatic effect, and evidently no manager cared to undertake the risk of production.

Zriny.—Körner's tragedy from Hungarian history—*Zriny*—was also analysed with extracts by Gillies in 1820;[1] and translated in full by G. F. Richardson[2] in his *Life and Selections from Körner*[3] in 1827; and its last scene was translated in Taylor's *Historic Survey*[4]

[1] *Black Mag.*, VIII. 543-61.

[2] *G. F. Richardson*, 1796?–1848. Assistant in British Museum in Department of Minerals. Published several useful geological handbooks. Was less successful in his efforts in general literature. His only work from German beside Körner's Life was a translation of Bouterwek's *History of German Literature*, completed shortly before his death. He committed suicide in 1848.

[3] *The Life of Carl Theodore Körner* (written by his father), with selections from his poems, tales and dramas. Translated from the German by G. F. Richardson (London, Hurst, 1827. Second ed., 1845).

[4] III. 430.

(1828-30). Richardson prefixed to his translation a few remarks on the tragedy, admitting the defects natural to a young and inexperienced writer, but pointing out many merits. Gillies also expressed admiration of the play. W. Taylor says of Körner that he imitates the style of Schiller without attaining to his pathetic force.

Of the longer translations Gillies's is the best. Richardson's verse is usually fluent and his version reads well enough, but compared carefully with the original it will be found that he often misses the finer shades of meaning, and sometimes makes real blunders —*e.g.*:

> " Darf ich's ? Darf ich das fremde Leben fordern ?"
> =" And can I, dare I, ask for life to come ?"
> (III. 8),

where the sense really is " can I demand another to sacrifice *his* life, as I am willing to do my own ?"

In

> " I was the only hero of my time,
> Though noble men have lived within my century,
> And valiant warriors were opposed to me"

for

> " Die Welt, die flammende hätt'ich bezwungen
> Wär'ich der einzige Held in meiner Zeit ;
> Doch grosse Männer lebten mein Jahrhundert
> Und grosse Helden standen wieder mich"

he quite misses the point.

Gillies, as usual, translates accurately:

> " If I, like my precursors stood alone,
> Even all the world before me would have kneeled,
> But, in my century, mighty spirits rose,
> And kindred heroes were opposed to me."

W. Taylor's short extract is well translated. None of the translators succeeded in reproducing the harmony of Körner's verse.

Dramatic Works

Besides *Zriny* Richardson translated *Joseph Heyderich*, an unimportant dramatic prose sketch in one act; several prose tales,[1] and a number of Körner's poems. Körner being in the first place a lyric poet, these lyrics are the most important part of the work, and on the whole the best done; but they do not come in for discussion here. The sketch of Körner's life and its sacrifice in the liberation of his country is translated from that by his father, to which Richardson adds some remarks of his own. Richardson gives rather higher praise to Körner's works than later criticism would consider they deserve, but we may perhaps concur with him in saying that "when we consider the various studies, pursuits and avocations of the author . . . and that he was snatched away at the early age of twenty-two, we cannot refuse our highest admiration of an instance of early genius, probably unrivalled and certainly never surpassed in the annals of literary distinction." He concludes with some verses of his own addressed to "the memory of Germany's soldier-poet." This attempt to give a comprehensive survey of the life and works of a German poet is unique, and therefore interesting. It is only a pity that it was not undertaken by a translator of greater power. However, Richardson's work evidently led to an interest in Körner. Some more of his poems were translated in that and the following year, and a few original poems on Körner's death appeared in various periodicals. One, by "E. H."—*On the Death Day of Körner*[2]—was written on the occasion of reading a letter sent by the elder Körner to Richardson, as the translator of his son's works.

[1] *Vide* Chap. VIII. [2] *Black. Mag.*, XXII. 730; 1827.

FRANZ GRILLPARZER (1791-1872).

With the exception of *Sappho* no complete play of Grillparzer appeared in English during his lifetime; but he takes a prominent place in the German studies of such reviews as *Blackwood's Magazine*, the *Foreign Review*, etc. Gillies devoted several of his "Horæ Germanicæ" to Grillparzer's plays, of which he was a consistent admirer, speaking of him frequently as the best writer of the new school of German tragedy and superior to Müllner—at that time a greater favourite in Germany, and, so far as he was known, in England.

Carlyle, on the contrary, found nothing but mediocrity in Grillparzer. In the article on German Playwrights in the *Foreign Review*[1] he relegates him to the rank of fourth-rate dramatists, denying him any but a feeble vein of poetic talent and all dramatic power. Of all his dramas Carlyle has a few words of praise for *Sappho* alone. Though a remark here and there is just and well-founded, most of Carlyle's assertions are much too sweeping and show that he was blind to many of Grillparzer's merits. It is surely untrue to say that "he cannot impart poetic life to any character or object," or that his talent is "essentially prosaic." One needs to think of the character of "Medea," and of many passages in *Sappho* or *Des Meeres und der Liebe Wellen*. Sarah Austin, on the contrary, in an article on "the New German School of Tragedy,"[2] lays special stress on "the richness of poetry" in Grillparzer, though it tends, in her opinion, "to heighten the undramatic effect of his pieces."

Die Ahnfrau.—According to Goedeke[3] Gillies made a translation of *Die Ahnfrau* for Covent Garden.

[1] III. 94; 1829. [2] *Black. Mag.*, XVIII. 286; 1825.
[3] VIII. ii., p. 387. Refers to *Conversationsblatt*, No. 62, 25 Mai, 1820; this paper is not in Brit. Mus.

Gillies does speak in his *Memoirs*[1] of having translated the play as *The Ancestress*, just after Müllner's *Schuld*, under the auspices of Mr. Harris of Covent Garden; but he makes no further allusion to it. Apparently it was never acted,[2] nor printed in book form. Extracts were given with an analysis of the play in "Horæ Germanicæ," II.,[3] taken from Gillies's MS. He has changed the light, short, trochaic lines of the original, imitated from Calderon, to blank verse, and the play loses a great deal of its peculiar character and beauty by this change of form. Otherwise the translation is faithful and correct and reads well. Here is the first speech of Bertha in the opening scene of the play, a good example of the general style of the whole:

The night
In truth is fearful: cold and dark, my father,—
Even as the grave. The let-loose winds are moaning
Like wandering ghosts. Far as our eyes can reach,
Snow covers all the landscape, mountains, fields,
Rivers and trees. The frozen earth now seems
A lifeless frame, wrapt in the shroud of winter;
Nay, heaven itself, so void, so starless, glares,
As from wide hollow eyeballs, blackly down
On the vast grave beneath."

("Eine grause Nacht, mein Vater!
Kalt und dunkel wie das Grab," etc.)

In the short extract from *Die Ahnfrau* (Act III.) in Sarah Austin's article, she has closely reproduced the form of the original in the mixture of rhymed and unrhymed trochaic lines, thus giving a more faithful picture of it than Gillies. For instance:

"Yes, I am, unhappy maiden,
Yes, I am what thou hast said!
He whom all with curses name,
Whom awaits a death of shame,

1 *Memoirs of a literary veteran*, II. 250.
2 There is no note of it in *Genest.*, 1819–20.
3 *Black. Mag.*, VI. 247; 1819.

Whom the peasant fearing evil,
Prays 'gainst as against the devil;
He whom fathers to their children,
As a terrible example,
Show, and warning whisper, 'Tremble,
Lest thou ever him resemble.'
Yes, I am, unhappy maiden,
Yes, I am what thou hast said.
He, whom blood-stained thickets fear,
He, whom murderers hold dear,
He, the robber Jaromir!"

("Ja, ich bin's, du Unglücksel'ge
Ja, ich bin's den du genannt"; etc.)

It is a pity Mrs. Austin did not translate more of the play in the same style.

The writer of the article in *Blackwood* (VI.) speaks with much praise of "this most beautiful and soul-subduing tragedy," and greets Grillparzer as the most promising of the younger dramatists of Germany. "We are yet acquainted with only two of his plays, the *Sappho* and *The Ancestress*, and each in its way appears to us a masterpiece." A very different criticism is given by Carlyle,[1] who calls it "much the worst play of Grillparzer's; a deep tragedy of the Castle Spectre sort, the whole mechanism of which is discernible and condemnable at a single glance." The climax is described thus: "There is a frightful uproar everywhere through that night; robbers dying, musketry discharging; women shrieking, men swearing, and the Ahnfrau herself emerging at intervals, as the genius of the whole discord. But time and hours bring belief as they always do. Jaromir in the long run likewise succeeds in dying; whereupon the whole Borotin lineage having gone to the Devil, the Ancestress herself also retires thither—at least, makes the upper world rid of her presence—and the piece ends in deep stillness. Of this poor Ancestress, we

[1] *For. Rev.*, III. 100; 1829.

shall only say farther: wherever she be requiescat ! requiescat !"

It is easy enough to turn any tragedy, and specially a "Fate-tragedy" thus to ridicule, but it would be more worthy of as serious a critic as Carlyle to discuss it in a different tone, and seek its beauties and merits rather than only its weaknesses. His bête-noir, Voltaire, spoke thus of *Hamlet* and *Othello*.

Sappho.—In the translation of *Sappho*[1] by Bramsen we have the first, and for many years the only complete, translation of a drama of Grillparzer. This *Sappho* is a very fair piece of work, showing adequate knowledge of German and good command of English; the language is usually clear, and though it does not succeed in reproducing the harmony of Grillparzer's iambics, the verse runs smoothly enough. But there are some examples of mistranslation, *e.g.*:

> "Then all my love was nature's and my country's,"

for

> "Da noch ein Zauberland mir Liebe war,
> Ein unbekanntes, fremdes Zauberland."

And in Sappho's speech beginning:

> "Dem Schicksal tust du Unrecht und dir selbst"

(Act I., sc. iii.) there are several examples of such translating as loses or distorts the whole force of the original meaning, *e.g.*:

> "No, not in vain the sacred Nine have chosen
> For their reward the cold and barren laurel;
> Though it can boast no fragrance, and no fruit,
> Yet when it circles round the poet's brow,
> He feels it recompense privations past."

---

[1] *Sappho*, a Tragedy in five Acts. Translated from the German of F. Grillparzer (London, Black, 1820). For references to German comments on translations of *Sappho* vide Goedeke, VIII., ii., p. 394. The papers mentioned are not available in England.

for:

> "Umsonst nicht hat zum Schmuck der Musen Chor
> Den unfruchtbaren Lorbeer sich erwählt,
> Kalt, frucht—und duftlos drucket er das Haupt
> Dem er Ersatz versprach für manches Opfer."

The important line:

> "Und Leben ist ja doch des Lebens höchstes Ziel"

is quite omitted, and the two last lines:

> "Und ewig ist die arme Kunst gezwungen
> Zu betteln von des Lebens Überfluss,"

are not well given as:

> "It leaves us still dependent upon those
> Who boast the superfluities of life."

In Gillies's analysis of *Sappho* in No. XXI. of the "Horæ Germanicæ" he makes no allusion to any earlier translation, which looks as if Bramsen's had not been widely known. Gillies thinks the character of *Sappho* will be more congenial to English feelings than that of *Die Ahnfrau*. "Its chief beauties are the just conception and delineation of character, the admirable portraiture of the workings of the human heart . . . and the rich vein of poetry adorning and vivifying the whole."[1] He criticises justly the weakness of the catastrophe, but says he does not wish to carp at the faults of a young and inexperienced writer where there are so many beauties to admire.

Gillies's translation is more carefully done than Bramsen's; he never deviates from the text as in the examples given above, and almost always keeps more exactly Grillparzer's expressions or images, *e.g.*:

"Nur ja kein Korn des Goldes zu verlieren"
="That not one honeyed syllable be lost" (Bramsen).
="To lose no grain of all the golden store" (Gillies).

[1] *Black. Mag.*, XIX. 404; 1826.

The following passage from the end of Phaon's first long speech (Act I., sc. iii.) shows both translations at their best:

"But I alone arose and wandered forth
Into the silent solitude of night,
Where Nature's pulse seemed slowly slumbering;
There did I stretch my amorous arms for thee!
Then—as the silver radiance of the moon
Played on my forehead, and the night-breeze cooled
The fever of my brow—then wert thou mine;
Then wert thou truly mine! 'Twas then I felt
They near approach, and Sappho's image swam
Upon the light and lovely clouds of heaven."
(Bramsen.)

"I only rose and silently went forth
Into the lonely realm of holy night;
There 'midst the pulses of sweet slumbering nature,
Within her magic circle's strong enchantment,
Did I outspread my arms in search of thee;
And when light snow-flakes from o'er hovering clouds,
The tepid breath of zephyr, mountain mists,
The pale moon's flood of silver radiancy,
Together blending, floated round my brow,
Then wert thou mine, thy presence then I felt,
And Sappho's image swam on each bright cloud."
(Gillies.)

Sappho found favour with most English critics. Even Carlyle saw in it "some poetic merit . . . and a degree of grace and simplicity, a softness, polish and general good taste little to be expected from the author of *Die Ahnfrau*." He considered it the most faultless of Grillparzer's poetic productions, but weak and thin as a drama.[1] A critic in the *Monthly*[2] hails *Sappho* as an augury of improving taste in Germany, and of reaction against the "Gothic school." It is, he says, classical not only in story but also in spirit and conduct, and is marked by a well-sustained interest throughout. He praises the translation as simple and correct. A

[1] *For. Rev.*, III. 105; 1829. [2] XCIV. 353; 1821.

long review of *Sappho* in the *London Review* also greets it as a happy reaction against the exaggerated horrors of the older dramatic school. "We know no dramatic poem with which *Sappho* can be justly compared; its attributes are peculiarly its own; its passion is refined beyond that of ordinary humanity: its personages hover in mid-air between men and angels; it interests only our purer and more exalted feelings, and we turn from it with feelings of deep regret, as those who have been holding converse with sublimity. . . . For richness, playfulness and elegance of fancy; for luxuriant beauty of imagery; for soft and soothing yet impressive majesty of verse we know no modern poem that can surpass it."

It is curious to find H. Crabb Robinson among those who disliked *Sappho*. During his second visit to Germany in 1818 he notes seeing Frau Jagermann performing "with ill effect" the part of Sappho in "Grillparzer's disagreeable tragedy of that name."

Der goldne Vliess was not translated until 1879. Its length seems to have frightened some people, as for instance Carlyle,[1] who said he had not time or patience to read it through. The *Literary Gazette* of May, 1821, gives a short account of the *Golden Fleece* as performed at Vienna. A few lines—including Medea's last speech to Jason—are correctly translated. There is a much longer account of it by Gillies in *Blackwood*,[2] 1828, with well-translated extracts from *The Argonauts* and *Medea*, and the opening scene of *The Guest*. He does not give any direct criticism of the tragedy, but his careful analysis and extracts allow the reader to judge for himself.

König Ottokars Glück und Ende.—An analysis of this play with extracts forms No. XXIV. of the "Horæ Germanicæ." Gillies considers it superior in every dramatic requisite to Grillparzer's former plays. "In

[1] *For. Rev.*, III. 105; 1829.
[2] XXVIII. 155-176.

it he has restrained the luxuriance of his imagination, adopting a style, usually esteemed more dramatic, and something of the quaint, but energetic, simplicity of the period to which the play belongs. Indeed, the whole spirit of the age breathes through the tragedy."[1] The extracts are excellently translated in the same metre as the original.

In an article by Carlyle in the *Foreign Review*[2] *König Ottokar* is alluded to as a much more "innocent piece" than *Die Ahnfrau*—whatever that exactly means—and "a comparatively harmless tragedy." Ottokar's soliloquy beginning: "Ich hab' nicht gut in deiner Welt gehaust" (Act V.) is well translated. Carlyle adds: "Such a passage as this makes us regret the more to condemn Grillparzer."

Ein treuer Diener seines Herrn.—This play did not find a place in the "Horæ Germanicæ" in *Blackwood*, but it was reviewed by Gillies in the *Foreign Quarterly*[3] as inferior to Grillparzer's earlier plays, especially *König Ottokar*; the story is said to be undramatic and the catastrophe disappointing, but the characters well drawn. Gillies gives the opening scene as the best detached specimen of the author's powers. The translation is executed with a good deal of spirit, though there are a few bad lines.

These are—as far as I have discovered—the only mentions of Grillparzer's earlier plays before 1830. His later ones fall outside our period.

Besides these better-known dramatists, several plays of less important authors found mention in *Blackwood* and the *Foreign Quarterly*.

In the "Horæ Germanicæ" these are:

Raupach's (1784-1852) *Darkness, or the Venetian Conspiracy*;[4] dealing with the same subject as Byron's

[1] *Black. Mag.*, XXII. 300-16; 1827.
[2] III. 94; 1829.
[3] VI. 520; 1830.
[4] *Black. Mag.*, VIII. 384-94; 1821.

Doge of Venice. None of Raupach's German historical dramas, nor the Cromwell trilogy—in spite of the English subject—were noticed in England. Neither were any of his numerous comedies.

Fouqué's romantic drama *The Pilgrimage*.[1] The extracts are unsigned, but they are not by Gillies.

F. Schlenkert's Rudolf von Habsburg,[2] given as a specimen of the "Historisch-Romantische-Gemälde." The articles and extracts are by Sarah Austin.

E. v. Houwald's (1778-1845) *The Light Tower*,[3] a two-act tragedy. The extracts are given in blank verse; the original is in the rhymed measure imitated from Calderon.

Uhland's[4] *Ernest, Duke of Suabia*—one of his few plays. The writer regrets that this "excellent poet" should have achieved so little in the drama.

In the *Foreign Quarterly*, besides what has been already mentioned, we find:

A critical sketch of *Graf von Platen's* Comedy, *Der romantische Œdipus*.[5] The critic doubts the success of this polemic in dramatic form. A passage from Act V. is translated in blank verse.

In the same number *Karl Immermann's* historical drama *Kaiser Frederick II*.[6] is reviewed as showing considerable power, some originality and skill in the delineation of character. Short extracts are given in blank verse.

In the following year a sketch appears of Michael Beer's *Struensee*,[7] with part of two scenes translated. The writer considers that it is much too long, the dialogue heavy and the verse halting, but that some skill is shown in the development of the characters.

These notices are probably all by Lockhart.

[1] *Black. Mag.*, IX. 481-97; 1821.
[2] *Ibid.*, XI. 38-49; 1822.
[3] *Ibid.*, XIII. 3; 1823.
[4] *Ibid.*, XXI. 214-26; 1887.
[5] IV. 670-3; 1829.
[6] IV. 661-4; 1829.
[7] VI. 516; 1830.

CHAPTER VIII

Works of Fiction

A. 1790-1815; B. 1815-1830; C. COLLECTIONS OF ROMANCES.

No branch of German literature had so widespread and lasting a popularity in England as fiction. Novels and tales were translated and read, when interest in the more serious literature of Germany was at its lowest ebb. Many of the translators, and probably most of the readers, were women. This fiction-translating falls into two periods: (A) from *c.* 1790-*c.* 1815; (B) from *c.* 1815-1830; with culminating points about 1798 and 1826.

A. 1790-1815.

Werther[1]—which has been discussed already—stands out before all others, and may be said to have opened the mine of German fiction. Amongst the large mass of other German stories translated in the last decade of the eighteenth century—many quite worthless in themselves and wretchedly translated—it is only possible to mention a few. Probably not nearly all have survived. Also there are many, without author's name, with only the vague title "A German Story," meaning perhaps actual translation, perhaps adaptation, or suggested plot. Or the phrase may have been sometimes used merely as an advertising device.

Most of the tales chosen were of the most thrilling horror and extravagant improbability. Soon they

[1] *Vide* Chap. V.

came to be imitated in England; Horace Walpole's *Castle of Otranto*, Mrs. Radcliffe's novels and many others, preparing the way for Lewis's *Monk* (1795). Mrs. Shelley's *Frankenstein* shows strong German influence as late as 1818.

Those who enjoyed these German tales did not mind the wildness of their plots. The *Analytical*,[1] speaking of the *Black Valley*, from Veit Weber's[2] *Sagen der Vorzeit*, evidently expresses a current point of view: "The story is improbable but highly interesting. . . . The German in giving unbounded license to his imagination is frequently extravagant; but there are few readers who will not easily pardon those violations of probability which amuse his fancy with pleasing and splendid visions, or which thrill his soul with grateful terrors." The same Review[3] praises the *Sagen der Vorzeit* in general as having considerable merit as "dramatic novels," and the *Sorcerer*[4] in particular as "a highly impassioned and romantic tale." The translator of these tales (1795) was a J. Powell. In 1806 he published a longer romance in two volumes from the *Sagen der Vorzeit—I.: Wolf, or the Tribunal of Blood*. The translation of this is very poor, and that of the earlier tales not much better, though highly praised by the reviewers.[5]

The Necromancer (1794), from *Der Geisterbanner* of Lorenz Flammenberg,[6] was another harrowing tale. The *Analytical*[7] says: "It will afford a delightful treat to those who are pleased with tales that freeze the blood and harrow up the soul, but it might be hazardous to readers of delicate nerves." The translator was a

[1] XXII. 507; 1795.

[2] Pseudonym of Leonhard Wächter. [3] *Ibid.*, 53.

[4] Reviewed in *European Magazine*, XXIX. 260; 1796, and *Critical*, XVII. 113; 1796.

[5] Scott knew these *Sagen der Vorzeit*. From one of them he borrowed the plot of his *House of Aspen*.

[6] Pseudonym of K. F. Kahlert.

[7] XX. 52; 1794.

German, Peter Teuthold; and his English, though fairly correct, sometimes betrays him.

In 1796 was translated a novel by Julius Grosse, *The Genius, or the Mysterious Adventures of Don Carlos de Grandez*, with the sub-title *Horrid Mysteries*, also of the "terrible school"—"ill-connected scenes of supernatural horror."[1] **The Dagger*, by the same, translated anonymously in 1796, is considered by the *Monthly*[2] as much superior to *The Genius*,[3] and called "an interesting and pathetic tale, well meriting perusal."

The anonymous *Count Donamar, or the Errors of Sensibility* (1797) is an example of the "Schauerroman" in extreme.[4]

Many of these translations were made at second-hand from the French, as for instance *Maurice*[5] (1797), by F. Schultz. Most of the reviewers objected to its licentiousness.[6] A great part of it was borrowed, without acknowledgment, by a Mrs. Gunning in a novel called *Delves*. Many of the novel-writers of this time—Mrs. Radcliffe in particular—seem to have used pretty freely plots and ideas suggested by the popular "German story." It was an inexhaustible source of material for sensational fiction.

A much-admired branch of German fiction was the "Räuberroman." The most famous specimen of this class, by Goethe's brother-in-law, C. A. Vulpius's (1762-1827) *Rinaldo Rinaldini*, was translated about

[1] *Month. Rev.*, XXII. 93; 1797. [2] XIX. 207; 1796.

[3] *The Genius* (from *Der Genius aus den Papieren des Marquis C. von Grosse*) was reprinted in two vols., under the title *Horrid Mysteries*, by Holden in 1927. It is preceded by the original translator's (Rev. P. Will) preface and an interesting introduction by Montague Sumner on the novels of this period, "the revival of Gothic romanticism." But it is curious to find a modern reprint of one of them.

[4] *Month. Rev.*, XXVII. 94; 1798.

[5] **Maurice*, a German tale, by Mr. Schultz, from the French (London, 1796).

[6] Cf. *Crit. Rev.*, XXII. 238; 1797. *Anal. Rev.*, XXIV. 109. *Month. Rev.*, XXII. 97; 1797.

1800[1] by J. Hinklei, presumably a German. His translation seems somewhat above the average. The *British Critic*[2] holds the vitiated taste of the author's time and country responsible for "the miserable jargon of philosophy, magic, ghosts and what not in a work which, from the plot, might have been made an interesting performance." It was also reviewed unfavourably in the *Monthly Magazine*, but favourably in the *European Magazine*.[3]

But no German romance enjoyed quite the celebrity of Zschokke's *Abällino*, translated as *The Bravo of Venice*[4] by "Monk" Lewis.[5] Lewis was early attracted by the novels and romances of the German school. These tales of horror, extravagance and mystery gave full play to his romantic imagination, and he adopted their spirit in his original prose and verse. He wrote *The Bravo of Venice* while staying at Inverary Castle in 1804, and dedicated it to his friend, the Earl of Moira. This little romance of double identity is perfect of its kind and very characteristic of the German school. Lewis treated his original pretty freely, adding all that had to do with one personage, Mondaleschi, and almost the whole of the last chapter; and omitting or abridging several passages.

[1] **The History of Rinaldo Rinaldini, captain of banditti*, translated from the German of Vulvius [*sic*] by J. Hinklei, Esq. I have not been able to find a first edition of this book. A third edition of 1831 is in Edinburgh. A translation in the Romanticists' and Novelists' Library (1841) gives no translator's name. Vulpius here is correctly spelt. Morgan (p. 533) gives an adaptation of Hinklei's translation as appearing in N.Y., 1810.

[2] XVI. 440.

[3] *European Magazine*, XXXVIII. 284; 1800. In *Monthly Magazine*, XII. 603; 1801.

[4] *The Bravo of Venice*, a Romance translated from the German by M. G. Lewis (London, 1805).

[5] Shelley read it in 1808 (see Dowden's *Life*, I. 42). Shelley's early romance *St. Myne* is made up of two German romances of unknown authorship. Medwin (*Life*, I. 118) alludes to seeing translations of German tales in manuscript when he visited Shelley at Oxford.

The *Critical*[1] calls the *Bravo* a " Germanico-terrifico-Romance "; says the history is interesting, the language glowing with animation, the dénouement rapid and surprising, and the effect " electric," every chapter containing a shock. The *British Critic*[2] thought it worthy of a much longer review than most novels, because of the popularity of the author and the claims of the German novel itself. It praises it on every ground—for entertaining character, well-sustained interest of plot, bold and nervous language and unexceptionable moral.

The *Bravo* having fallen into the hands of Harris, manager of Covent Garden, it struck him as of good effect for the stage. At his suggestion Lewis made out of it a melodrama, *Rugantino*. The plot, abounding in stirring incident, mystery and romance was exactly suited to Lewis's taste, and he made a very effective piece, produced on October 25th, 1805, with popular caste, and splendid scenery and decorations. It had a great success and was often given.[3]

Rugantino was printed for the first time in Oxberry's *New English Drama*, IX. (1820), and again in Cumberland's *British Theatre*, XXXIV. (1829).

A German feminine *Abällino* was translated into French, but not into English.

In 1806 Lewis published a romance from the German in four volumes entitled *Feudal Tyrants*,[4] a typical specimen of its kind. " It belongs to that class of writing so highly popular about the end of the last century, in which incident succeeds incident with stirring rapidity, arousing the mind by an endless succession of ingenious scenes in which, though commonsense, probability and even good taste are at continual warfare with the narrative, yet we wander on through every extravagance pleased for the time

[1] V. 252; 1805. [2] XXV. 201. [3] *Genest.*, VII. 712.

[4] *Feudal Tyrants or the Counts of Carlsheim and Sargans.* A Romance taken from the German, by M. G. Lewis (London, Hughes, 1806).

and amused."[1] It is really rather an English tale imitated from the German than an actual translation, and probably quite as original as many others which Lewis gave to the public as his own.

There was another class of German stories popular in England which were quite different from the "Schauerromane." They were simple, sentimental, and moral tales, depicting family life, or country manners and customs. An early example of these is *Henrietta von Gerstenfeld, a German story* (1789), a two-volume novel in the form of letters, of which the scene is laid in the Seven Years' War. On the title-page of the first part the novel is ascribed to Wieland, but not on that of the second part. A remark in the review in the *Critical*[2] is significant of the growing popularity of German fiction at this moment: "Is it in consequence of our common ancestry that we feel a congenial warmth for everything of German origin, or do we approve of their writings because of the strong sound good sense which is observed on every page?"

The **Mountain Cottage*, translated from *Die Alpenhütte* of C. H. Spiess by Miss Plumptre (1798), was a simple tale of family life. As also the anonymous *Hertford and Clara*, badly translated by a German, recommended in the *European Magazine*[3] as "giving a picture of domestic felicity and natural pleasures in preference to the fictitious enjoyments of fashion," and in the *Critical*[4] as "exemplary, entertaining and with excellent moral."

Some historical tales were translated—the Secret Tribunal being a favourite subject. Two novels treating of it by Professor Kramer[5] appeared in 1794.

[1] Vide *The Life and Correspondence of M. G. Lewis*, II. 43.

[2] LXIII. 389; 1787. See also *Europ. Mag.*, XIII. 338; *Anal. Rev.*, I. i., 209; *Month. Rev.*, LXXVII. 79 and LXXX. 168; 1787.

[3] XVII. 200; 1790.

[4] LXVIII. 682; 1789.

[5] *I.e.*, C. B. E. Naubert (1755–1817), writer of over a hundred vols. of novels.

The first is *Alf von Deulmen*,[1] a long romance, mostly in the form of letters, fairly translated by a Miss A. E. Booth, and preceded by an account of the foundation and history of the Tribunal taken from the French. The second is *Hermann von Unna*, an historical tale of the fifteenth century, dealing with the proceedings of the Tribunal. The *Critical*[2] gives a long account of *Hermann von Unna* with extracts, calling it "a singular and interesting novel, giving a striking picture of the manners of the age it treats." The *Monthly*[3] praises it also. Scott knew both these stories, and praises them in the preface to his *Götz* as "excellent romances."

P. Will translated an *Essay on the Secret Tribunals* from the *Sagen der Vorzeit* (III.) in the *German Museum* (I. 43), 1801.

German biographical novels were popular from the appearance of the *Swedish Countess* (1752) and *Fräulein von Sternheim* (1776) until quite a late date.

A. von Knigge's *Geschichte Peter Klausens* (1784), translated anonymously in 1793 as *The German Gil Blas*,[4] seems to have been fairly well known. The Advertisement, consisting of a short criticism and eulogy of the work, is interesting as a contemporary English view of this class of novel, showing what qualities were sought for and found in them, and why they were popular. "Baron Kniegge . . . appears to have a thorough knowledge of men and manners, exhibiting a critical and moral picture of almost every condition in human life, each situation offering a useful lesson. The variety of character, the diversity of adventures and descriptions, with the pleasant vein of criticism that runs through the whole work renders

[1] *Alf von Deulmen, or the History of the Emperor Philip and his Daughters*, translated from the German by Miss A. E. Booth, 1790.

[2] XIV. 68; 1795.

[3] XV. 21; 1794.

[4] *The German Gil Blas, or the Adventures of Peter Claus*, translated from the German of Baron Kniegge [*sic*] (London, 1793).

it as instructive as amusing, keeps the imagination alive, while at the same time the author, under the ingenious disguise of natural and interesting fiction inculcates the purest morality." The translation is rather free, but gives the substance of the German correctly. The style, though sometimes stiff and awkward, is above the average of the translations of the time. Much of the novel treats of the manners of the day, as, for instance, this rather amusing description of the Court beauties:

"In the morning, when I went to the office of finance, those pale beauties appeared at their windows, their eyes sunk and their charms out of repair. This was the moment when they quitted their beds of down, their chamber-maids carefully informing them of the interesting scandal of the neighbourhood to amuse the first hours of the morning. At noon the skilful architect raised the edifice of a transparent toupee, in which was intermingled the spoils of a hundred heads. Miraculous boxes furnished them with blushes, and a strong but fine wire thread tied in a beautiful row of ivory teeth, in the place of those destroyed by high-seasoned viands and heating liquids. Small shoes contracted their feet within narrow bounds; four hours' labour at the toilet was hardly sufficient to put these moving puppets in a state to appear."

The inevitable comparison with the *Gil Blas* of Le Sage was rather a drawback for Knigge's novel, found by all to be "but a poor imitation of a great original."[1]

Another novel of Knigge's was translated in 1799—*The History of Amtsrath Gutman, written by himself.*[2]

The year 1798 brought the translation of a novel of another member of the "Illuminati," Nicolai's *Sebaldus Nothanker*,[3] a satirical novel, very famous in its time, treating of philosophical and religious ques-

[1] *Month. Rev.*, I. 212; also *Anal. Rev.*, XV. 458.

[2] Reviewed in the *Critical*, XXVIII. 240; 1800. And *British Critic*, XIV. 670, which censured it for the "anarchical doctrines" typical of the school of the "Illuminati."

[3] *The Life and Opinions of Sebaldus Nothanker*, translated from the German of Friedrich Nicolai, by Thomas Dutton, A.M. (London, 1798).

tions of the day. The character of the work will have made it popular among certain circles in England; though much of the force of the satire must have been lost through ignorance of German customs and conditions. Two years before its translation the *Monthly Magazine*,[1] in an article on "Celebrated Men now living," spoke of Nicolai beside Klopstock and Voss, and praised *Sebaldus Nothanker* as "a spirited attack on the ramparts of superstition, ecclesiastical tyranny and the exploded systems of false philosophy." W. Taylor reviewed the translation in the *Monthly*,[2] giving long extracts, but not very much criticism. The *Analytical*[3] regards the work more particularly as a representation of manners than in its philosophical aspect, and praises it as a fictitious tale, which may serve to give us a more intimate acquaintance with general characters, opinions and customs of Germany. The *British Critic*[4] alone has nothing but censure for the work of "this illuminated bookseller." His opinions will naturally have been obnoxious to the very orthodox *Critic*.

Dutton's translation was highly praised by Taylor, and with justice. It is much above the ordinary level, being faithful to its original and simple and direct in style.

A. von Kotzebue.—The fame of Kotzebue as a dramatist led to the translation of several of his tales and novels, which in turn became almost as popular as his plays. The Advertisement to three volumes of *Novelettes* from Kotzebue (1807) speaks of them as worthy of the first dramatist of his age. The translation of these tales is very bad. But not quite as bad as that of another collection in four volumes, **The Pastor's Daughter and other romances*, published in the preceding year (1806). Here we have epithets such as "the ever-with-hope-deceiving disease," "red-wept

[1] V.; 1797.
[2] XXII. 248; XXVI. 583; 1797.
[3] XXVI. 75; 1797.
[4] XI. 680; XII. 543; 1798.

eye," "the poor-by-man-deserted-betrayed-creature," etc.

In 1807 appeared a volume of **Historical, literary and political anecdotes from the German of Kotzebue*, probably by the same translator. The *Critical*[1] calls them "in general unamusing, dull and unmeaning."[2]

Some earlier translations had been rather better than these—for instance, *The sufferings of the Family of Ortenberg* (*Die geprüfte Liebe*) (1799), by Peter Will, highly praised in the *Critical*.[3] An historical novel, *Ildegerte, Queen of Norway*,[4] translated by Benjamin Thompson (1798), was very popular, as also *The Escape*[5] (1799), an exciting narrative of an escape from the dungeons of the Inquisition, by the same translator.

Another tale, the **Constant Lover, or William and Jeannette* (*Die geprüfte Liebe*) (1799), was enthusiastically reviewed in the *Critical*:[6] "Such are the talents of this wonderful author, that we can scarcely wish him to correct more, lest he should write less." But this was in the heyday of Kotzebue's popularity. A few years later, in a review of his *Travels in Italy*,[7] the same periodical speaks of "the pompous trifles of this strutting sentimentalist!" Kotzebue's day was soon over, and his novels were forgotten even sooner than his plays.[8]

A. H. Lafontaine (1758-1831).—A novelist, the popularity of whose novels in England may almost be compared to that of Kotzebue's plays, is August Lafontaine. He was a Saxon clergyman, an extraordinarily prolific writer of novels and tales, famous in their own day, but now almost entirely forgotten. From about 1798 to about 1813 scarcely a year passed without a translation of one or more of

[1] XI. 183; 1807.
[2] See also *Brit. Crit.*, XXX. 454.
[3] XXIX. 352; 1800.
[4] *Crit. Rev.*, XXVI. 117.
[5] *Europ. Mag.*, XXXVI. 253; *Brit. Crit.*, XVII. 315.
[6] XXVI. 117; 1799.
[7] VII. 83; 1806.
[8] For Kotzebue's autobiographical works, see Chapter IX.

his novels into English, most of them by women, one or two at second-hand through French, but the greater part of them more or less freely from the original German.[1] Nearly all belong to the class of novel called in German the "Familienroman," the history of the same family being often continued from one novel to another. *Saint Julien* (translated twice, 1798 and 1799) and the *Family of Halden* (1799) form together a work to which Lafontaine gave the general title *Familiengeschichten*. In the Advertisement to the *Family of Halden* Lafontaine is called "the German Fielding." The *Monthly*[2] has a long account of Lafontaine's novels from the pen of W. Taylor, who mentions the *Family Histories* as works of "singular merit," which interested him to a degree rarely experienced since Richardson and Fielding. The same periodical in another place says his works are "never without interest."[3] Most of the contemporary reviews of Lafontaine's novels seem to have been equally favourable. There is one exception in a review in the *Critical*[4] of *Henrietta Bellman* (1804), alluding also to the *Six Novels* by Mrs. Parsons (1804). Only if the number and rapidity of his productions be a merit will this critic allow him any.

A novel of Lafontaine's, the *Man of Nature, or Nature and Love*, erroneously ascribed to Miltenberg, was translated by a William Wennington in 1799. The translator's preface is dated from Vienna; and he appears to have lived some years in Germany.[5]

[1] See catalogue of Brit. Mus. Two translations not in Brit. Mus. are, **Clara du Plessis and Clairant*, vide *Month. Rev.*, XXVII, 94; 1798. **New Moral Tales* (1803), vide *ibid.*, XLI. 330; 1803. And Morgan, *Bibl. of Ger. Lit.*, pp. 317-8.

[2] XXIV. 565; 1797.

[3] English novelists borrowed from him. *E.g.*, Lafontaine's *Barneck und Saldorf* is the source of Campbell's *Gertrude of Wyoming*.

[4] VI. 215; 1806.

[5] In the *German Museum* (1801) there is a short tale from Lafontaine—*Hulkem*, and an extract from a political novel—*Rudolf of Werdenberg*.

The translations of Lafontaine's novels vary from very mediocre to fairly good. Wennington's is certainly among the worst, being very stiff and foreign in idiom and not always even grammatical. Many of the translators were women, authoresses of numerous original works now forgotten: Mrs. Parsons, for instance, wrote no less than sixty volumes of novels. R. Holcraft included one tale of Lafontaine's—*The Haunted Castle*—in his *Tales from the German*. He calls him "the clearest and purest of all German novelists." So even in 1826 his reputation still lived.

In 1811 appeared a novel translated by Henry Crabb Robinson from Anton Wall (*i.e.*, Christian Leberecht Heyne). *Amatonda*[1] is a Persian fairy-tale, absolutely different in style and character from any of the stories of which we have been speaking. The original is now forgotten, and Robinson's translation was from the first a failure, though it was praised by Coleridge in a letter to the translator. Crabb Robinson has given in his Diary a long account of this translation, and of his visit to the author. In this alone lies any interest *Amatonda* may have today.

B. 1815-1830.

We now come to the romances of the Romantic School, many of which were as popular in England as the earlier "Schauerromane."

F. H. de la Motte Fouqué (1777-1843).—The most important name is that of de la Motte Fouqué. Speaking of him in the introduction to his *German Novelists*, 1827, Roscoe states: "Few modern writers of Germany have become greater favourites with the English reading public, or have received more gratifying proofs of its admiration in numerous versions from their

[1] *Amatonda—A Tale from the German of Anton Wall* (London, Longman, 1811). Two short tales from Anton Wall appeared in the *German Museum*, III.; 1801.

productions." And though *Blackwood*[1] expresses surprise that Roscoe should have called Fouqué a favourite in England—" one of his tales has been a good deal read, but the Baron's name is wholly without power in England except among our German literati; . . . *Undine* is nothing but waterworks "—yet we are inclined to think that Roscoe's remarks better represent the general opinion.

The first translation of *Undine* was made by George Soane in 1818.[2] He purposely took many liberties with his original, adding and expunging freely, with the intention of adapting the tale to the taste of English readers. The *Monthly*[3] criticised it rather severely. There was a project to give another translation both of *Undine* and *Sintram*, to be printed in a handsome form, and the editor of the *Monthly* wrote to W. Taylor (September 19th, 1820) suggesting that he should undertake the translation of one or both of them. But Taylor's opinion of both works was unfavourable; and partly because of this the project was abandoned.

The next translation was made in 1830.[4] The anonymous translator makes fewer actual alterations than Soane, but catches even less of the poetic tone of the original, and his style is often pompous and involved—*e.g.*, " und wenn sie die treue Seele in mir spüren " becomes " and when once they perceive my being invested with the vital principle which is animating me." Soane is generally more simple and direct, though sometimes less accurate—*e.g.*, " der weisse Hengst, der den Ritter trug, war schlankeren Baues, als man es sonst bei Streitrossen zu sehen gewohnt ist" = " the white steed on which the knight rode was of slender make, as is the custom with war-

[1] XX. 852; 1826.

[2] *Undine, a Romance*, translated from the German by George Soane, A.B. (London, Simpkin and Marshall, 1818).

[3] LXVIII. 184; 1820.

[4] *Undine, a Romance*, translated from the German (London, Simpkin and Marshall, 1830).

horses" (Soane) = "the white steed on which the knight was mounted was of a more slender make than steeds of war commonly are known to be" (1830). On the whole, however, Soane's is the more readable version.

The pieces in verse scattered through *Undine* Soane translated freely, with different metres. The 1830 translator did them more literally. Neither version is very successful.

Undine at once became popular in England. The *London Magazine*[1] calls it: "The brightest fiction of modern times, an airy unsubstantial dream, but a dream of uncommon brilliancy." The *European Magazine*[2] gives high praise both to the original and Soane's translation, and it speaks of *Undine* as "more popular in England than any other foreign work, even *Faust*." The *Monthly*,[3] at much greater length, dwells specially on its allegorical significance, commenting also on the general dissimilarity of taste and feeling between English and German Romance. It pleads for the same liberality of feeling and impartial criticism towards German writers as they show to us. Southey called *Undine* "the most graceful fiction of modern times." And Coleridge is known to have read it several times in the original and in translation.[4]

Undine gained immensely in popularity in England by being dramatised[5] and produced at Covent Garden on April 23rd, 1821, as *Undine, or the Spirit of the Waters*.

[1] III. 524. [2] LXXIX. 443; 1821. [3] CIII. 184; 1820.

[4] Stokoe, *German Influence*, etc., p. 131, says that Coleridge read an English translation of *Undine*, by E. Littell of Philadelphia, 1824. But this is only an American reprint of Soane.

[5] The author's name is nowhere mentioned. It is known that Scott once had the intention of dramatising *Undine*, as he wrote to D. Terry, November 10th, 1819 (Lockhart's *Life*, IV. 315): "There is a tale in existence, by dramatising which I am certain a most powerful effect might be produced; it is called *Undine*, and has been translated into French by Mlle. Montolieu, and into English from her version; do read it and tell me your opinion: in German the character of Undine is exquisite. The only objection is that the catastrophe is

The scenery and staging seem to have been beautifully done; the public was pleased, and the "melo-dramatick Romance" was given twenty-six times.[1] Among the many alterations made in its adaptation for the stage, the most important is the substitution of a happy ending. Through these changes the figure of Undine appears to have lost a good deal of her original character, and, as one critic remarked, "the theatrical nymph Undine has little to do with the Maid of that name."[2]

The two translations of *Undine* here mentioned are now superseded by many more modern ones, for the story of *Undine* has become really naturalised in England and is read and enjoyed by many who do not even know that it is of German origin.

Fouqué's *Sintram* was translated anonymously in 1820.[3] The translator is now known to have been J. C. Hare.[4] In the Preface he speaks at great length

---

unhappy, but this might be altered." But I found no further mention of the dramatisation in Lockhart, or elsewhere. Scott alone speaks of an English *Undine*, done from the French. He probably mistook Soane's for such. Stokoe (*German Influence*, etc., p. 80), notes that the White Lady in the Monastery is an unskilful adaptation of *Undine*. The *Dresdener Abendzeitung*, 5 Juni, 1821, speaks of the English dramatisation of *Undine*.

[1] *Genest.*, IX. 109. [2] *Lond. Mag.*, III. 524.

[3] *Sintram and his Companions*, a romance from the German of Frederic Baron de la Motte Fouqué, author of *Undine*, etc. (London, Ollier, 1820).

[4] *Archdeacon Julius C. Hare* (1795–1855) spent a year at Weimar with his parents, 1804–5, and early made acquaintance with German literature. In 1812 he went to Trinity College, Cambridge, and gave himself up to classics; in 1818 he was elected Fellow, and in 1822 made classical lecturer. He read much German. In 1826 he took Orders, and in 1832 accepted the family living of Hurstmonceaux and went to live there. His house is said to have been one vast library. H. Crabb Robinson (*Diary*, II. 293), mentions calling on Hare, and says he had the finest collection of modern German authors he had ever seen in England. His fine collection of pictures is now in the Fitzwilliam Museum, Cambridge. Hare intended following his *Sintram* by further translations from Fouqué, but never did so. In 1847 he published hexameter translations from Goethe and Schiller.

of the beauty of Fouqué's works and especially of *Sintram*, comparing it in some points to *King Lear*. (The comparison seems rather far-fetched.) Hare hopes that very soon Englishmen may be enabled to read the best German works of the imagination in the original. In the meantime it is desirable, he says, that they should be translated for their benefit, and still more for that of the " fair sex, on whom the works of imagination possess a so much greater influence." (Hare did not think it at all desirable that the " fair sex " should themselves learn German and other modern languages : " The place where woman is most beautiful is the home, and this applies to things of the mind, as well as to those of the body "!)

Hare adopted a somewhat curious system of translating. His aim, he says, has been to render the original with the most scrupulous fidelity. The success of his method can best be judged by a few examples taken at random.

1. " He had learnt nothing of the wild breaking up of his knight " (for " er hatte nichts von dem wilden Aufbruch seines Ritters vernommen ").

2. " Furiously at length he tore himself up " (for " tobend riss er sich endlich in die Höhe ").

3. " 'Whither ?' *cried* Sintram suddenly *back* " (for " 'Wohin' ? rief Sintram plötzlich zurück ").

4. " 'I must now look the pilgrim into his wondrous face' " (for " 'Ich muss dem Pilger ins wunderbare Gesicht schauen' ").

5. " With flighty leaps " (for " mit flüchtigen Sprüngen ").

It will be agreed that here the translator goes rather farther than " the difference in idiom between the two languages " will allow!

Here is a longer specimen:

" Where the sea-coast rises highest and most head-long beneath three half-decayed oaks—human sacrifices are said to have been offered there in the heathen time—stood Sintram, leaning upon his drawn sword, alone and exhausted, beneath the night now again lightened by the moon, and looked out upon the distant wanderings of the waves, and stiffened deadly pale, like a fearful magical image, shone upon here and there by pale rays which trembled through the branches of the trees. Then some one raised himself up on his left side with half the trunk of his body out of the high yellowed grass, and laid himself down again" (chap. xii.).

Also, in spite of his scruples as to absolute fidelity, Archdeacon Hare is often incorrect in the translation of even the simplest idioms. *E.g.*, "er liess das Sammetgezelt aufschlagen" = "he let his satin tent be struck," instead of "he caused his tent to be pitched." "Ein paar" he always translates by "a pair," instead of "a few," and "Baumgarten" by "garden-trees" instead of "orchard." Some of his new compounds are "storm-wind," "fearfully-over-mighty," "his now-altogether-quiet-steed"—and of his coined forms "wildlier," "wonderfullest."

Hare has pushed the principle of literal translation much farther than any respect for the genius of the language into which the translation is made allows, and the result is usually a miserable jargon, not always even intelligible. Hare had criticised Soane's *Undine* as "labouring under all the disadvantages of a translation professedly loose." Soane revenged himself by a deservedly scathing criticism of *Sintram* in the preface to his *Minstrel Love*: "I know not who the translator may be, but a more unfitting person for the task could hardly have been selected. That he is imperfectly acquainted with the German is the least of his disqualifications; he writes in a dialect which is not always English as to single words, and very seldom indeed as to idiom; what is still worse, he fancies, nay actually asserts, that this barbarous jargon is beneficial . . ." After giving several pages of examples and extracts Soane concludes: "These are a few only of the advantages of a translation professedly literal, and certainly they deserved a triumph, for it must be confessed that a more complete victory over the

English language has never yet been obtained by any-one."

Not many reviews noticed *Sintram*; and any that did thought it much inferior to *Undine*. The *British Critic*,[1] which had reviewed *Undine* very favourably in Mme. Montolieu's French translation, does not think *Sintram* deserving of nearly as much admiration. But this sagacious critic pronounces the translation a satisfactory one. The *London Magazine*[2] considers Hare's system of translation utterly mistaken, but praises much of *Sintram* as "characteristic and fine," though remarking in it (with a good deal of truth) a certain straining after effect, a theatrical tone and a certain exaggeration and unreality of sentiment.

No other translation of *Sintram* appeared before 1830.

Soane's translation of *Sängerliebe* as *Minstrel Love*[3] (1821) has been already mentioned. The Preface is long and exceptionally interesting. Having dis-posed of Hare's *Sintram*, he goes on to discuss the nature of translations in general, concluding that in the case of Fouqué, a literal translation is not desirable: Soane himself has acted on this principle, and altered without scruple. His translation reads fairly well. He then goes on to speak of the character of Fouqué's writings. "The Baron moves in a world of his own, which is for the most part beautiful and consistent with itself, however opposite to our visible world. . . . His characters are dream-like and unsubstantial and act on a code of feelings, pure in the extreme, but not recognised in daily life . . . yet, there is a moral beauty in them which has seldom if ever been equalled." He then discusses at some length the value of this work of imagination, condemned by modern critics as contrary to "Nature." Soane concludes that near-

[1] XVI. 205; 1821.
[2] II. 65; 1821.
[3] *Minstrel Love*, from the German of the author of *Undine*. By George Soane, A.B. (London, 1821).

ness to common life is not necessarily "Nature," and that if a work is in unison with itself it need not harmonise with things without which are perpetually changing; popular legends were the *truth* of one age, and as such are real. We should judge creations of fancy, not by nearness to nature, but by their inner harmony, and truth to themselves, and a writer such as Fouqué by these standards.[1] The *Monthly*[2] praises Soane's *Minstrel Love* more than *Undine*, as showing taste and feeling, and good judgment in the alterations. But it calls his remarks in regard to *Sintram* "strange and unfounded"; and considers *Minstrel Love*, the best of all Fouqué's works, as giving a bright and picturesque picture of the olden times.

Another "Ritterroman" of Fouqué's, *Der Zauberring*, was translated as *The Magic Ring*[3] in 1825. The anonymous translator's preface, addressed to a German gentleman,[4] recalls their common meeting with Fouqué at Charlottenburg, and their subsequent discussion of his works, and specially of a possible translation of *The Magic Ring*. The translator upheld that a *remainement* of the work would be much more suitable for English readers than a literal translation. But his friend upheld the contrary; he allowed himself to be persuaded, and so the translation is as literal as it is correct.

The Magic Ring met with very contrary criticisms. The *Monthly*[5] calls it an admirable imitation of an old romance, with no anachronism of sentiment or character, with enchanting descriptions and polished diction. The *Monthly Magazine*[6] disapproves altogether of such imitations of old romances, which drag

[1] Soane illustrates his argument by a popular legend of Arndt, *The Nine Mountains at Rambur*, given in his own words.

[2] LXXIX. 202; 1822.

[3] *The Magic Ring*, a romance from the German of Frederick, Baron de la Motte Fouqué (Edinburgh, 1825).

[4] Freiherr von Amschburg, Berlin, translator of Scott.

[5] CVIII. 395; 1825.

[6] I. 298; 1826.

literature down into the musty records of the past, characterising them rather appositely as " an unceasing repetition of knights, armour, tournays, battles, bruises, and brutality; castles, priests and beautiful damsels."

Several shorter tales of Fouqué's appeared in the various collections of German romances in 1826 and 1827. Roscoe included two in his *German Novelists—II.* (1826): *The Field of Terror, or the Haunted Field* and *The Mandrake*. His estimate of Fouqué's stories is interesting and the specimens he chooses are good examples of the qualities he praises in Fouqué's art. The translations show the same examples of careless mistakes as in *The Ghost-Seer* and other parts of the work.

Carlyle in his *German Romance* (1827) gives the first translation of *Aslauga's Knight*. His remarks on Fouqué are made in a more critical tone than Roscoe's. He comments specially on the certain narrowness of Fouqué's vision, owing to his possession by one idea only: " A few notes, some of them in truth of rich melody, but still a very few, include the whole music of his being."

In *Blackwood*[1] (1821) Gillies translated a short story from Fouqué—*The Field of Terror* (also in Roscoe, but not as well done) calling it " one of the numberless fairy-tales which Fouqué has thrown off with the grace of a genuine master."

Stokoe (p. 85) mentions a projected translation in 1828 of *Die Fahrten Thiodolfs des Isländers* by a friend of Scott. But nothing seems to have come of this.

Karoline de la Motte Fouqué (1773-1831).—Not only Fouqué himself, but also his wife, Karoline, was popular with English novel readers. Gillies translated a tale of hers—*Der Cypressenzweig*, as *The Cypress-Crown*—in *Blackwood* (1820).[2] It appeared again (wrongly attributed to Fouqué himself) together with the Baroness's *Der Abtrünnige, eine*

[1] VIII. 131. [2] VI. 535.

Vision (1817) as *The Turn-Coat, a Vision* and P. Gottwalt's *Christmas* in a little volume of three tales published in Ghent in 1820.[1] They are of interest only as a curiosity. The translation was made by a German "but a novice in the English language," for the benefit of English friends who could not read them in the original. The translations may be a praiseworthy effort from a novice, but the English is decidedly strange. The last two tales are somewhat better; the translator was learning.

Another short tale of Baroness de la Motte Fouqué's, *Scharfenstein Castle*, was included by Gillies in his *German Stories* (1826). The translation, needless to remark, is very different from the above.

A longer novel, *The Outcasts*[2] (from *Die Vertriebenen*), had been translated by Soane two years before. It is an historical novel treating of the England of Queen Elizabeth's reign, written probably in imitation of Scott. Soane sets it far above the generality of German romances for its striking scenes and happy sketches of character. But he points out as faults (1) traces of the old disease of mysticism and sentimentality; (2) the adventuring on English ground, with whose customs the authoress is unfamiliar; (3) too great minuteness of detail in the descriptions.

Soane has, as usual, translated pretty freely, but his version reads well. He has added some notes as explanations of references, etc. Most of the English periodicals noticed the work favourably.[3] Only in the *Westminster Review*[4] is the novel absolutely condemned as "the incomparably dullest work of its kind we ever remembered to have encountered. . . .

[1] *An Essay of Three Tales*, translated from the German language (Ghent, 1820).

[2] *The Outcasts, a Romance*, translated from the German by George Soane (London, Whittaker, 1824).

[3] *Literary Gazette*, August, 1824. *European Magazine*, LXXXV. 583; 1824. *Monthly*, CIV. 105; 1824.

[4] I. 556; 1824.

It gives a picture of English history at once crude, coarse and fade."

A. von Chamisso (1781-1835).—Chamisso's tale of the shadowless man first became known in England under the name of la Motte Fouqué, and as such was translated in 1824.[1] It appeared with excellent plates by Cruikshank, and soon became popular. The anonymous translator (whose identity was discovered long before that of the real author) was Sir John Bowring,[2] the well-known linguist and traveller. The translation which he tells us he undertook at the suggestion of Adelung, is not always quite accurate—*e.g.*, we find " glance " for " Anblick "; " with wild impatience " for " mit grimmigem Durst." But on the whole it is well done. It has been reprinted several times, even as late as 1910,[3] and thus takes its place beside more modern translations.

It was, of course, reviewed as a work of Fouqué's, and considered by the *Monthly*[4] to be inferior to his other tales. The critic remarks justly that the interest grows up to a certain point, but flags very much as it draws near an end. The *British Critic*[5] also notes the poorness of the conclusion, but considers that in the earlier part Fouqué has written with his usual singular power and originality.

[1] *Peter Schlemihl*, from the German of La Motte Fouqué, with plates by George Cruikshank (London, Whittaker, 1824).

[2] *Sir John Bowring* (1802–1872), one of the best linguists of his day. He learned French from a refugee priest, Italian from itinerant vendors; Spanish, Portuguese, German and Dutch from mercantile friends. He afterwards learned enough Swedish, Danish, Russian, Serbian, Polish and Bohemian to be able to translate from them. He studied Arabic and Magyar, and during a residence in the East made considerable progress with Chinese. He published anthologies of poems from Russian, Serbian and some other languages. He travelled abroad for commercial purposes, but not as much in Germany as in other countries. In 1824 he became joint editor of the *Westminster Review*.

[3] In *St. Martin's Library of Standard Authors* (London).

[4] CVI. 201; 1825.

[5] XXI. 172; 1824.

J. L. Tieck (1773-1853).—Tieck's best-known novels—*Franz Sternbald's Wanderungen*[1] and *Genoveva* found no English translator; but several of his shorter tales appeared either in the collections of romances or alone. Two—*Die Gemälde* (1821) and *Die Verlobung* (1822)—were translated as *The Pictures* and *The Betrothing*[2] in 1825 by Connop Thirlwall.[3] They are preceded by a long introduction, in which Thirlwall treats of German conditions and literature from the Thirty Years' War down to his own day—the years of degeneration, the era of French imitation, the revival under the influence of English literature, the new spirit aroused by the Wars of Liberation, and the varying contemporary currents of thought. Thirlwall knew what he was writing about, and shows insight and clear judgment; and he was able to discuss the tales in their proper setting. *The Pictures*, he says, treats of the conflict of opinions aroused by the opposite tendencies in the art of the time—the classic and the romantic; *The Betrothing*, of the false tendencies, perversions and exaggerations of religious feeling at the moment. He notes the charm of Tieck's language and the dramatic concentration in the composition of the

[1] A translation of *Sternbald* is mentioned as announced in the Press in the *Month. Rev.*, IV. 15 (1826), but I have found no further allusion to it.

[2] *The Pictures* and *The Betrothing*, novels translated from the German of Lewis Tieck (London, Whittaker, 1825).

[3] *Bishop Connop Thirlwall* (1797–1875). As a child he showed very precocious talent, and is said to have read English, Greek and Latin at four! He learned French, Italian, German as an undergraduate at Trinity College, Cambridge. Fellow of his College, 1818. Made several tours abroad; published his two tales from Tieck anonymously in 1824; called to the Bar in 1825, took Orders in 1828; a friend of J. C. Hare's, and with him translated Niebuhr's *History of Rome* (1828). He had a thorough knowledge of modern German theology, which was practically unknown in England at that time. In 1840 he became Bishop of St. David's. He took a keen interest in public affairs, and supported several unpopular causes in the House of Lords, including the Disestablishment of the Protestant Church in Ireland. He was well known as an historian.

two little tales. He makes at the end a comparison between Tieck and Goethe. The translation is good, but the style is sometimes rather stiff.

In Roscoe's *German Novelists—IV.* there are four tales from Tieck, two of which—*The Faithful Ekhart* (*Der getreue Eckart*) and *Auburn Egbert* (*Der blonde Eckbert*)—appear again (with a slightly different title) in Carlyle's *German Romance—II.*, though as a rule Carlyle has tried to avoid duplication. Roscoe also has three others of a rather more fantastic character—*The Runenberg* (*Der Runenberg*), *The Elves* (*Die Elfen*), and *The Goblet* (*Der Pokal*) translated by him for the first time.

Roscoe warns his readers not to be startled at the supernatural exhibitions Tieck delights in conjuring up. These appear in full force in several of the tales chosen by Roscoe. A critic of Roscoe's collection in the *Monthly*[1] who disapproves altogether of Tieck as a novelist, though admitting his worth as a scholar, says: "He is a complete exemplar of all the most extravagant horror-mongers who infest the literature of Germany, and here he is at his worst." There may be a germ of truth in these remarks; but they estimate Tieck very unjustly; and also Hoffmann. For Carlyle Tieck is "a true Poet, a Poet born as well as made. A still imagination reigns over all his poetic world. His peculiar province is the 'Mährchen,' and there he reigns without a rival." Yet Carlyle does not dare to predict for him a very flattering reception in England, his merits not being such as to force themselves on the reader, and since he loses, perhaps more than most, in translation.

In 1830 a translation of a literary novel of Tieck's, *Ein Dichterleben* (treating of Marlowe and Shakespeare), was published in Leipzig, presumably the work of a German.[2] It is fairly correct, but very poor in style,

[1] IV. 136; 1826.

[2] *The Life of Poets*, by Lewis Tieck, Esq., translated from the German (Leipsic, Fleischer, 1830).

with long and involved sentences. It has neither preface nor notes.

Novalis, pseudonym of F. L. von Hardenberg (1772-1801).—A word may be said here about Tieck's friend, *Novalis*. His short career was practically unknown in England until a review of his works by Carlyle in the *Foreign Review*[1] in 1829. It is an interesting and sympathetic study. The facts of Novalis's life are taken from Tieck's preface to his works, from which several extracts are translated. Carlyle also translates some passages from the *Lehrlinge zu Sais*, the third of the *Hymnen an die Nacht* and two extracts from *Heinrich von Ofterdingen* (the description of the "Blue Flower" at the beginning, and Heinrich's Dream of Matilda and the river). This novel shows, in Carlyle's opinion, that Novalis had other aspects beside the mystic, and could write in the most common style; and also not without originality. In the second extract he remarks a trace of that simple sublimity, that soft still pathos, which are characteristic of Novalis, and doubtless the highest of his specially poetic gifts.

E. T. A. Hoffmann (1776-1822).—E. T. A. Hoffmann is well represented in the various collections of German stories. Holcraft included *Das Fräulein von Scudéry*, in his *Tales from the German* (1826). Gillies, unaware of this, included the same tale in his collection; but afterwards, he had no regret, "since a good story may bear to be twice told." Both translations are done pretty much on the same plan; but there are minor differences. The French words and expressions (of which there are many, the scene being laid in France) Gillies leaves in French, while Holcraft translates them into English. Gillies's version is the better of the two; but the tale reads agreeably in both. Gillies also included

[1] IV. 97-141.

from Hoffmann *Rolandsitten, or the Deed of Entail*[1] (from *Das Majorat*). Another translation of this as **The Entail, or the Mysteries of the Manor-House* appeared in *The English Fireside, an Almanack for the year* 1829.[2] A review of Hoffmann's work in the *Foreign Quarterly Review*,[3] which discusses at great length the question of the supernatural in Fictitious Composition, gives an analysis of *Das Majorat* with long extracts. The whole essay is worth reading. Gillies—anonymously—is also the translator of a longer novel of Hoffmann's, *Das Elixiere des Teufels* as *The Devil's Elixir*.[4] The *Literary Gazette*[5] recommends it as an excellent translation "to those who like this class of tale—we do not." But *Blackwood*,[6] in a long article, praises both the translation and the tale itself as "our chief favourite among numerous works of a man of rare and singular genius. . . . Ghosts, spirits, etc., in spite of all philosophy and reason say, will ever hold our minds and never be entirely banished; therefore we delight in such works as this. . . . The author marries dreams to realities with admirable art."

Soane devotes Volume II. of his *German Romance* (1826) to a tale from Hoffmann, *Meister Floh* (1822), as *Master Flea*. It was too wild and disconnected to please the English public. The *Monthly Magazine*[7] says "it is the most indescribable production we have ever read. It may be a satire on men or fleas—we cannot tell." One rather sympathises with the reviewer.

[1] It is suggested in a recent book on Emily Brontë, *All Alone* . . ., by Romer Wilson (London, Chatto and Windus, 1928), that the whole framework of *Wuthering Heights* was borrowed outright from *The Entail*, and an interesting parallel is drawn between the two (see *All Alone* . . ., pp. 248, 249).

[2] See Goedeke, VIII. ii., p. 490. I have not been able to find this publication.

[3] I. 60-98; 1827.

[4] *The Devil's Elixir*, from the German of E. T. A. Hoffman (Edinburgh, Blackwood, 1824).

[5] August, 1824, p. 54.

[6] XV. 55; 1824.

[7] II. 323; 1826.

Works of Fiction

Carlyle in his interesting character sketch of Hoffmann in his *German Romance—III.* (1827), concludes by saying that in Hoffmann there are materials for a great poet, but that no poet has been fashioned out of them; both in Art and Life he found no Truth adequate for his guidance. Carlyle has given in fluent translation *The Golden Pot*[1] as most likely to interest the English reader, and as exhibiting a true picture of the author's individuality. Several of Hoffmann's best novels were not translated at all before 1830.

J. K. A. Musæus (1735-1787) was known in England as early as 1791 by a volume of *Popular Tales* (see p. 247). He appears again in a curious collection of tales and legends, some imitated or translated from the German, entitled *The Odd Volume* (1826), etc.[2] Roscoe translated *The Dumb Lover* (*Stumme Liebe*) in his *German Novelists*, and Carlyle translated it much better in *German Romance—I.* Most of this first volume is devoted to Musæus; the two other tales from him being *Libussa* and *Melechsala*.

Of all the other romance writers—*e.g.*, Laun, Langbein, Pichler, Kruse, etc.—whose tales are in these collections, it is impossible to speak here in any detail. Many, though famous in their day, are well-nigh forgotten. Mention is made of some of them in the later part of this chapter.

Jean Paul Friedrich Richter (1763-1825).—Carlyle is usually said to have been the first to introduce Jean Paul to English readers. This is not quite true. He had several forerunners. Almost thirty years before, two extracts from Jean Paul's *Hesperus*[3] ap-

[1] *Der goldne Topf aus Fantasiestücke in Callot's Manier*, Bd. II.

[2] Part I. contains *The Elopement*; Part II. *Legends of Number Nip* (a mistranslation from Rubezahl; zahl = zagel = tail). *A Legend of Number Nip* also appeared in *Tales and Legends* by the authors of *The Odd Volume* (1828), and *The Elopement* had appeared twenty-five years earlier in *The German Museum*, III. (1801).

[3] (1) Victor at the Parsonage. (2) Paltry extra-syllable concerning Sacred Music, from the XIXth Dog's Post-day. *Hesperus*, II.

peared in the *German Museum—II.* (1801), sent by an anonymous correspondent, and not badly translated, considering the difficulty of Jean Paul's style.

The next attempt to introduce Richter was made by H. Crabb Robinson in his *Amatonda* (1811), where one of the characters is said to be Richter himself. To this allusion, Robinson appends an account of his original called "the German Sterne"; though with this comparison Robinson himself disagrees, making an interesting contrast between the two.[1] As Richter's principal characteristic, he aptly points out "the exuberance of *matter* and the inability or disinclination to give *form* to it." The few fragments Robinson gives at the end (he does not say where they are from) as "specimens of Richter's style, imagery, and turn of thought," are well chosen and well translated. Charles Lamb liked them, and said they were the finest things he had ever seen from the German.

These first presentations of Richter reached few readers, and were soon forgotten,[2] not leading to any further interest in him in England. Not for ten years do we find the next mention of his name. A letter in *The London Magazine*,[3] dated Grasmere, October 18th, 1821, giving a short life and critique of Richter, mentions him with Kant and Schiller as one of the writer's three favourites in German literature: and subjoined is a translation of two specimens from the *Flegeljahre*.[4] The author was de Quincey, and in 1824 in the same magazine came *Analects from J. P. Richter* by the author of *The Confessions of an*

[1] H. C. R.'s *Diary and Reminiscences*, I. 360.

[2] Carlyle did not even know of them. Writing in 1830 he says: "It is some *six* years since the name of . . . Richter was first printed with English types" (*For. Rev.*, V. 1).

[3] IV. 606.

[4] *The happy life of a parish priest in Sweden ; Last Will and Testament ; The House of Weeping.*

English Opium Eater,[1] and in a later number *The Dream of the Universe*,[2] signed "X. Y. Z." These translations of de Quincey's—considering again the many difficulties in Jean Paul—are very good. A later writer in *Blackwood*[3] says: "All the world has read the eulogy of J. P. Richter by an English Opium Eater in the *London Magazine*, and his exquisite translations." These articles brought Jean Paul for the first time seriously to the attention of English readers.

Before coming to Carlyle, we must mention one other translator, R. Holcraft, who included *The Death of an Angel* and *The Moon*[4] in his *Tales from the German*, 1826. Holcraft has been less successful here than with easier writers, and there are many mistranslations.

In 1827 Carlyle published the first complete translations from Richter—*The Life of Quintus Fixlein* and *Schmetzle's Journey to Flaetz*—in the third volume of his *German Romance*. They are preceded by a short sketch of Richter's life, together with a long discussion of his characteristics as an author. The same year saw Carlyle's review of Doering's *Life of Jean Paul* in the *Edinburgh Review*;[5] and 1830 a review of *Wahrheit aus Jean Paul's Leben* in the *Foreign Review*.[6] This last article, and much of the earlier articles, is reprinted in Carlyle's *Critical Essays—III*. Carlyle pleads for a deeper study of Richter's works, for "though difficult to understand, they always have a meaning, and often a deep and true one." He ventures to hope that, though a first judgment may be unfavourable, curiosity will be awakened, and a second and truer judgment based on ampler grounds and maturer reflection will follow. Carlyle's expectations

[1] IX. 117. [2] *Ibid.*, 242. [3] XXII. 466.
[4] Episodes from *Quintus Fixlein*. [5] XLVI. 178-251.
[6] V. 1-52. Passages are translated from the *Vorschule der Aesthetik*, *Quintus Fixlein*, *Hesperus* and *Siebenkäs*.

were hardly fulfilled, for in spite of his efforts, Richter did not, and never has, become a popular writer in England.

Carlyle justly remarks that Richter is the most untranslatable of Germans. He has brought him into English in as nearly as possible his original form. The following sentence will show how carefully Carlyle keeps the exact images of Richter:

"And now the Moon, as it were the hanging seal of his last night's happiness, dips down into the West, like an emptied bucket of light, and in the East, the other overrunning bucket, the Sun, mounts up, and the gushes of light flow broader and broader."

"Jetzt taucht sich der Mond (gleichsam das hängende Siegel seiner gestrigen Wonne) am Abend als ein ausgeleerter Eimer des Lichts, und am Morgen ging der zweite übervoll geschöpfte Eimer, die Sonne, in die Höhe, und die Güsse des Lichts flatterten immer breiter."

Karl Theodor Körner (1791-1813).—Kŏrner—the soldier-poet of the Wars of Liberation—is the author too of some prose-tales, and of these several were translated.

There are three translations of *Hans Heiling's Rocks, a Bohemian Legend*: (1) *Blackwood*,[1] 1820; (2) *London Magazine*,[2] 1821; (3) G. F. Richardson's *Life and selections from Körner*, 1827.[3] That in the *London* is the poorest of the three; Richardson's is not always accurate—*e.g.*, "gelernt hab' ich etwas Ordentliches" = "I have learnt something in a common way"; "ausreden" = "to talk on"; "in der Hoffnung, ihren Getreuen *daher* wandern zu sehen" = "in the silent hope that she might see her lover wandering *there*"—which just loses the point. Richardson makes little additions of his own. The translation in *Blackwood* is more faithful, and the best of the three.

Holcraft, in *Tales from the German* (1826), has two from Körner—*Woldemar* and *The Harp*—and the

[1] VIII. 625. [2] III. 342.
[3] For account of this work see *Kŏrner* in Chap. VII.

Literary Gazette[1] declares that "Körner, heretofore unknown as a prose writer, sustains here the reputation he has gained as a writer of patriotic poetry." *Woldemar* and *The Harp* were translated again in G. F. Richardson's *Life of Körner* in the following year. Holcraft makes some mistakes—*e.g.*, "Zaudern" = "fear" (confused with "Zagen"), but on the whole he is much more accurate in his work than Richardson, who often translates very carelessly.

A translation of some interest is that of J. J. Engel's *Lorenz Stark*,[2] translated by a German, and published by a German firm in London in 1826. It forms a sharp contrast in its character to most of the other tales of the time, a contrast intentional, as is shown by the translator's Postscript. Gans, apparently a German living in England, was angry at the unjust and one-sided ideas prevailing there on the literature of his country: "A book or play has only to be announced as 'from the German' to arouse expectations of goblins, spectres and chimeras dire; a display of sickly sentiment, overwrought delicacy and sophisticated morality. German mysticism and German sentimentality are almost proverbial." How this prejudice can exist in the face of works like those of Lessing, Goethe, etc., all wholly free of such unfounded charges, Gans confesses himself unable to understand, but he thinks it may be ascribed in a great measure to the influence of Kotzebue's *Stranger* and *Pizarro*, which—introduced under the mistaken protection of the great Sheridan—were regarded by the vast portion of the public, unacquainted with German literature, as the very models of German taste and perfection in writing. When afterwards the voice of impartial criticism was raised against these pieces, the censures

[1] 1826, p. 227.

[2] *Lorenz Stark, a Characteristic Picture of a German Family*, by J. J. Engel. Translated from the German by I. Gans (London, Treuttel and Würtz, 1826).

were unfortunately extended from them to the whole German school. Since then an idea of gloom and mystery has been associated with the idea of German literature, aroused by *Lenore*, some tales of Tieck and romances of Fouqué, which idea is prejudicial when imputed to the whole literature of a great and intellectual people. With the intention of correcting these erroneous impressions, he has decided to present the British public with a series of works of the class of *Lorenz Stark*; equally free as it is from horrors on the one hand and false sentiment on the other; showing truth of feeling, simplicity of design, and knowledge of the human heart; a faithful and living portrait of German life and manners before the French Revolution. Gans concludes with a short biographical notice of Engel and a list of his works. Judging by the English of these remarks and also of the translation, Gans must have been for many years in England.

It seems doubtful whether *Lorenz Stark* was ever as popular as the tales to which it was an intended antidote. It may be free from the aforementioned faults, but it has that of dullness. The *Monthly*,[1] after expressing surprise at not finding a ghost, robber, or a drop of blood shed from beginning to end of this German tale, says: "It is quite a novelty in the literature of Germany, for it presents a simple and expressive view of everyday life in that country, without any of the sentimentality of Kotzebue, or the theatrical exaggeration of Pichler." But it finds the story feebly told and the conversations stiff and dull.

Gans may have been discouraged by the reception given to *Lorenz Stark* from publishing any more of the series, for no more appeared.

[1] IV. 538; 1827.

C. COLLECTIONS OF GERMAN ROMANCES.

The earliest collection of German stories in translation appeared in 1791. They are translated from Musæus's *Volksmärchen der Deutschen* under the title of *Popular Tales of the Germans.* No translator's name is given.[1] As introduction there is a half serious, half burlesque dialogue between the Reviewer attacking the Tales and the Publisher defending. Musæus is here alluded to indirectly as the original author of the Tales.

The translator makes readable stories. He knew German well, and translated correctly, though often adapting freely. His collection of stories compares very favourably with many of a much later date. The *European Magazine*[2] reviewed the *Popular Tales* as "being of a very original cast and displaying much shrewd humour, laughing satire, and extensive learning." The *Gentleman's Magazine*[3] recommends them to "all those who value genuine humour, originality, whim, and anecdote." To the *Analytical*[4] they are "entertaining and interesting." To the *Monthly*[5] alone, "monsters of fiction, extravagant in the extreme, having little humour, satire, or sentiment."

M. G. Lewis's *Romantic Tales*[6] (1808) has many free adaptations from German tales, ballads, etc. He admits he would find it difficult to say exactly what portion is his own. He tells which tales are of German origin, but does not specify sources. *Amorassin, an Oriental Romance*, is the most interesting. One of the verse pieces, *The Dying Bride*, is partly translated

[1] *Popular Tales of the Germans*, translated from the German in two volumes (London, Murray, 1791). *Lit. Gaz.* (1826, p. 508) refers to them as by Beckford. The Bodleian catalogue gives J. Beresford. The Brit. Museum catalogue neither name.

[2] XIX. 350.

[3] LXI. ii., 1126.

[4] X. 217.

[5] V. 467; 1791.

[6] *Romantic Tales*, by M. G. Lewis, author of *The Monk*, etc., in four volumes (London, Longman, 1808).

from Herder's version of a Lithuanian ballad given in his *Volkslieder*. Both the *Annual Review*[1] and *The Gentleman's Magazine*[2] speak of the Tales as interesting and entertaining, and happily free from the licentiousness of Lewis's earlier works. But the *Critical*[3] thinks that these same earlier works displayed a genius capable of much higher things than these tales, many of which it characterises as a "farrago of nonsense."

Lewis's *Tales of Terror* (1800) also have adaptations from German; all in the spirit of the "Schauerroman."

W. Taylor's *Tales of Yore*[4] (1810) has translations from both French and German. The only German authors mentioned are Wieland (*The Religion of Psamnius* and *Koxkox and Kikequetzel*) and Meissner. Another story, *Sir Libeo*, is abridged from a German version of *Li beaus disconnus*, and is thus a double translation. The choice of these tales shows Taylor's constant predilection for Wieland. Otherwise they have no particular interest. It was a work really unworthy of Taylor's powers, and few but immediate friends knew it came from his pen. The *Critical*[5] reviewed it coldly. Robberds[6] speaks of it in 1843 as a scarce book, having had a ready enough sale.

**Tales of Wonder, Humour and Sentiment* (1818), by Anna and Annabella Plumptre, are said to be "original and translated"—some probably from German sources; but none such are mentioned. Annabella Plumptre also published **Domestic Stories from the German of various authors*.[7] (No date.)

Three volumes entitled **Popular Tales of the Northern Nations* (Bohte) appeared in 1823. They are reviewed

[1] VII. 616. [2] LXXIX. i., 141. [3] XV.; 1808.
[4] *Tales of Yore*, in three volumes (London, Mawman, 1810).
[5] XVIII. 443; 1810. [6] *Memoir*, II., p. 316.
[7] See D.N.B., XLV. 436. I could not find a copy of the work itself.

in *Blackwood*[1] as a disappointing publication likely to do more harm than good to the cause of German literature; for in the choice of pieces there is no discrimination, absolute trash being selected, and excellent ones (*e.g.*, of Hoffmann) being left untouched. Translation is said to be miserable—bald in style and even grammarless. The tales are selected from various writers—Veit Weber, Grimm, Laun, etc. The sources are not exactly given. Most are terrific or horrible.[2]

Between 1823 and 1826 appeared the now famous collection of Grimm's *Märchen* by Edgar Taylor,[3] with Cruikshank's illustrations.[4] The tales of the first series were selected and translated by Taylor and a circle of friends (1823), the first suggestion coming from the delight children took in a few of the tales when narrated. The Preface gives some account of the sources of the tales, quoting a good deal from the original notes of MM. Grimm. Taylor sent this first volume of tales to Walter Scott, who acknowledged them on January 16th, 1823 as follows: "I have often wished to see such a work undertaken by a gentleman of taste sufficient to adapt the simplicity of the German narration to our own, which you have done so successfully." The volume was praised by several periodicals[5] and went to a second edition the same year.[6] Encouraged by its success, Taylor prepared the second series alone. In this the tales have rather more the general character of fairy-tales, and less of German peculiarities; but the design

[1] XIV. 293. [2] *Month. Rev.*, CIII. 40; 1823.

[3] *Edgar Taylor* (1793–1839). He was a barrister in partnership with one of the brothers of T. Roscoe; prospered by the law, but in his later years gave much of his time to literature. A cousin of Sarah Austin; translated with her *Lays of the Minnesingers* (1825). This and the *Popular Tales* are his only translations from German.

[4] *German Popular Stories* from the *Kinder und Hausmärchen*, collected by MM. Grimm from oral tradition, two vols. (London, 1824–6).

[5] *Month. Mag.*, LIV. 331; 1823. *Europ. Mag.*, LXXXIII. 259; 1823. *Lond. Mag.*, VIII. 91.

[6] See *Lit. Gaz.*, March, 1823, p. 164.

is the same. Two or three of this second series are not by Grimm, *e.g.*, *The Nose* from Zwehrn, and the *Elfin Grove*, an abridgment of Tieck's *Phantasus*.

The *Monthly*[1] reviewed both volumes unfavourably, remarking that there were domestic sources of native legends to be used instead of German, and that the stories lacked antiquarian research and illustration. But this is an unfair objection to make to what was intended mainly for enjoyment. Besides there are notes to many of the tales; so the volumes have some critical value. The general public made none of these objections and were content to be pleased with the charm of the tales, and the simple yet picturesque manner of telling. Soon there were several editions, now very scarce. But reprints appeared in 1869 and in 1876, and Grimm's *Fairy Tales* have become a children's classic in English as in German.

In 1827 there appeared a translation of three fairy-tales[2] from the German of Albert Ludwig Grimm (a South German and no relation of the brothers Grimm, who were Hessians). The translation was suggested by Taylor's volumes. The anonymous translator has been fairly successful and on the whole the stories read well, and in style are "Volkstümlich." I have found no evidence as to how they were received.

The demand for German stories in England[3] about this time seems to have been insatiable, and was supplied by no less than five collections (including E. Taylor's) in the one year 1826; for which reason Carlyle postponed publishing his until 1827.

Richard Holcraft's *Tales from the German*[4] con-

[1] CIII. 40; 1823. And II. 448; 1826.

[2] *Fairy Tales*, from the German of A. L. Grimm, containing *The Black Guitar*, *The Two Foundlings of the Spring* and *The Avenging Cudgel*, with illustrations by Cruikshank (London, Tilt, 1827).

[3] See Max Batt, *The German Story in England*, *c.* 1826. *Mod. Phil.*, V. (1907).

[4] *Tales of Humour and Romance*, selected from popular German Authors and translated by Richard Holcraft, B.A. (London, 1826).

tained translations from Körner and Richter, then scarcely known in England; also from Hoffmann, Schiller, Langbein and Lafontaine.[1] Holcraft had a very fair knowledge of German and German literature, and made better translations than others of the time, though not without mistakes, *e.g.*, "joined" for "überraschte," "dispersed" for "entwischte" and—still worse—"in deep distress" for "mit unendlicher Heiterkeit." There are a good many misprints in the volumes. The *Literary Gazette*[2] praises the translation and says a few words about several of the stories, but gives no criticism of interest. Of Holcraft himself nothing appears to be known.

The plan of Roscoe's[3] collection[4] is wider, including ancient legends and tales from folk-books, as well as from modern writers. Volume I. gives *The Pleasant History of Reynard the Fox* (here Roscoe has used an old English version); *Howleglass the Merry Jester*; and the *History of Dr. Faustus, the renowned Arch-Sorcerer*. Volume II. gives *Local Popular Traditions* out of collections of stories by Otmar, Gottschalk, Eberhardt, Büsching, Grimm and Lothar. Among those from Otmar is *Peter Klaus*, the original of Rip van Winkle, and from Gottschalk *The Mouse Tower*, of which the story is familiar to us in Southey's *Bishop Hatto*. Roscoe's selections from Grimm's *Märchen* are not representative; almost

[1] For translations of and remarks on most important writers in all these collections, see under their names in earlier part of this chapter.

[2] April, 1826, p. 227.

[3] *Thomas Roscoe* (1791–1871), a well-known author and translator. His father had a fine library of Italian and other foreign books (mentioned in Irving's *Sketch-book*), so the boy was early attracted to the study of foreign literatures. He published *Italian Novelists* in 1825 and *Spanish Novelists* in 1832. His best-known work is a translation of Benvenuto Cellini's *Memoirs*.

[4] *The German Novelists*, tales selected from Ancient and Modern Authors in that language, from the earliest period down to the end of the eighteenth century. Translated from the originals with critical and biographical notes by Thomas Roscoe (London, Colburn, 1826).

all being local legends of a rather gruesome variety, while he gives none of the lighter and more charming tales. But he was perhaps limited in his choice by not wishing to repeat those already given by Taylor (from whom, however, he borrows one specimen). Roscoe's translation is not as good as Taylor's. The tales from Fouqué are also in this volume. Volumes III. and IV. give translations from modern authors—Schiller, Tieck, Musæus, Engel and Langbein. Roscoe says that his chief aim has been to give "amusing narrative and novelty of incident." But his critical and biographical notes form a great part of the interest of this collection, and must have given much useful and new information. In Volume I., for instance, he gives a short history of the origin and development of the legend of Reineke Fuchs; of the different versions of *Eulenspiegel* with a characterisation from Görres, and an account of the various traditions extant in German with regard to Dr. Faust.[1] In the introduction to the second volume he gives some account of each collection of "Volksagen," of their aims and method. To some of the modern authors he gives extravagant praise. "The spirited and elegant tales" of Langbein and Engel, for instance, are now wellnigh forgotten, other and better Novellen having followed them. His comments on Fouqué and Schiller (quoted before) are more just.

Roscoe's volumes testify to much painstaking work, and give a good idea of the various kinds of German story. Unfortunately, the selecting of the stories and the compiling of the introductions got more care than the translating (*vide* Schiller's *Geisterseher*).[2] Other examples of bad translating are: "preparations" for

[1] Among the testimonies to the historical Faust he quotes rather an interesting work written by an Englishman in Wittenberg in 1594 (see I. 268).

[2] Chap. VI.

"Vorstellungen"; "and when I openly declared how much I needed compassion" for "und wenn ich's aufrichtig sagen soll, ich brauchte Bedauerung"; "free-life" for "Freygebigkeit"; "reproach" for "Auswurf," evidently confused with "Vorwurf," etc. The style is unequal; now good, now awkward and slovenly, the whole showing haste.

The *Monthly*[1] analysed Roscoe's volumes at length, with many extracts, giving praise to the selection and arrangement, but blame to the translation. Of the German story in general this critic says: "Putting aside a few pieces of a very high merit, its all-pervading character is one of unbounded extravagance, both of fancy and feeling. The German novelist sups full of horrors and has only a nightmare for the result. . . . He has the complacent conviction that he must be soaring in the elevation of genius only because he has quitted the region of common-sense. . . . He mistakes frothy rhapsody for sentiment, voluptuous impurity of the heart for workings of the finer passions, affectation for pathos, buffoonery for humour, ribaldry for wit."

Soane's[2] *Specimens of German Romance*,[3] without introduction or notes, came out anonymously, but he was generally known as the author. Except Hoffmann's *Master Flea*, the stories are taken from now almost forgotten authors—van der Velde, Laun, Naubert and the Dane, Oehlenschläger. Soane's original intention was to carry on the work through many

[1] IV. 136; 1826.

[2] *George Soane* (1790–1860) graduated from Pembroke College, Cambridge; knew French, German and Italian well; published several translations from these languages, as well as original works. In 1821 he supplied the extracts from *Faust* to illustrate Retsch's drawings. In 1822 he began a metrical translation of *Faust*, but completed only about six hundred lines. The publisher sent the advance sheets to Goethe, who gave high praise (see Hauhart, *Faust in England*, pp. 92-3).

[3] *Specimens of German Romance*, selected and translated from various authors (London, Whittaker, 1826).

more volumes and thus present a complete cycle of German romance. Had he known these three volumes were to be the limit of his labours, he might, he says, have made a somewhat different choice. Each volume has a frontispiece by Cruikshank—as extravagant and grotesque as the tales themselves. According to a critic in the *Literary Gazette*[1] " the tales are what they profess to be—romance, which in spite of its imagination gone mad and its extravagance of adventure, has a strongly excited interest, not often to be found in the more chastened pages of sober literature. . . . The volumes bid fair to rebuff the too general accusation against German tales being only those of horror." The *Monthly Magazine*[2] did not approve of the choice of the stories but praised the translation. A critic in the *Monthly*[3] made an interesting comment: " The general features of the tales are curiously illustrative of the modern national mind of Germany . . . they show the contradiction between the sedateness and phlegmatic decency of German private life, and the wild flights of fancy and glowing and voluptuous delineations of character which they like in their literature."

As usual, Soane translates pretty freely, often simplifying his task by rather summarising than translating. But actual inaccuracies are few and his style is pleasant.

Gillies's *German Stories*,[4] besides tales from the authors mentioned on the title-page, contains two or three ghost stories, anonymous.[5] They are, he says, but a small portion of a series long accumulated on his shelves, and are now printed in consequence of the

[1] 1826, p. 355. [2] II. 323 ; 1826. [3] II. 464 ; 1826.

[4] *German Stories*, selected from the Works of Hoffmann, de la Motte Fouqué, Pichler, Kruze and others, by R. P. Gillies, Esq. (Edinburgh, Blackwood, 1826).

[5] One tale, the *Siege of Antwerp*, is said to have been adapted as a melodramatic play at Covent Garden. It is not mentioned by Genest as such.

increasing interest lately excited in favour of German stories. He comments shortly on each story, and gives a short characterisation of the German novel in general.

Gillies's translations are generally better than those which had appeared before, reading like originals, yet keeping many of their peculiar German characteristics. The *Literary Gazette*[1] thinks it the best publication of the kind since the collection of 1791. The *Monthly*[2] says that no one could be better fitted than Gillies for the carrying out of such a task, since he combines with an eminent degree of good taste a lively partiality for just such extraordinary and fantastic tales as these, strongly resembling the *Arabian Nights*.

Gillies's *Stories* led to an interesting article in *Blackwood*,[3] based on the work of Gillies, whose judicious choice of stories and admirable mode of translation will, it is hoped, set the precedent for raising the standard in that department. As principles which should guide the selector in his choice of German stories this writer lays down: (1) Let him abstain from novels of manners, which are coarse and coarsely delineated. Lafontaine and Langbein and all their following are utterly unfit for importation, for besides being extravagantly silly, they are too intensely local to bear transportation. (2) Let him avoid tales of sentiment; Richter stands absolutely alone in this department and he is all but untranslatable. (3) Let him confine himself to novels of incident and regular plot; only avoiding the monstrosities of the supernatural with which they abound. With regard to the translations this writer considers there is absolute need for reform in this department; "most are so villainous in point of style that no one can read them." Other translators should take pattern by Gillies, and not only avoid downright errors and slovenliness, but also *think*

[1] November, 1826, p. 508. [2] IV. 526; 1826.
[3] XX. 844; 1826.

in English. He also considers that they should apply the principle of rifacimento on a much larger scale, adapting the stories to English taste, and improving where they can.

Whether translators should adapt freely or translate literally was a question much disputed at the moment. Gillies himself, though he has here anglicised his authors by translation, thinks they would be made more acceptable to English readers by a "rifacimento." A critic of the *Stories* in the *Monthly Magazine*[1] takes the opposite view, upholding that the only use for translations is the exhibition they afford of the varieties of human thought and human manners, and that the plan of adaptation goes to annihilate this utility. The truth of this argument applies perhaps less to these tales than to writings of more lasting value.

Carlyle worked on this principle of the real interest of a foreign literature lying just in its peculiar and national characteristics; "I ask readers," he writes in the preface to his *German Romance*,[2] "to remember one thing—that these are *German* novelists, not English ones, and their Germanhood I have recognised all along as a quality not as a fault. . . . Every nation has its own form of character and life; and the mind which gathers no nourishment from the everyday circumstances of its existence will be but scantily nourished. Of writers who belong to all nations, or more properly speaking to none, there is no want in Germany as elsewhere, but they have no interest for us." Carlyle hopes that this little publication may assist to forward an acquaintance with a literature and people well worthy of study. Also that it will excite to a more general learning of the German language, whose difficulties have been much exaggerated. Carlyle

[1] II. 656; 1826.

[2] *German Romance*, translated by T. Carlyle. Two vols. (Edinburgh and London, 1827). (The original edition is prized by collectors, as the tales from Fouqué and Hoffmann have never been reprinted).

worked hard at these volumes through 1825 and 1826, as he mentions in a letter to John Carlyle, December 1st, 1825: "For myself I have gone along with exemplary industry for several weeks; translating daily at my appointed task, and turning neither to right hand or to left, as if I were a scribbling, smoking, sleeping and dyspeptical automaton." In the selection of pieces Carlyle says he has had no easy task, since time has not yet exercised its separating influence on the thousands of German novelists. He notes also that the real strength of German literature does not lie in its novelists; as was foolishly thought by many English readers at that time. He divides German novel writing into six Modes: (1 and 2) the "Mārchen," shown here by Musæus (prosaic) and Tieck (poetical); (3) the Chivalry Romance, whose great representative is Fouqué; (4) the Fantasy-Piece, whose originator is Hoffmann; (5) the Novel, in English sense, as shown in Richter's two pieces; (6) the Art Novel, of which the greatest is *Wilhelm Meister*.[1] Carlyle gives examples of each of these modes, Richter occupying the whole of the third volume, and *Meister* the fourth.[2]

Carlyle's sketches of the life and works of each author are interesting and have more critical value than those of Roscoe. He was not, however, entirely satisfied with them himself, as one can judge from passages in his letters, where he complains of the difficulty of getting the necessary materials, etc. The *Monthly*[3] never viewed favourably the importation of German stories in such numbers, and here it wishes

[1] *Vide* Chap. V., p. 128.

[2] An example of the "Æsthetic Novel"—said to be most popular but little known in England—is analysed with translated extracts in the *For. Rev.*, V. 337; 1830. It is *Die Bildhauer*, by Karoline von Woltmann. A literary hoax, *Walladmor*, brought out in German as a translation from Scott, really an imitation of Scott's novels, was translated (anonymously) by De Quincey, 1825 (*vide* Chap. X). Rev. *West. Rev.*, III. 273; 1825.

[3] V. 157; 1827.

that a translator of such ability should have turned his attention to the sounder portions of German literature rather than this "trash of fiction." It considers the memoirs far the most valuable and attractive portion of the work. The *Literary Gazette*[1] doubts that English taste will ever become reconciled to the "sentimentality of Richter" or the "mysterious mysticism of *Wilhelm Meister*," but welcomes the volumes as a venture on new lines.

A great part of the interest of Carlyle's work certainly lay in the biographical and critical sketches, that of Goethe being the first at all adequate account of him in English.[2] But in the accuracy and vigour of the translations it is also much superior to its predecessors.

[1] 1827, pp. 35, 53.

[2] During the writing of *German Romance* Carlyle had many conversations with H. Crabb Robinson about Weimar, Goethe, etc. On May 14th, 1827, Carlyle sent Robinson a copy of the work with a letter (*vide* J. M. Carré, *Revue Germanique*, Janvier, 1912).

CHAPTER IX

A.—Miscellaneous Prose Translations; B.—German Miscellanies

A

In this chapter are put together translations of prose works, other than fiction, from minor writers. They are of very various character, and it is impossible to classify them more particularly. They are arranged as far as possible in chronological order, but the works of the same author are kept together.

BARON FREDERICK TRENCK[1] (1746-1794).

An autobiographical work which aroused enormous interest in England was the account of the life and adventures of Baron Trenck, political prisoner of Frederick II. Translated into English, with some omissions, by T. Holcroft in 1788,[2] only a couple of years after its appearance in Germany, it went through numerous editions. A fourth volume—not translated by Holcroft—was published in 1793.[3] Trenck was guillotined in Paris in 1794.

[1] Not to be confused with his cousin, Franz (1711–1747), who died at Gratz. *Memoirs of the Life of the Illustrious Francis Baron Trenck, translated from the original German* (Owen), appeared already in 1747. It is thus a very early translation, but it can hardly rank as literature.

[2] *The Life of Baron Frederic Trenck—containing his adventures, his cruel and excessive sufferings during ten years imprisonment at Magdeburg, by command of the late king of Prussia, also Anecdotes, Historical, Political and Personal.* Translated from the German by T. Holcroft (London, Robinson, 1788).

[3] Vide *Month. Rev.*, XII. 388; 1793. *Anal. Rev.*, XVI. 248; 1793.

Two other translations of *Trenck* appeared the same year as Holcroft's.[1] The first, containing only two-thirds of the original, by an artillery officer,[2] was—to judge by the reviews—full of mistakes. One reviewer says it was taken from a mutilated French version; but the title-page says "translated from the original German," and the translator announces that he undertook the work as "an exercise in the German language."

The second **Life of Baron Trenck*, from the German (Murray, 1788) was reviewed in the *European Magazine*.[3] A letter from "Viator" in the same number[4] expresses great interest in the work, the writer saying that he met Trenck at Aix, and heard much of the story from his own lips. At Glasgow in 1809 appeared **The Life and surprising adventures of Baron Trenck*, abridged, to which is added "an account of his more recent transactions." Several shorter abridgments were published as chap-books (1802, 1820, 1826). Trenck's *Memoirs* were republished as late as 1893 in Routledge's World Library. Of the three 1788 translations, Holcroft's was much the most complete and the only one generally known.[5]

R. P. Gillies tells of reading this work, and of the great impression which it made on him:[6] "Another book which I first perused in my tenth or twelfth year, namely, the *Memoirs of Baron Trenck*, made a great impression on my boyhood, which has lasted with me through life. It was no paltry pamphlet about Trenck; it was the complete edition in four volumes by Holcroft. . . . Not all the speeches of C. J. Fox,

[1] *Anal. Rev.*, III. 140; 1789.

[2] **Memoirs of Baron Trenck* . . . by an Officer in the R.A. (London, Egerton, 1788).

[3] XII. 287; 1788.

[4] P. 320.

[5] I found no copy of either of the other two. Holcroft's is the only English translation given in a *Bibliographische Übersicht der Trenck Literatur*, by J. Petzholdt (Dresden, 1866).

[6] *Memoirs of a Literary Veteran*, I., chaps. ix., x.

much as I admired them in after years, nor any other demonstrations of the liberal party made such an indelible impression on my mind as that old book. I conceived from it not only a hatred of oppression and tyranny, but a lurking suspicion of all crowned heads without exception."

J. J. K. ENGEL (1741-1802).

A translation, or rather adaptation of a dramatic treatise by Engel, was made in 1807 by Henry Siddons[1] as *Practical Illustrations of Rhetorical Gesture and Actions*.[2] Siddons has adapted freely to suit the special conditions of the English stage. The work was accompanied by engravings "expressive of the various passions and representing the modern costume of the London theatres." It must have been approved in some dramatic circles; for a new and improved edition of it was published in 1822. The *Monthly*—though it had given a long and favourable account of a Dutch translation[3] of the original in 1792[4]—judged it very severely in the English translation.[5]

In the following year appeared a volume of *Essays and Tales*[6] from the German of the author[7] of the *Essays*

[1] *Henry Siddons* (1774–1814) was the son of the famous actress, Mrs. Sarah Siddons, and nephew of Charles Kemble. He was an actor himself, and also author of several plays. His talent was admired by Scott.

[2] *Practical Illustrations of Rhetorical Gesture and Action, adapted to the English Drama*, from a work on the subject by M. Engel, Member of the Academy of Berlin, by Henry Siddons (London, 1807).

[3] *De Kunst der Nabootsing door Gebaarden* (Haarlem, 1791).

[4] IX. 52; 1792.

[5] LVIII. 373; 1809.

[6] *Essays and Tales; Moral, Literary and Philosophical*, by M. Engel, author of *Essays on Dramatic Gesture and Action*, from the original German by Thomas Horne (London, Coxhead, 1808).

[7] These (as also the tales in Roscoe's *Novelists*, IV.) are given in Brit. Mus. Catalogue under "Moritz Erdmann Engel," the *Essays on Dramatic Gesture* under "J. J. Engel." But both should be under "J. J. E." The "M" before his name on title-page stands, as frequently, for "Mr." or "Monsieur."

on Dramatic Gesture, by T. Horne.[1] Horne, in the Preface, says Engel must be numbered after Goethe, Wieland [*sic*], etc., among the writers who are "the flower and chivalry of German Literature. . . . His diction is classical, his imagery beautiful and his sentiments refined." After this panegyric the fifteen essays and tales contained in the volume fall rather flat. Some are philosophical dissertations, others humorous tales and dialogues. There is at least variety—*e.g.*, *Dissertation on Death*, *Toby Witt*, *The Receptacle for Lunatics*, *Remarks on the Moral Excellence of Poetry*, etc. The translation is good enough. The *Monthly* confesses to being disappointed in the *Tales* after the panegyrical Preface.

F. MATTHISSON (1761-1831).

In 1799 appeared Matthisson's *Letters written from various parts of the Continent*, translated by Miss Anne Plumptre. The letters are taken from a collection published at Zürich in 1795. They contain interesting descriptions of travel, and many anecdotes of Klopstock, Herder, Wieland, Bürger and other German writers. These will have interested English readers just at this moment when German literature was at the height of its popularity in England. The *Monthly*[2] had already reviewed the original with translated extracts, in 1797. In 1800[3] it noticed the translation as "on the whole well executed, with good notes. The *Letters* were also praised as amusing and interesting in the *European Magazine*[4] and the *Critical*.[5] Miss Plumptre's translation has many inaccuracies due to ignorance of German manners and literature.[6]

[1] *Cf.* Schiller's *Fall of the Belgian Republic*, chap. vi.

[2] XXIII. 522.

[3] XXXI. 108.

[4] XXXVI. 41.

[5] XXVII. 67.

[6] Matthisson's *Poems* were very favourably reviewed by W. Taylor in the *Month. Mag.*, V. 1794. Many were afterwards translated in the various collections of German lyrics before 1830.

Miscellaneous Prose Translations

E. M. ARNDT (1769-1860).

A translation of the second part of Arndt's *Geist der Zeit* as the *Spirit of the Times* (1808)[1] takes its place among anti-Napoleonic literature. The translator is the Rev. P. Will, but he does not here give his name in full. He proclaims himself a German by birth, long resident in England, "that hospitable country where all the intended victims of the modern Attila are sure of meeting with a safe asylum."

The *Spirit of the Times* aroused considerable attention in England; the original being printed by Boosey in London (1813), as Arndt mentions in his second edition Preface. The *Monthly*[2] had reviewed the original in 1806, and reviewed the translated work in 1809.[3] It regrets that the translator has not included the remarks on Great Britain, and not increased the strength of the epithets on the French nation.

AUGUST WILHELM SCHLEGEL (1767-1845).

We now come to two works of much greater interest as literature. In the first decade of the nineteenth century, until the interesting account given of him in Madame de Staël's *De l'Allemagne* (1811), little was known in England of A. W. Schlegel. Once known, it was natural that he would be better received there than by Madame de Staël's own countrymen. Schlegel's attacks on rules long sacred to French critics roused much indignation in France. In England, on the contrary, as Black remarks in the Preface to his translation of *Vorlesungen über dramatische*

[1] Arndt's *Spirit of the Times*, translated from the German by the Rev. P. W., being the work for the Publication of which the unfortunate Palm of Erlangen was sacrificed by Napoleon the Destroyer (London, 1808).

[2] XLIX. 524; 1806.

[3] LX. 108.

Kunst und Litteratur[1] many scholars would be ready to accept Schlegel's views, while his unsparing attack on the literature of the enemy would be no disadvantage to him in their eyes. His enlightened interpretation of their own greatest poet gave his work an additional interest for the English, and many allusions can be found to the *Lectures* in the original German. Proof of Black's[2] capabilities as a translator is given by the inclusion of his translation (slightly altered and revised according to the latest German edition) in Bohn's *Standard Library* (1846). His avowed endeavour was always to discover the true meaning of the author, and he was justified in saying that he had seldom mistaken it.

A very few inaccuracies are small blemishes in an otherwise careful piece of work. It keeps only rather too close to the German for ease in English. The following interesting passage—on Æschylus' *Prometheus*—is a good example of the general style.

" *The Chained Prometheus* is the representation of constancy under suffering, and that the never-ending suffering of a god. Exiled to a naked rock on the shore of the encircling ocean, his drama still embraces the world, the Olympus of the gods and the earth of mortals scarcely yet reposing in a secure state above the dark abyss of the Titanic Powers. The idea of a self-devoting divinity has been mysteriously inculcated in many religions, as a confused foreboding of the true ; here, however, it appears in a most alarming contrast with the consolations of revelation. For Prometheus does not suffer on an understanding with the power by whom the world is governed, but he atones for his dis-

---

[1] A *Course of Lectures on Dramatic Art and Literature*, by Augustus Wilhelm Schlegel, translated from the original German by John Black (London, 1815).

[2] *John Black* (1783–1855). Attended Edinburgh University ; made German translations for Sir David Brewster's Encyclopædia, and contributed articles on Italian and German literature to the *Universal Magazine*. In 1810 went to London and translated foreign correspondence of *Morning Chronicle*, of which he afterwards became editor (1817–1843). Translated some German works of travel and W. von Humboldt's *Political Essay on the New Spain* (1812). He was an early patron of Dickens.

obedience and that disobedience consists in nothing else but the attempt to give perfection to the human race. It is thus an image of human nature itself, endowed with a miserable foresight and bound down to a narrow existence, without an ally and with nothing to oppose to the combined and inexorable powers of nature but an unshaken will and the consciousness of elevated claims. The other poems of the Greek tragedians are single tragedies; but this may be called tragedy itself: its purest spirit is revealed with all the annihilating and overpowering influence of its first unmitigated austerity."

("*Der gefesselte Prometheus* ist die Darstellung standhaften Leidens, und zwar des unsterblichen Leidens eines Gottes," etc.—*Vorlesung*, VI.)

W. Taylor reviewed the *Lectures* in the *Monthly*[1] as "on the whole deserving to be considered as forming an epoch in the history of literature." He then goes through the Lectures one by one, bringing up special passages for praise or blame. The Lecture on the structure of the Greek drama he regards as specially noteworthy, but criticises Schlegel severely, with a good deal of justification, for his undervaluation of French comedy and of Diderot, and for a cursory and deficient view of the German theatre. It is characteristic of Taylor's own deficiency of judgment that he considers Kotzebue "unfairly depreciated." The *Edinburgh Review*[2] begins by some general remarks on German writers, some justifiable, others betraying a good deal of insular prejudice. But to all the faults mentioned the reviewer says the present work forms an absolute exception. "The author's views in general are ingenious and just; his speculative reasonings on principles of taste as satisfactory as profound. . . . His fault is that he sometimes carries love of theory and spirit of partizanship farther than is allowable." The critic praises especially Schlegel's remarks on Shakespeare. Those on German literature he considers much more questionable, and takes great exception to Schlegel's not recognising *Werther* as the greatest of Goethe's works,

[1] LXXXI. 113; 1816. [2] XXVI. 67; 1816.

to his praise of *Egmont* "which seems to us insipid and preposterous," and of *Nathan the Wise*, "unintelligible except to the wise," and to his preference of *Wallenstein* over *The Robbers*. These last remarks are interesting as showing views of German literature still current in England in 1816.

No other work of A. W. von Schlegel was translated in full into English. But the *Monthly*[1] in 1828 gave a long account of his *Vorlesungen über die Theorie und Geschichte der bildenden Künste* (1817) with translated extracts.[2]

FRIEDRICH SCHLEGEL (1772-1829).

In 1818 was published an anonymous translation of the *Vorlesungen über Geschichte der alten und neuen Litteratur*[3] by the younger of the Schlegels, Friedrich Wilhelm. The translator appears to have been J. G. Lockhart,[4] the biographer of Scott. Before going to Germany in 1816 or 1817 Lockhart had made the acquaintance of Blackwood, the publisher, who paid him £300 for a work in translation to be done later.

[1] VII. 182.

[2] Nathan Drake included several pieces from A. von Schlegel's criticism of Shakespeare (in Black's translation) in his *Memorials of Shakespeare, or Sketches of his Character and Genius by various writers*. 1828.

[3] *Lectures on the History of Literature, Ancient and Modern*, from the German of Frederic Schlegel (Edinburgh, Blackwood, 1818).

[4] *J. B. Lockhart* (1794–1854) was a good classical scholar and read French, Italian and Spanish. While at Balliol he began to read German too, and led by interest in the literature, he determined to visit Germany. The date of his tour is rather uncertain; and there are scarcely any records of it. The only mention of it by himself gives the date of his return as October, 1817. We know that while at Weimar he met Goethe (see *Peter's Letters*), whom he later defended against the sneers of the *Edinburgh Magazine*; also that he attended Fichte's lectures, as proved by sketches of Professor and students in an old note-book. In May, 1818, he met Scott, who was interested in his talk of Goethe at Weimar. These lectures are his only big piece of translation from German. (See A. Lang's *Life of Lockhart*.)

Lockhart selected F. Schlegel's *Lectures*, and the translation appeared in 1818, the year after his return from Germany.[1] A short translator's preface says that these Lectures—delivered in Vienna, 1812—are the first work of Frederick Schlegel's to be translated into English, though the name of his elder brother is now as much respected in France and England as in Germany. Schlegel's own preface is omitted, as also several passages throughout the work, most of them dealing with religious questions. Not only in omissions, but also in actual translation, Lockhart has treated his original pretty freely. But he always gives the substance of Schlegel's ideas correctly, and needless to say his style is good, his work reading like an original. Here is a longer specimen—a passage characteristic too for Schlegel:

"We often think of and represent to ourselves the Middle Ages as a blank in the history of the human mind. An empty space between the refinement of antiquity and the illumination of modern times. We are willing to believe that art and science had entirely perished, that their resurrection after a thousand years' sleep may appear something more wonderful and sublime. There as in many other of our customary opinions we are at once false, narrow-sighted and unjust; we give up substance for gaudiness and sacrifice truth for effect. The fact is that the substantial part of the knowledge and civilization of antiquity never was forgotten, and that for very many of the best and noblest productions of modern genius, we are entirely obliged to the inventive spirit of the Middle Age."

(" Man schildert und denkt sich das Mittelalter oft wie eine Lücke in der Geschichte des menschlichen Geistes," etc.—*Vorlesung*, VII.)

The work was noticed in all the leading periodicals. The *Monthly*[2] had reviewed it already in the original (1816), giving a synopsis and translated extracts from

[1] A. Lang does not record the actual publication of the work, but it seems indisputable that this translation (1818) is that by Lockhart. It corresponds to the description of the " earlier translation attributed to Lockhart " in the preface of the new translation in Bohn's Library. In view of all the other evidence the remark in the D.N.B. (XXXIV. 48) that Lockhart's work was not published till 1838 must be a mistake or a misprint.

[2] LXXI. 507; 1816.

Lectures IV., VI. and VII.; and calling it a "neat, welcome and agreeable compendium of general literature," but considering that the author does not show talents of as high an order as his brother. In 1819[1] in the same review the translation is highly praised as being "executed with honourable facility and satisfactory elegance." The *British Critic*,[2] after quoting Madame de Staël's critique of F. W. Schlegel, says: "It is a book we can heartily recommend to the scholar, as a guide to his researches in tracing out the connections of literature in various ages and nations. . . . There is no portion of the wide field of literature on which the author is not prepared to speak with understanding and effect." The *Westminster*,[3] in a general review of F. W. Schlegel's works, written some years later, says his translated *Lectures* may be expected to have some influence in England. But this reviewer is specially anxious to warn readers against the "latent poison" hidden in a work otherwise interesting and valuable. It is, he says, "jesuitical" in its political bearing, and aims at perpetuating the dominion of despotism and bigotry.

A review of the *Lectures* of much greater value and interest appeared in *Blackwood*,[4] showing the new attitude towards the more serious literature of Germany, largely due to the influence of *De l'Allemagne* and expressing itself primarily in *Blackwood*. The writer of this article boldly asserts at the start "that the last fifty years have produced in Germany more great and valuable literary works than the last hundred years among all the nations of Europe." The authors of Germany, he considers, are pretty free from the overweening self-complacency of French and English writers, for the reason that besides being writers of eminence they are also scholars of eminence; they read before they think of writing; their books may sometimes

[1] LIX. 148.
[2] XI. 533; 1819.
[3] III. 321; 1825.
[4] III. 497; 1818.

be too full of learning, nevertheless they well repay our study. He goes on to discuss the philosophy of Schlegel's *Lectures*—the particular subject of the article—praising it specially for combating the tendency of the age to revolution and for showing plainly that greatness of character can be preserved only by endeavouring to cherish and keep alive the spirit of our ancestors. Schlegel's religious belief, expressed always openly, but with a liberality in pleasing contrast with the bigotry of many French and Italian Catholics, he regards as specially interesting to English readers. After quoting at length from the chapters on Homer, the Crusades, the Reformation, etc., he concludes: "On the whole we consider this work as by far the most rational and profound view of the history of literature yet presented to Europe. Comparing it with ideas in England, wc must admit that another nation has got the start of us in point of reflection."

A second edition of Lockhart's translation was published (anonymously) in 1841. A new, more complete and more faithful one was made for Bohn's Library (1846).

J. J. VON GÖRRES (1776-1848).

Two years after Schlegel's *Lectures* Black translated *Germany and the Revolution*[1] from Görres, a work belonging more properly to political history than to literature, but remarkable as being the only one by which Görres appears to have been known in England, and also as a sign of the interest beginning to be taken about this time in things German.

A few remarks in Black's preface are worth quoting:

"Germany is a world within itself, to which the South of Europe and even this country are in a great measure strangers. The difficulties

[1] *Germany and the Revolution*, by Professor Görres, late editor of the *Rhenish Mercury*; translated from the original German by John Black (London, 1820). It was also printed in the *Pamphleteer*, Vol. XV.

which the acquisition of the language presents even to English people are such that the knowledge of it is yet rare, and from this ignorance of the language proceeds an ignorance of the state of the country and the feelings and opinions of the people."

Görres's work, Black considers, will afford just the needed information about Germany.

The *London Magazine*[1] reviewed the work with many extracts, and the *Monthly*[2] noticed it in conjunction with the *Memoir of Sand* (1819) "both being works which throw light on the pursuits and opinions of the patriotic party in Germany." A *Memoir of Andreas Hofer*, translated by C. H. Hall (1820), may be mentioned here.

One of Görres's Oriental studies—*Das Heldenbuch von Iran* (1820) was also noticed in the *Monthly*[3] with several passages translated.

W. Taylor in the *Historic Survey*[4] translates two stories from Görres's prose translation of old Persian Sagas, the *Shah-Named*, and compared Görres's with the rimed English version of Champion.

A. F. VON KOTZEBUE (1761-1819).

It was natural that the rage for Kotzebue's dramas should lead to translations not only of his much less noteworthy novels and tales (as already mentioned) but also of his autobiographical works. The public were interested not only in the dramatist but in the man. Some twenty years later the sensation caused by his murder led to the publication in England of further biographical recollections of Kotzebue. It is interesting to contrast the remarks made at the earlier and the later date.

In 1798 Kotzebue's autobiographical romance, **Die Geschichte meines Vaters, oder wie es zukam dass ich geboren wurde*, was translated anonymously and (judging by the extract given in the *Critical*)[5] very badly, as the

[1] I. 181; 1820. [2] LXI. 141. [3] LXIII. 449; 1820.
[4] III. 383 and 388. [5] XXIII. 233; 1798.

History of my Father.[1] The *Critical* had reviewed a French version of the same in a former number. The *Monthly*[2] compares it to Voltaire's *Candide.*

In 1800, just when the popularity of *Pizarro* was at its height, Miss A. Plumptre published a translation: Kotzebue's *Life and Literary Career,*[3] of which, she says, short abstracts have already been published in various ways and under various forms. The sketch of Kotzebue's life and works is taken from a collection of Miscellaneous Pieces—*Der Wildfang*, and from some anecdotes, etc., at the end from *Die jüngsten Kinder meiner Laune.* Miss Plumptre gives a list of the plays already translated or acted in England. This *Life* was very popular with all the admirers of Kotzebue.[4] W. Taylor took over large portions of it in his chapter on Kotzebue in the *Historic Survey*, calling it "*Miss* Plumptre's excellent translation"—rather higher praise than it deserves.

Two years later *Das merkwürdigste Jahr meines Lebens*, a continuation of Kotzebue's Autobiography, was translated by B. Beresford[5] and reached a second edition in 1806. Beresford made his translation from

[1] **The History of my Father, or how it happened that I was born.* A Romance in twelve chapters (Treppass).

[2] XXX. 94; 1799.

[3] *Sketch of the life and literary career of Augustus von Kotzebue with the Journal of his Tour to Paris till the close of the year* 1790, written by himself; translated from the German by Anne Plumptre. To which is subjoined an Appendix, including a general abstract of Kotzebue's works (London, Symonds, 1800).

[4] Reviewed in *Europ. Mag.*, XLI. 455; 1801. *Month. Rev.*, XXXIV. 78; 1801.

[5] *The most remarkable year in the Life of Augustus von Kotzebue, containing an account of his exile into Siberia and of other extraordinary events which happened to him in Russia,* written by himself; translated from the German by the Rev. Benjamin Beresford, English lecturer to the Queen of Prussia (London, 1802). B. Beresford (sometimes confused with a Rev. James Beresford, also a writer of verse, but who was never in Germany) also made translations from German lyric poets which were published in Berlin in 1801, and reprinted in London in 1821 as *Specimens of the German Lyric Poets.*

the original manuscript of the work, furnished him by the author himself. The *Annual Review*;[1] the *British Critic*[2] and the *Monthly*[3] gave a long account of it, describing it as entertaining and interesting, and likely to arouse the warmest interest in England. But his *Travels in Italy* (1804) the *Critical*[4] called "four volumes of dullness and impertinence, full of pompous trifles of a strutting sentimentalist."

From the days of the height of his popularity dates a volume of *Beauties of Kotzebue*,[5] collected by W. C. Oulton.[6] The frontispiece is a portrait of Kotzebue. The short biographical sketch at the beginning contains little criticism. Kotzebue is, of course, placed above all other German dramatists; but Oulton will not admit him to be on the same level with Shakespeare. The mere fact of it being necessary to prove Kotzebue's inferiority to Shakespeare shows the extraordinary position he held at that moment in England! A summary and short critique of about twenty plays follow and then extracts from them under various headings—*e.g.*, Ambition, Duelling, Love, Remorse, etc.[7]

[1] I. 74; 1802.
[2] XIX. 430.
[3] LXVIII. 75; 1805.
[4] VII. 83; 1806.

[5] *The Beauties of Kotzebue*, containing the most interesting scenes, sentiments, speeches, etc., in all his admired dramas, freely translated, connected and digested under appropriate heads, alphabetically arranged, with biographical Anecdotes of the Author; a summary of his dramatic fables and cursory remarks, by Wally Chamberlain Oulton (London, 1800).

[6] *W. C. Oulton* (1770–1820), a native of Dublin; educated there at a private school. As a schoolboy wrote farces and other dramatic essays, performed at the Fishamble Street Theatre. Went to London in 1786. Wrote many plays—i.e., *Hobson's Choice*, and a *History of the Theatres of London*; translated Gessner's *Death of Abel* in verse in 1811.

[7] There is another volume with the same title, *Beauties of Kotzebue*, by Alfred Howard, Esq., bound with *Beauties of Fenelon*, by the same author. There is no date on title-page. Brit. Mus. Catalogue gives 1834. It contains prose extracts from his travels, two short tales and selections from his plays. It is curious to find a book of this kind brought out so many years after the rage of enthusiasm for Kotzebue was over.

Miscellaneous Prose Translations

A revival of interest in Kotzebue soon followed the sensation caused by the news of his murder by Sand (1819), defender of the "Burschenschaft" movement. Notices of his death appeared in many of the leading periodicals, with sometimes a short account of his life and work; the criticisms were generally very different from those before 1800. The *Monthly*,[1] for instance, says that as a dramatist he is comparable to Goldoni in Italy or Cumberland in England, but certainly does not deserve first rank.

Already in August or September, 1819, Whittaker published a *Memoir of Charles Lewis Sand* translated from German with a narrative of Kotzebue's death, a defence of the German Universities against the attacks of Kotzebue and an introduction and notes by the Editor, a witness of the extraordinary sensation caused in Germany by Kotzebue's death. Here, too, we see the change twenty years had brought about in Kotzebue's reputation in England; his dramas are now judged "more artificial than natural, more melodramatic and picturesque than profound in knowledge of the human heart, or happy in concoction of incident or illustration of manners." This editor asks why English audiences are not made to relish the plays of Schiller, Goethe and Lessing instead of these "melodramatic follies."

In the following year (1820) Boosey published a short life of Kotzebue in seven chapters, taken from Kramer's recent *Lebensgeschichte Kotzebues*. The translation is fair, but an allusion to Goethe's *Geschwister* as the *Brothers and Sisters* shows that the translator did not know German literature at first hand.

Seven years later, Miss Plumptre's and B. Beresford's translation of Kotzebue's *Autobiography*[2] was reprinted

[1] XLVII. 325; May, 1819.

[2] *Sketch of the Life and Literary Career of Augustus von Kotzebue, with the Journal of his Exile to Siberia* (London, Hunt and Clark, 1827).

with some omissions and a new Introduction as Volumes IX. and X. of a series in *Autobiography*.[1] The introductory chapter again shows the newer critical attitude towards Kotzebue; admitting that his fame as a dramatist has greatly passed away, that his autobiographical works lack critical weight and solidity, and that he shows neither profound reflection nor deep insight into human nature; yet notwithstanding claiming a place in this collection for his extraordinary and unique experiences, and his shrewd and animated observations.

Taylor's chapter on Kotzebue in the *Historic Survey*, written just at this time, shows little of this new attitude. But Taylor's exaggerated admiration for Kotzebue is well known, and he represents an older generation. He had been the first in England to understand German literature, but he had not kept up with its later developments.[2]

TRAVEL.

Many German books of travel were translated from time to time,[3] but not strictly belonging to literature, they are not included here.

A few only are worth mentioning, as the work of writers important in other connections; as for instance F. von Stolberg's *Travels through Germany, Switzerland, Italy and Sicily*, translated by T. Holcroft in 1796, and then popular, as proved by many reviews with long extracts.[4] The *Monthly*, which had already given an

[1] *Autobiography, a collection of the most amusing lives ever published, written by the parties themselves.*

[2] *A Volume of Historical, Literary and Political Anecdotes and Miscellaneous Pieces*, from the German of Kotzebue (Lettermen, 1807), is not in the Brit. Mus. The *Brit. Crit.* (XXX. 454) says that some are interesting and entertaining, some trifling and a few contemptible, and that the translation indicates carelessness or ignorance and sometimes both.

[3] Miss Anne Plumptre was specially active in this line.

[4] *Brit. Crit.*, XIX. 360; XX. 148. *Anal. Rev.*, XXVI. 545. For Stolberg, see G. M. Baker, *Graf Friedrich Stolberg in England. Mod. Lang. Notes,* XXI. 232; 1906.

account by W. Taylor of the original,[1] reviewed the translation favourably in 1797. The readable translation is often incorrect in small points, and not always accurate in German titles and other details, but well brought out, with good index and maps.

We may also add a few books of travel in England by Germans translated afterwards into English; not very valuable or deep studies, yet not altogether without interest as showing how the England of that time appeared to a more or less superficial foreign observer. Again the comments of English critics on this picture of themselves are sometimes amusing. K. P. Moritz's *Reisen eines Deutschen in England im Jahre* 1782 was translated "by a Lady" in 1795 as *Travels through various parts of England.*[2] A book of travels in England—*England, Schottland, Irland und Wales: Erinnerungen an Natur und Kunst aus einer Reise im Jahre* 1802-3 (Dresden, 1804), by C. A. G. Goede, was twice translated in abridged form (1) as *The Stranger in England*, etc., (2) *Memorials of Nature and Art*, etc., by T. Horne (1808). Horne's translation was reprinted in 1821 with a different title: *A Foreigner's opinion of England.*[3] The *Monthly* thinks the work might be useful for travellers from the minute accuracy of detail, but that the author's views are superficial and his judgment often defective. The *British Critic* goes farther and says "it is full of offensive absurdities and total ignorance of English customs." With the value of Goede's views in general we are not concerned here. A few remarks of interest as to German literature in England in 1802 have been quoted in the introductory chapter.

[1] XVIII. 535.

[2] Reprinted in *Voyages and Travels*, II. (1808). Vide *Anal. Rev.*, XXII. 24; 1795.

[3] Only these two are in the Brit. Mus. For Horne's earlier translation see *Month. Rev.*, LVI. 29; 1808, and *Brit. Crit.*, XXXII. 86; 1808.

DEVOTIONAL LITERATURE.

German devotional or religious works were a good deal read in England. These again do not belong to literature proper, but a few may be mentioned. Some German sermons were translated, the most important collection being that of the sermons of the Swiss divine, Zollikofer, translated by the Rev. W. Tooke (1804-1812). Tooke followed these in 1814 by *Devotional Exercises and Prayers* from the same author.

A little collection of translated German Prayers and Hymns[1] was made by a Miss Knight,[2] a lady at Court, and dedicated to the Royal Princesses. It was privately printed in 1812, but not published till 1832. Most of the book is taken up with prayers translated from a Dr. Seiler. At the end there are five hymns taken from different authors, among them a couple from Gellert.

In 1830 another clergyman, E. J. Burrow,[3] published a somewhat similar volume to Tooke's (1814)—*Hours of Devotion for the Promotion of true Christianity and Family Worship*, taken from Zschokke's *Stunden der Andacht*—but at that time the German author was not known. Burrow says he was induced to undertake this translation by the popularity of a work entitled *Reflections on the works of God* from the German of C. C. Sturm. These are examples of some of the different kinds of German devotional literature which

[1] *Translations from the German in prose and verse* . . ., by Ellis, Cornelia Knight (Windsor, 1812).

[2] E. C. Knight (1757–1837) was educated at a school kept by a Swiss pastor, and thus early got to know some continental languages. She became companion to Queen Charlotte (1805), and afterwards to Princess Charlotte, daughter of George IV. After the latter's marriage in 1816 Miss Knight lived abroad, and died at Paris. Her didactic romance, *Flaminius* (1792), was translated into German. Her *Autobiography* (1861) is among the most valuable sources of information for the Court history of those days.

[3] E. J. Burrow (1785–1861), a divine, and miscellaneous writer, was a member of Magdalene College, Cambridge.

found favour in England. Of more serious German theological works little appears to have been known in England. J. C. Hare is said to have been the only Englishman who understood anything of German theology.

B

Collections of Miscellaneous Pieces from the German.

In 1795 the Rev. William Tooke[1] published two volumes entitled *Varieties of Literature from foreign literary journals and original MSS. now first published*, with the intention of "putting the public in possession of the state and progress of German literature on the Continent; . . . and at the same time furnishing them with an agreeable literary collection of a superior order." Among the translations made from German are several papers on scientific subjects from Dr. Bahrdt and Professor Tiedemann; some tales from Meissner; Schiller's *Spiel des Schicksals* as *Sport of Fortune* (without Schiller's name); and numerous dialogues from Wieland as the author's favourite among German writers[2] (these under Wieland).

In 1798 Tooke, encouraged by the favourable reception given to the *Varieties*, published a further volume, **Selections from Foreign Periodicals*; pieces on a great variety of subjects—travels, anecdotes, etc.—none of literary interest.[3]

[1] W. Tooke (1744–1820) is best known as the historian of Russia. In 1783 he translated a *History of Russia* from the German, and in 1800 published his own *History of Russia*. From 1774 to 1792 he was English chaplain at St. Petersburg, and while there made frequent visits to Germany and Poland. After 1792 he devoted himself to literature.

[2] *Cf.* his translation of *Peregrinus Proteus*, chap. iii.

[3] For two pieces see Rabener and Wieland.

The year after Tooke's *Varieties of Literature* appeared a somewhat similar work of Scotch origin, entitled *The German Miscellany*,[1] translated and edited by Alexander Thompson[2] of Perth. It contains a comedy of Kotzebue: *The Indians in England*, and several pieces from Meissner's sketches—*e.g.*, the *Nut-Shell*, a tale, *Bianca Capello*, a dramatic narrative, and the *German Theatre at Venice*.[3] Several of these were unfinished, the translator intending to publish more volumes of the same kind, which, however, never appeared. The translation is moderately good, compared to the common level of work at that time. None of the tales, etc., are of particular interest now, though they were then found "well-chosen and entertaining"[4] and "amusing and instructive."[5] A longer review in the *European Magazine*[6] contains some interesting remarks showing how, in the opinion of some people in England at any rate, and partly by the influence of public affairs, German literature was ousting French from public favour.

"The literature of Germany seems for some time to have taken the lead among the nations of Europe. The French were interrupted by the din of arms, and indeed have always exhibited too vain and volatile a character to make progress in the severer labours of the mind. . . . La Fontaine and Voltaire arouse momentary amusement, Klopstock and Gessner lasting delight and admiration. . . . Under these circumstances a judicious selection from works of German authors must be an acceptable present to the English reader. . . . This fruitful field is much cultivated at present."

---

[1] *The German Miscellany*, consisting of dramas, dialogues, tales and novels, translated from that language by A. Thompson (Perth, 1796).

[2] *Alexander Thompson* (1763–1803). He resided in Edinburgh. He was the author of several poems—i.e., *Whist* and *The Paradise of Taste*, and he left unfinished a *History of Scotch Poetry*. Besides this miscellany he also translated Kotzebue's comedy, *The East Indian*, and wrote *Six Sonnets from Werther*.

[3] An anecdote also given in *Varieties of Literature* in a much better translation. Tooke is altogether a translator much superior to Thompson.

[4] *Month. Rev.*, XXII. 359; 1797.

[5] *Crit. Rev.*, XX. 357; 1797.

[6] XXXIV. 386; 1798.

Most reviewers specially praised the *Nut-Shell* and *In what language should an author write?* (Meissner). *Bianca Capello*—of which only the introductory scenes are given—does not seem to have found so much favour. But it probably suggested the translation of the historical account of the heroine by P. Siebenkees.[1]

A much more interesting and larger German Miscellany appeared in monthly numbers from 1800-01. This was the *German Museum*,[2] whose aim was "to make English readers more intimately acquainted with thc literary labours of Germany, and to pourtray the national character and manners of that country." The three volumes contain a most miscellaneous collection of pieces: whole dramas, novels and tales, biographies of German authors, selections from all kinds of periodicals, catalogues of works published on the Continent, German songs with music and English translation—and so on. Among the contributors were B. Beresford (from whose *German Erato*, 1801, all the songs are taken) and Peter Will. The dramas translated are Babo's *Strehlitzes* and Leisewitz's *Julius von Tarent*, and some scenes from Möser's *Petitioners*. Among prose pieces are: extracts from Rabener's *Satires*; a fable of Lessing; tales from Wieland, Meissner, Lafontaine, Musæus and others; Schiller's *Criminal from lost honour* and some short Essays, and two extracts from Richter's *Hesperus*—interesting as probably the first appearance of Richter in English. In verse (besides the lyrics from the *German Erato*),

[1] *The Life of Bianca Capello, Wife of Francesco de Medici, Grandduke of Tuscany*, translated from the German original of P. Siebenkees by C. Ludger (London, 1797). See *Crit. Rev.*, XXIX. 359; 1800. Also *Month. Rev.*, XXIV. 371; 1797.

[2] *The German Museum, or Monthly Repository of the Literature of Germany the North and the Continent in General* (London, printed for C. Geisweiler and the Proprietors, 1800–1).

appear some of Gessner's idylls; E. von Kleist's idyll *Irin*; Bürger's *Wild Huntsman*, and Schubart's *Wandering Jew* (in prose)—interesting as the original version of the translation given by Shelley in the notes to *Queen Mab*. This gives some idea of the range of the volumes.[1] The more important pieces have all been touched on in their own place. Apparently the publishers intended continuing the monthly numbers indefinitely, but they ended after May, 1801. The venture probably fell a victim to the general reaction against the immense popularity of German literature, which culminated about 1801.

Some little collections from German appeared from time to time after this date, giving both German and English text; but these belong rather to a study of the German language in England than to one dealing with German literature. There is, by W. Render,[2] translator of *Werther* and some other works, one collection worth noting as about the earliest example of a text-book for students. It bears the double title *Recreations and Ergoezzungen*,[3] and is intended to be "an interesting selection from Natural, Moral, Political and Theological History, with the object of uniting the study of language with the acquisition of useful and instructive general knowledge." It contains all sorts of stories and anecdotes; and geographical and statistical and other information; German on one side,

[1] It is curious to note that the general favourite of the moment, Kotzebue, does not appear at all.

[2] *William Render*, native of Germany, came to England about 1790; settled in London; taught German and other languages in several rich families; and about 1800 he became "teacher of German" at Cambridge, Oxford and Edinburgh. He made a translation of *Werther* (1802); also several translations from Schiller and Kotzebue; publishing later several grammatical works.

[3] *Recreations, instructive and amusing: Ergoezzungen, lehrreich und angenehm*, in English and German, by Dr. Render, Professor of Languages, and author of various grammatical and philological works (London, Symonds, 1806).

English on the other, not always identical, even if meant to be so ! Gray's *Elegy* is given at the end with a fairly satisfactory literal German translation—not without one or two amusing mistakes; *e.g.*, " the simple annals of the poor " becomes " die simpeln Quaalen der Armen."

CHAPTER X

A Short Account of Some Early Translators and Critics of German Literature[1]

THOMAS HOLCROFT[2] (1745-1809).

Thomas Holcroft—one of the most prolific writers and translators of his day—was born in London in 1745. His father was a cobbler and itinerant merchant, and the boy was by turns pedlar, stable-boy, shoemaker, schoolmaster, prompter in a Dublin theatre (1770-1), actor in strolling companies (1771-8) and literary hack. He had no education except what he managed to pick up for himself. In spite of such adverse surroundings he managed to educate himself well and to learn German, French, and Italian. In 1778 he got a position at Drury Lane, and here his first comedy was performed.

In 1783 he visited Paris, where he became a friend of M. Bonneville, author of "Le Théâtre allemand," of whom he had a high opinion. But they quarrelled afterwards when M. Bonneville visited England. While in Paris in 1784 Holcroft wished to translate *Le Mariage de Figaro*. Being unable through government censorship to obtain a copy of the play, he and

[1] Two important names have been omitted from this chapter: S. T. Coleridge (1772–1834) and H. Crabb Robinson (1775–1867), there being nothing to add to what Mr. Stokoe has said, *German Influence*, etc.; S. T. C., chap viii.; H. C. R., pp. 53-60. For a long and interesting account of H. C. R.'s relations with Goethe, see J. M. Carré, *Goethe en Angleterre*, pp. 50-52, 87-100.

[2] *Vide* D.N.B., and *Memoirs of Thomas Holcroft*, written by himself (1810), and continued to time of his death from diary, notes and other papers by William Hazlitt (1816). Reprinted abridged in *Traveller's Library* (1852).

a friend visited the theatre nightly until they knew the text by heart. Holcroft then translated it from memory, and it was given at Covent Garden on December 4th, 1784, as *The Follies of the Day*, Holcroft himself taking the part of Figaro; but, it is said, he did it badly.

After this Holcroft brought out many original comedies (of which the most popular was *The Road to Ruin*), poems, novels, translations from French and German; and he contributed to many magazines.

In 1788 he translated the *Memoirs of Baron Trenck*, in 1789 Lavater's *Physiognomy*, in 1790 *The German Hotel*, and in 1796 Stolberg's *Travels*. In 1789 appeared also his translation from the French of the works of Frederick II., in twelve or thirteen volumes. Holcroft long projected, but never carried out, a work on the subject of war and despotism, of which Frederick the Great was to have been the hero.

During the French Revolution, convicted of high treason, he spent two years in Newgate. In 1799, in straits for money, he sold his books and pictures and went to Hamburg. While there he made an attempt to set up a literary journal—*The European Repository*—containing notices of foreign literatures and anecdotes of celebrated characters. But it only reached a second number. While at Hamburg Holcroft visited Klopstock, Voss, Sander and other German literary men. It was during this time abroad that he made his translation of *Hermann und Dorothea*. After a stay of a year or so at Hamburg, Holcroft went on to Paris, where he remained for two years. On his return he published *Travels in France* (1804).

In 1805-6 his *Theatrical Recorder* came out in monthly numbers. It contained several translations from French and German, mostly made by his daughter, Fanny Holcroft.

Holcroft died in 1809 after a long illness, at the age of sixty-three.

None of Holcroft's translations have real literary merit, *Hermann und Dorothea* being the poorest. But they show at least great perseverance and industry; and his prose translations of travels, etc., are written with ease and fluency and make pleasant enough reading. He wrote too much and too easily to do anything really good, either in original work or translation. His knowledge of German was pretty thorough, and, if not always very accurate, his translations do not contain many serious blunders. His *Memoir* gives no particulars as to how or when his knowledge of German was acquired.

WILLIAM TAYLOR OF NORWICH (1765-1836).

G. Herzfeld, at the beginning of his valuable essay on Taylor,[1] says: " Der Erste, der durch seine ganze Vorbildung, durch sein kritisches Urteil wie durch sein Formgefühl der eigentliche Herold und Bahnbrecher der deutschen Litteratur in England wurde, ist William Taylor von Norwich." And even Carlyle, who cannot be accused of too great a partiality for Taylor, admitted that "in respect of general talent and acquirement, he takes his place above all our expositors of German things." His name has occurred very frequently in the course of this study; and we propose to give here a short summary of his career, in as far as it is connected with Germany and things German. It may be useful to have such a summary in English, even though it contain no facts not already given in the above-mentioned essay of Herzfeld. To this readers are referred for a complete survey and criticism of Taylor's German activities.

[1] *William Taylor von Norwich.* Eine Studie über den Einfluss der neueren deutschen Litteratur in England; Von Georg Herzfeld (Halle, 1897). *Vide* also *Memoir of William Taylor of Norwich,* by J. W. Robberds, F.G.S. Two vols. (London, 1843). And for a good criticism of W. Taylor's work, Stokoe, *German Influence,* etc., pp. 38-43.

William Taylor was born at Norwich in 1765; his father, a well-to-do merchant, his mother belonging to an old Norwich family. The boy, an only child, received a very careful education, with special attention to the classics, foreign languages, and English style. At the age of fourteen he was sent by his father to travel in Holland, France and Italy, with a view to getting, for business purposes, a good knowledge of the languages of these countries. French and Italian letters written home during this journey show how quickly and correctly he learned.

In 1782 he was sent abroad again, this time to Germany, which was to have a much greater influence on his career. He spent several months at Detmold, studying German language and literature with Pastor Roederer, and was able after five months to read the *Messiah* in the original. He also mentions reading Lavater. Besides reading he also practised writing German, and always kept the habit, acquired during these early visits to the Continent, of thinking in whatever language he was using—a habit very useful to him when he came to interpret the thoughts of others.

In July, 1782, Taylor left Detmold, passing through Göttingen, Weimar, Leipzig and Königsberg on the way home. He visited at Weimar, Schloezer and Angelica Kaufmann. He does not appear to have visited Goethe, though he had an introduction to him.

After his return home Taylor applied himself, as was his father's wish, to business, but did not in the meantime neglect literature. He tells of reading with his friend Sayers Goethe's *Proserpina*, Voss's *Luise*, Klopstock's *Dramas* and Stolberg's *Odes*, many of which pieces he afterwards translated.

He also took an active part in the social and intellectual life of Norwich, where there was more intellectual activity at that time than in most other provincial towns of the same size. Specially among the Dissenters, to which Taylor's family belonged, there was a wide tolerance and open discussion of literary and political subjects. With the outbreak of the French Revolution Taylor became one of its enthusiastic adherents and wrote from Paris, which he visited in the spring of 1790, of "a nation of heroes obeying by choice a senate of sages." But he later became much disillusioned; as may be seen by his account of a second visit to Paris twelve years later (1802). In 1790 the "Revolution Society" in Norwich to which Taylor belonged was suppressed by the Government, and Taylor turned his attention again from politics to literature. In that year he made his famous translation of *Lenore*, not printed till 1796 in the *Monthly Magazine*. It is commonly regarded as the best of the many *Lenore* translations of that time,[1] and is interesting as having suggested to Scott his translation, the starting-point of his whole poetical career.[2] The correspondence between Taylor and Scott on the subject of this translation and that of *The Chase* is given by Robberds.[3]

About the same time Taylor was at work on his two most important pieces of translation—*Nathan der Weise* (1791) and *Iphigenie* (1793). These have been fully discussed elsewhere.[4] In 1795 followed his translations of Wieland's *Dialogues*,[5] both less successful and less noteworthy than the other two works. More interesting are his two *Dialogues*,[5] imitated from Wieland, in the *Monthly Magazine* (1796 and 1798). But one feels rather with Carlyle that "these paganising dialogues had never much worth, and now have scarcely any."

In these years began Taylor's very important activities

[1] *Vide* G. Herzfeld, *W. Taylor*, pp. 19-22. W. W. Greg, *English Translations of Lenore. Mod. Q. of Lang. and Lit.*, V., August, 1899; and Stokoe, *German Influence*, etc., p. 65 *ff.*

[2] A. R. Hohlfeld, *Scott als Übersetzer*; *Koch's Studien z. vergl. Litt.*, 1903.

[3] *Memoir of W. Taylor*, I. 96-100.

[4] For references *vide* Chaps. III. and VII.

[5] *Vide* Chap. III.

as a critic. In 1793 he contributed his first article to the *Monthly Review*, edited by Dr. Griffeths. For this and the *Monthly Magazine* (begun in 1796 by Dr. Aiken) Taylor wrote for about thirty years. He also contributed articles for a shorter time to the *Critical Review* and the *Annual Review*. The articles he contributed to these various periodicals covered a wide range of subjects, one of those most frequently treated being the contemporary literature of Germany.[1] From 1795-9 the foreign department of the appendix to the *Monthly Review* was principally confided to W. Taylor, and his longer articles in the same periodical formed the groundwork of the *Historic Survey*. To the *Monthly Magazine* he contributed many of the best of his shorter translations (afterwards reprinted in the *Survey*), *e.g.*, *Lenore*, the *Lass of Fair Wone*, or *The Parson's Daughter* (Bürger's ballad, *Des Pfarrer's Tochter von Taubenhain*), *Odes* of Klopstock, Stolberg and Ramler, Voss's *The Devil in Bann*, etc.

In 1798 Robert Southey came to Norwich; and after his departure a friendly correspondence began between him and W. Taylor, lasting over many years. German literature is not seldom the subject of these letters. We find, for instance, criticisms by Taylor of several of Schiller's later dramas, on their first appearance. In a letter of October 28th, 1805, he exclaims of *Wilhelm Tell*: "It is an admirable tragedy . . . worthy of the only competitor Shakespeare has yet had. . . . Oh, why is not Coleridge at home to translate it?" Another frequent subject of discussion was the use of hexameters in English; and it is known that Southey was led to use them in his *Vision of Judgment* through Taylor's influence.

In 1810 Taylor published anonymously his *Tales of Yore*, many of them borrowed from German models—

[1] Robberds gives a complete list of articles contributed each year.

a work of little interest, which few at the time connected with Taylor.

Between 1815-18 Taylor reviewed many German works of importance—*e.g.*, A. W. Schlegel's *Lectures on Dramatic Art*; F. W. Schlegel's *History of Literature*; *Faust*; Gellert's *Life*; Werner's *Martin Luther*, etc.; and later, in the *Monthly* (1823), Goethe's *Memoirs* (*i.e.*, *Dichtung und Wahrheit*), *Wilhelm Meister*, Wieland's *Graces*, and others.

In 1819, after his father's death, he planned another visit to Germany, but the plan fell through.

Among his activities as an exponent of German literature must not be forgotten the help and encouragement he was always ready to give to young men interested in the subject; among them Robert Harvey of Catton, near Norwich, translator of Kotzebue's *Falsche Schaam*, 1799; and Lessing's *Minna* (as *Love and Honour*); C. R. Coke, translator of Wieland's *Krates and Hipparchia*; and, most noteworthy, George Borrow, of whom Taylor writes in March, 1821: "A Norwich young man is construing Schiller's *Wilhelm Tell* with me with a view to translating it for the press.[1] His name is G. H. Borrow, and he has learned German with extraordinary rapidity; indeed, he has the gift of tongues, and though not eighteen understands twelve languages."

Between 1828-30 Taylor published the great work so long planned (it is first mentioned in a letter to Southey, June 1st, 1810)—the *Historic Survey of German Poetry*,[2] the first history of German literature in English, and, in Carlyle's words, "if no map of intellectual Germany, at least some first attempt at such." Its defects are apparent to any reader; composed, as it is, of detached papers and pieces of translation made at various times during thirty years, without

[1] This was never carried out.

[2] *Historic Survey of German Poetry interspersed with various Translations*, by William Taylor of Norwich (London, 1828–30).

combination of purpose or design, put together by Taylor at the end of his life when neither physical nor mental powers were fresh. Hence the inherent defect of want of unity and cohesion. It was also out of date even at its first publication. Not only was most of the book actually written many years before, but Taylor himself, who had never revisited Germany since he was a boy, had not kept pace with the later developments of German literature, and his views and standpoint were to a great extent those of a past generation. Carlyle—the representative of the new generation—wrote a damning critique[1] of the *Historic Survey* in the *Edinburgh Review* of 1821, condemning it as "a mere aggregate of dissertations, translations, notices and notes . . . bound together by the book-binder's pack-thread and no other tie whatsoever." That Carlyle's criticism had some justification cannot be denied; but, as is clearly shown by both Robberds and G. Herzfeld, his condemnation was much too sweeping, and often does not touch on the real defects of the work. In points of detail Carlyle often accuses Taylor quite unjustly, betraying a very careless reading of the text on his own part, while in general he made demands of Taylor which, under the circumstances, he could not have been expected to fulfil. The "Blütezeit" of German classical literature was scarcely over; and to draw from it "a picture of the national mind of Germany," would have been impossible then even in Germany itself, still more so in England.

Among the real defects in Taylor's work may be mentioned: the entirely inadequate treatment of German literature up to the eighteenth century; the admission of long disquisitions on subjects interesting to Taylor, but quite extraneous to the matter; the amount of quite unnecessary detail, and the admission of long pieces of translation out of proportion to the whole. The best part is that treating of the newer

[1] Reprinted *Miscellaneous Essays*, III. 283 *ff*.

literature, especially the chapters on the Swiss school, on Klopstock, Herder, and Wieland. Goethe is inadequately and unsatisfactorily delineated; while one-tenth of the whole work is devoted to Kotzebue, still to Taylor in 1828, one of the greatest German dramatists.

Of the translations which form such a large part of the work, those of Taylor's own are almost all good. Even Carlyle says of them: "Apart from the choice of subjects which, in probably more than half the cases is unhappy, there is much to be said in favour of these. Compared with the average of British translations they may be pronounced of almost ideal excellence; compared with the best translations extant—for example, the German Shakespeare, Homer, Calderon—they may still be called better than indifferent. One great merit Mr. Taylor has: rigorous adherence to his original; he endeavours at least to copy with all possible fidelity the turn of phrase, of tone, the very metre, whatever stands written for him. With the German language he has now had a long familiarity, and what is no less essential, and perhaps still rarer among our translators, has a decided understanding of English." This is high praise from the hostile Carlyle, and certainly deserved.

Of the translations not his own, included in the work, some are good—*e.g.*, an anonymous version of Schiller's *Ideale*. Others only mediocre—*e.g.*, some lyrics by B. Beresford, and Miss Plumptre's *Autobiography of Kotzebue*. Here Taylor does not show much discrimination, for in his view all are "excellent"; nor did he always trouble to remove errors before reprinting.[1]

The *Historic Survey* was at first not unfavourably received,[2] though it could not boast of extensive or

[1] *Vide* also Leslie Stephen, *Studies of a Biographer*, II. 69-74 (1898).

[2] *E.g.*, review in *Month. Rev.*, IX. 543; 1828 and XV. 609; 1830. "Mr. Taylor's labours have the great recommendation of supplying what has long been a desideratum in our literature . . . and supplying us with a guide to a subject of which attraction grows every day. . . . Both design and execution merit encouragement."

rapid sale. But it was much injured by the criticism of Carlyle, already a respected critic, and after 1831 was little spoken of. Goethe, influenced by Carlyle, expressed a very unfavourable opinion of it in a letter to Zelter, August 20th, 1821.

From 1833 Taylor's bodily strength and mental powers rapidly declined and his last years were a sad ending to an active life. He died on March 5th, 1836.

THOMAS DE QUINCEY[1] (1785-1859).

It was during De Quincey's wanderings in Wales in 1802 that he was first introduced to German literature through meeting with a German, named De Haren, a man who carried about with him a library of German authors and was only too glad to read and discuss them with such an intelligent companion. "From him it was that I obtained my first lesson in German and my first acquaintance with German literature. Paul Richter I then first heard of, together with Hippel, a humorist admired by Kant, and Hamann, also classed as a humorist, but a nondescript writer, singularly obscure, whom I have never seen in the hand of any Englishman, except once of Sir William Hamilton. With all these writers Mr. De Haren had the means of making me fully acquainted in the small portable library which filled one of his trunks."

Three years later (1805), in Oxford, De Quincey began the study of German in earnest and soon made himself proficient in it, probably getting help from a German, Schwarzberg, with whom he studied Hebrew. From the first he was most attracted by the prose writers and metaphysicians. With the poetry he seems to have occupied himself little. He wrote some

[1] *Vide* article by Leslie Stephen, D.N.B., XIV. 385. H. H. Japp ("H. A. Page"), *De Quincey's Life and Writings*, new ed., 1890, and W. Dunn, *T. De Quincey's Relation to German Literature and Philosophy*, Strassburg, 1901 (not in Brit. Mus.).

years later: "The German literature is at this time beyond all question, for science and philosophy properly so called, the wealthiest in the world. It is an absolute Potosi, . . . a mine of which the riches are scarcely known by rumour in this country." He read at first Herder, Kant, J. P. F. Richter, and later Lessing and Goethe.

In 1809 De Quincey got to know John Wilson, and in the winters of 1814-15 and 1815-16 accompanied him on visits to Edinburgh, becoming there a prominent figure in the literary society of which Lockhart, R. P. Gillies and Wilson himself were members. "They did not at first know well what to make of this man with the boyish figure and the gentle voice, who, with quiet unassuming deliverance, speedily asserted a kind of right to say the final word, and who soon became a referee in knotty points of philosophy or scholarship. . . . All felt that a new influence was at work in their midst and they enjoyed it. . . . This new-comer who could cap Hamilton's most recondite quotations from Plato or Plotinus, from Kant or Richter . . . was worthy of study and of deference, both of which were so loyally yielded to him that he ever afterwards felt a love for Edinburgh as for a second Alma Mater."[1] Speaking in after years of the recollections of this time De Quincey speaks with especial affection and esteem of R. P. Gillies, regretting the "shadows of calamity of his later years"; while Gillies in his *Memoirs* speaks with equal admiration of De Quincey, and alludes to him specially as his first competent leader and guide in German literature.

In 1819 De Quincey became editor of the *Westminster Gazette*. He also wrote for the *Quarterly* and *Blackwood*—to the latter contributing an article on Herder in 1823[2] and analects from Richter in 1824. He also sent German articles to Knight's *Quarterly*

[1] *Life*, p. 138. [2] VII. 373.

Magazine. From 1821 he wrote for the *London Magazine* under the signature of X. Y. Z. Here appeared first in 1821 and 1822 the *Confessions of an English Opium Eater.* He translated Kant's *Essay on National Character* and other essays, all rather philosophical than purely literary. In 1824 appeared his famous review of Carlyle's *Wilhelm Meister.*[1] Japp, contrasting the contradiction in what Carlyle himself says of the work in the letters written before its publication and in the preface, considers his treatment of De Quincey's review as eminently unjust.[2] In 1824 De Quincey sent an article to the *London Magazine*[3] on *Walladmor*, the novel by Willibald Alexis, first published in Germany as a genuine translation from Scott, to meet the demand of a new work by "The great Unknown." De Quincey afterwards translated it, or rather took the German as a groundwork and "darned" it to his own wish. The result is a clever parody and caricature of the excessive incident and mystery of *Guy Mannering.*

In 1826 (November) De Quincey sent to *Blackwood* an analysis with an excellent partial translation of Lessing's *Laokoön*—continued till January, 1827. In February appeared *The Last Days of Kant.* This series of German prose classics was not continued.

In the later years of his life De Quincey accomplished little in the way of actual translation from German, but he never ceased to interest himself in German philosophy and literature. We hear of him at seventy climbing a hill "like a squirrel," discoursing the while of German literature.

[1] *Vide* Chap. V. [2] *Life*, pp. 202-9.

[3] X. 353; 1824.

German Literature

MATTHEW GREGORY LEWIS[1] (1775-1818).

In the introduction of the "Schauerromane" and the dramas of the "terrific school" of Germany into England M. G. Lewis played a large part. He was always powerfully attracted by the marvellous and extravagant, and in this inferior branch of German literature he found what best suited his nature and tastes. With the exception, perhaps, of Mrs. Shelley in *Frankenstein*, no English writer adopted so successfully in prose and verse the wild and bizarre character of the "German school," and his writings enjoyed an enormous popularity at the time. They are now forgotten, but they are interesting as illustrating a passing phase of taste, and for their influence on Scott's early attempts. It was Lewis who procured the publication of Scott's *Götz* in 1792.

Lewis was born in London in 1775. His earliest talent was for music, but he soon showed also a marked taste for literature. His father and mother were separated when he was about fifteen, but he kept on good terms with both, and visited his mother in Paris in 1792. Thence he went on to Germany, attracted by the reputation of Schiller and Goethe, and desirous of learning the language, to which he applied himself with great diligence. He writes to his mother from Weimar, July 30th, 1792: "I am now knocking my brains against German as hard as ever I can. I take a lesson every morning; and as I apply myself very seriously, I am flattered with the promises that I shall soon speak very fluently in my throat and that I already distort my mouth with considerable facility. The

[1] *The Life and Correspondence of M. G. Lewis*, Mrs. Baron-Wilson (London, 1839). Stokoe, *German Influence*, etc., pp. 68-170. J. M. Carré, *Goethe en Angleterre*, pp. 32-36. Account of life and works in introduction to *The Monk*, Gibbings and Co., London, 1913. O. F. Emerson, *Monk Lewis and the Tales of Terror*, *Mod. Lang. Notes*, XXXVIII. 3.

place is at present rather dull, most people . . . being gone to different places. . . . The few people who are still here are, however, extremely polite, and I doubt not that when I know a little of the language I shall find the place extremely agreeable. Among other people to whom I have been introduced . . . is M. de Goethe, the celebrated author of *Werter*, so you must not be surprised if I should shoot myself one of these mornings." This introduction to Goethe was a source of great interest and pleasure to the boy of seventeen, and he always entertained afterwards a deep respect for the great man. In after years *Faust* particularly engaged his attention, and Lord Byron, in a letter, mentions hearing Lewis one evening translate part "of that eccentric work" with great ease. But Lewis does not appear to have committed any of the translation to writing.

Lewis led a pleasant life in Weimar, hearing a good deal of music, and taking part in Court festivities. He writes on September 17th, "The music which I hear nowhere except at Court is almost entirely instrumental, of Haydn and Pleyel, and which can be got better in England than here; the little vocal music I hear is entirely from the Italian operas. But the Comédie will begin in October, and then perhaps I shall hear some German airs. . . . My situation is very pleasant here. Nothing can be more polite than the people belonging to the Court. The two duchesses are extremely affable and condescending; and we have nothing but balls, suppers and concerts." In a letter of December 24th he gives some amusing details of Court manners: "I continue to be well contented with this town. There are some things, to be sure, which are not quite so well ordered as in England: for instance, the knives and forks are never changed even at the Duke's table, and the ladies hawk and spit about the room in a manner most disgusting. But, as the Duchesses are very affable and everybody extremely obliging, I put up with everything else, and upon the whole amuse myself tolerably well."

From Weimar he sent his mother a small collection of German songs, with words he had translated for her. Perhaps some of these appeared later in the *Tales of Wonder*, but the greater number were apparently never printed. He paid also a short visit to Berlin, but did not stay long enough to know it well.

Lewis returned to England in February, 1793, and went to Oxford. But during his years there he was much away, and spent more time abroad learning foreign languages than reading Greek.

While staying at Bothwell Castle in 1793 Lewis sent his mother part of a translation of a German tragedy, saying he was sure she would like it, the style of the whole being exactly adapted to her taste. This was *The Minister* (Schiller's *Kabale und Liebe*). But he made no use of the translation for several years. It was during this same visit to Bothwell Castle that he wrote the ballad *Bothwell's Bonny Jane* which opens his *Tales of Wonder*, published many years afterwards. Just at this time he was, as he puts it himself, " horribly bit by the genius of authorship." At twenty he published his first work, *The Monk*, an accumulation of extravagance and horrors, written in ten weeks, which immediately became immensely popular in England and was even known abroad. From it he got his name of " Monk " Lewis.

In 1796 he produced the musical drama, *The Castle Spectre*; in 1799 the comedy of *The East Indian* (written at sixteen); and in 1804 *The Bravo of Venice*, from which in the following year he framed the melodrama of *Rugantino*.[1]

Three years before he had published his *Tales of Wonder* a collection of ballads, some by Scott (*Lenore*, and *The Wild Huntsman's Chase*); others of his own,

[1] *Vide* Chap. VII., p. 186.

borrowed freely from all possible sources—German, Scotch, etc. One morning paper wrote:

> "The Monk has published 'Tales of Wonder';
> The public calls them 'Tales of Plunder.'"

They all have some characteristics in common—wildness and "diablerie." The work was on the whole neglected by the public.

About the same time he published *Romantic Tales*[1] and *Tales of Terror*—of which many are taken from Italian, French, Spanish, and German models. They were spoken of in 1839 as "still read, and highly deserving of popularity."

His *Feudal Tyrants*[2] (1804) is a free imitation of a German work. Among the "Miscellaneous Poems" given at the end of Lewis's *Memoirs* there are a few translations from German. Two are anonymous: *The Tailor's Wife* and *Papa's Nose*. The only one of any interest is Goethe's *Das Veilchen*, but the flower—for no apparent reason—has been changed to a primrose.

In 1812, on his father's death, Lewis came into a large property in Jamaica, and in 1815 went out there to enquire into the condition of the negroes, doing much to improve their lot, and leaving arrangements in his will to ensure that his successors would do as he had done. In 1817 he went for a tour in Italy, visiting his friends Byron and Shelley at Genoa. In 1818 he visited Jamaica again, and died at sea on his way home.

J. C. MELLISH (1768-1823).

J. C. Mellish was one of the small band of Englishmen who towards the end of the eighteenth century took an intelligent interest in German literature. In 1795 he went to Weimar in the Consular service, married, and settled there for many years. He stood

[1] *Vide* Chap. VIII., p. 247. [2] *Vide* Chap. VIII., p. 219.

in friendly relation to the scholars and writers of Jena and Weimar, especially to Schiller. When Schiller gave up his town house in 1801 it was taken by Mellish. There are numerous mentions of visits to and from Mellish in Schiller's correspondence. In a letter to Noehden, August 24th, 1799, he speaks of him as "ein sehr gebildeter, in alter und neuer Literatur vollkommen erfahrener Mann."

Mellish took a keen interest in the contemporary literature of Germany, and wished to translate it for the benefit of his countrymen. His translations of Goethe's Masque, *Palæophron und Neoterpe* and of *Hermann und Dorothea* (never printed), have been already mentioned.[1] In 1800 he translated Schiller's *Maria Stuart* from the MS.; and the English translation appeared in 1801, before the German original.[2] It had no success at the time, and Schiller is said to have been much disappointed at its not being presented on the English stage. But the merits of the translation were recognised later, and it was reprinted in a slightly revised form in Bohn's Standard Library (1843).

Mellish also projected and began a translation of *Wallenstein*. In a letter to Goethe, July 24th, 1799, Schiller speaks with great praise of some fragments of the *Piccolomini*, and says that Mellish had written to a publisher on the subject of translating the whole. But nothing came of the project.

Mellish left Weimar in 1813 and went to Hamburg as British Consul. R. P. Gillies met him there in May, 1821, and speaks of him as "one of the very few of his order who have ever given their attention assiduously to the language and literature of the country in which they were stationed."[3]

Mellish kept up his interest in German literature to the end of his life; also his relations with Weimar.

[1] *Vide* Chap. V.
[2] *Vide* Rea, *Schiller in England*, pp. 77-82.
[3] *Memoirs of a Literary Veteran*, II., chap. xii.

In 1816 he visited Goethe at Weimar with his son (Goethe's godson), and the poet presented the boy with a copy of *Hermann und Dorothea* with a dedication to "Meinem theuren Pathen, dem der Vater der beste Dolmetsch dieses Gedichtes seyn kann."[1]

After leaving Weimar Mellish does not seem to have undertaken any big piece of translation. But in 1821 he contributed several lyric pieces to *Specimens of the German Lyric Poetry*, a reprint of Beresford's *German Erato*, with some additional poems translated by Mellish. If Mellish's contributions are compared with Beresford's, they will be seen at once to be, if not perfect, usually superior to these in literary taste, and in simplicity and directness of expression. Mellish died in London in 1823.[2]

ROBERT PEARSE GILLIES[3] (1788-1858).

R. P. Gillies was born in Scotland, studied at the University of Edinburgh and settled there in 1815, devoting himself to literary pursuits. He tells in his *Memoirs* of the position of foreign languages in Edinburgh during these years, and of his own attempts to become acquainted with German. "The knowledge of French," he says, "was superficial, of Italian rare; of German we remained so profoundly ignorant that in 1806 I am very sure all the booksellers' shops in Edinburgh could hardly have supplied more than a dozen volumes." A certain change was effected by the efforts of Henry Mackenzie, "the patriarch of our northern literature," and of De Quincey, who wintered

[1] See K. Meyer's Paper on Mellish, April 28th, 1888 (*Transactions of the Manchester Goethe Society*).

[2] K. Meyer in the above-mentioned paper says he died at Hamburg, but Rea gives London, which is much more probable. Mellish is spoken of in 1821 as "late Consul at Hamburg," so he had then retired. Meyer is incorrect in speaking of the Masque from Goethe as never printed, since it was printed twice (see Chap. V.).

[3] *Vide* D.N.B., and *Memoirs of a Literary Veteran*, by R. P. Gillies. Three vols. (London, 1851).

in Edinburgh 1815-6 and frequently visited Gillies, who found in him "the first friend who could profess to have a command over the German language and who was able *ex cathedra* to corroborate my notions of the great stores contained therein." But still in 1817 Gillies could find scarcely one book or one competent teacher in foreign literature. "Moreover," he adds, "we were of opinion that the German stores were exhausted already by such prodigious efforts as those of Holcroft, M. G. Lewis, B. Thompson, and a few more. . . . And this was in the year 1817, when the German press overflowed with productions most forcible and original, of which a few stray leaves are all that have found their way into England up to the present hour."

Gillies, however, managed to discover one German work—Wieland's *Werke*, in twenty or thirty volumes, and as teachers "two ancient gentlemen in extreme poverty," one a Russian Jew, the other a Frenchman who had lived in Germany and whose knowledge of German may be judged from his remark to Gillies: "I have von German book. Le voilà! mais il faut avouer, dare are some sentences vich I do not understand." Another teacher was a "Baron" Rabenstein, who visited Edinburgh as a teacher of foreign languages, and Gillies gives an amusing description of the lessons he took with him, until he found him out as a rank impostor. After these first experiences Gillies found a better teacher in a Dr. W. Gardiner, a man of good education, who had been English pastor at Danzig. Gillies studied with him and made rapid progress, but his favourite method was not very sound; he aimed at getting as soon as possible into the heart of the book, trusting that knowledge of the language would in some mysterious way come afterwards.

Through a friend, Consul Mitchell, Gillies had placed at his disposal a collection of German works of recent date: "The discovery of Aladdin's lamp," he writes, "could not have been more elating." His first piece of translation was that of Müllner's *Schuld*,[1] by which he introduced the German "Schicksalsdrama" into England. He went on to Grillparzer's *Ahnfrau* and then to many other pieces, most of which appeared in the "Horæ Germanicæ"[2] (1819-28) in *Blackwood*, edited by Lockhart. Gillies threw himself with great ardour into these essays and translations, and felt that through them a new literary world had been opened to him. "They were to me like a bridge across the dark waters, hitherto thought impassable, leading a way into a stupendous cavern, with its glittering stalactites and its various treasures guarded by Teutonic genii, who would be propitiated by one who came before them humbly but courageously." Though only partial translations appeared in *Blackwood*, Gillies actually translated many plays entire, as well as some prose pieces. He speaks of having a large collection of these to be used when time served; but most of them were scattered and never appeared in print.

In 1821 Gillies went to Germany, spending ten days at Hamburg, where he met Mellish. He mentions being much interested in hearing anecdotes of Lavater, whose *Physiognomy*, together with Baron Trenck's *Memoirs*, had been among the favourite books of his boyhood. He went on to Berlin, where he was most interested in the theatre, and thence to Dresden, whose scenery and people pleased him better. He was much struck by the interest shown by Germans in the literary world of England and specially in Scott, and contrasted it with the stolid indifference in England

[1] *Vide* Chap. VII.

[2] Gillies's own statement (*Memoirs*, II. 263) that all the "Horæ Germanicæ" were by him, except *Faust* and Fouqué's *The Pilgrimage*, is not exact. A few others were by other writers. *Vide* Max Batt, *Gillies and Blackwood's Magazine*, *Mod. Lang. Notes*, XVIII. 65-69; 1903, where a summary is also given of Gillies's opinions as expressed in *Black. Mag.*

towards the literary world of Germany. He noted also the number and excellence of the translations from English.

He met Tieck in Dresden, and at Weissenfels visited Müllner, " the first author whose works I happened to translate and who afterwards became one of my kindest correspondents and friends."

Gillies next visited Weimar, which he found " in a sad state of decadence," but he was much interested in seeing Goethe, who discussed with him some of his English translators—Sir Brooke Botheby and Mellish.[1] After leaving Weimar Gillies visited Erfurt, Gotha and Fulda, and then settled for some time at Frankfurt, where he set to work seriously at German; though the only teacher he could find at first was " illiterate and obtuse." However, he got help from books and later from a Dr. Becker of Offenbach and made great progress. Gillies's reading knowledge of German was very thorough, as can be seen from his translations. Blunders are very rare.[2] But apparently he never became fluent in speaking German, and writing it always remained somewhat of a labour.

In Frankfurt Gillies saw Müllner's *Schuld* performed. He remarked an extraordinary contrast between the English and German theatres and the behaviour of the audience, the German audience being much more serious.

After his return to England in 1825 Gillies lost most of his money. On the suggestion of Scott[3] he took up the plan of editing a journal devoted to foreign literature, including good translations. In February,

[1] For relation between Gillies and Goethe, *vide* article by J. G. Robertson, *Gillies and Goethe*, *Mod. Lang. Rev.*, IV. 89; 1908 and J. M. Carré, *Goethe en Angleterre*, pp. 55-56.

[2] Vide *Gillies and the Foreign Quarterly Review*, by Max Batt, *Mod. Lang. Notes*, XVII. 166-70; 1902. Batt accuses Gillies unjustly of a mistranslation in *Götz* (*Black. Mag.*, XV. 369). Here Gillies is quoting Scott's translation and the mistake is his.

[3] *Vide* Letter of Scott to Gillies, June, 1816.

1827, he left Edinburgh for London and founded the *Foreign Quarterly Review*, of which, however, he did not become the editor as originally intended. Cochrane was the first editor, but Gillies contributed a large number of articles—*e.g.*, on the Modern German Drama, Tieck's *Dramaturgische Blätter*, Heine's *Reisebilder*, Grabbe's *Poetische Werke*, H. von Kleist's *Werke* (1828), etc. Thus to Gillies belongs the honour of introducing to England writers whom Carlyle scarcely knew, and who were not known at all in France at this time. But as Batt says: "Gillies, as can be readily seen, is not always trustworthy in his literary judgments. While he shows good discriminative powers in recognising earlier than any other in England the genius of Heine and Grabbe, he errs woefully in asserting the superiority of Klingemann's or Müllner's dramas over Kleist's." He names also in the one breath such dramatists as Grillparzer with others absolutely worthless.

In 1826 Gillies published his well-translated German stories, with an interesting preface.[1]

Most of Gillies's best work in connection with German literature was done in these earlier years of his life. His later years were much broken by money troubles, and he spent months in prison for debt. From 1840 to 1847 he lived at Boulogne and while there translated Kant's *Kritik*.

In 1851 he published his *Memoirs of a Literary Veteran*. He was a friend of Wordsworth, Scott, Carlyle,[2] and other famous men of letters, which gives to these *Memoirs* a great part of their interest. Many passages also, especially in the first two volumes, are of special interest for our subject as showing Gillies's continual occupation with the literature of

[1] *Vide* Chap. VIII.

[2] In a letter to A. Carlyle, March 2nd, 1824, Carlyle speaks of Gillies—whom he had visited during the translation of *Meister*—as "a great German scholar," and having a fine library of books.

Germany,[1] and recording his opinion thereof, and giving vivid accounts of his meetings with literary men in Germany.

Gillies died in London in 1858.

[1] *E.g.*, vol. i., chap. xiv., Conversations on Revolution of Literary Taste in Europe. Gillies ascribes this revolution in great part to the "Kraftmänner" of Germany.

APPENDICES

APPENDIX A[1]

LIST OF WORKS TRANSLATED FROM THE MOST IMPORTANT GERMAN AUTHORS

Chamisso

Peter Schlemihl. [As Fouqué's.] 1824.

De La Motte Fouqué

Undine.

(1) *Undine, a Romance.* By G. Soane. 1818.
(2) *Undine, a Romance.* 1830.

Sintram. Sintram. [By J. C. Hare.] 1820.

Sängerliebe. Minstrel Love. By G. Soane. 1821.

Der Zauberring. The Magic Ring. 1825.

The Field of Terror. (1) By Gillies in *Black. Mag.*, VIII. 131; 1821.

The Field of Terror. (2) By T. Roscoe. *German Novelists*, III., 1826.

The Mandrake. By T. Roscoe. *German Novelists*, III., 1826.

Aslauga's Knight. By T. Carlyle. *German Romance*, 1827.

Gellert

Das Leben der schwedischen Gräfin von Guildenstern.

(1) *The History of the Swedish Countess of G.* 1752.
(2) *The Life of the Swedish Countess of G.* By the Rev. Mr. N. 1776.
(3) *The Life of the Countess of G.* By a Lady. 1776.

Die Zärtlichen Schwestern. The Tender Sisters. In T. Holcroft's *Theatrical Recorder*, 1805.

The Life and Moral Lessons of Professor Gellert. By Mrs. Douglas. Kelso, 1805 (from the French).

[1] Translator's name put in brackets if work was originally published anonymously. Translator unknown if no name given. Place of publication in each case "London" if not otherwise mentioned. Complete titles are given in the foot-notes.

German Literature

Gessner

Der Tod Abels.

(1) *The Death of Abel.* [By Mrs. Collyer.] 1761. (Prose.)

(2) *The Death of Abel.* A new translation[1] (1764–5). (Prose.)

(3) *The Death of Abel.* By the Rev. Thomas Newcomb.[2] Dublin, 1763. (Blank verse.)

(4) *The Death of Abel.* [By Rose Lawrence (*née* d'Aguilar).] In Gessner's *Works*, I., Liverpool, 1802. (Prose.)

(5) *The Death of Abel.* By F. Shoberl in Gessner's *Works*, 1805. (Prose.)

(6) *The Death of Abel.* By W. C. Oulton. 1811. (Blank verse.)

The Morning Hymn from the *Death of Abel* (Bk. II.). Translated in heroic couplets was circulated as a fly-leaf, *c.* 1770.

Specimen of *Death of Abel* (Bk. I.), in verse by W. Holloway, in *Europ. Mag.*, XXXVII. 228; 1800.

Imitations of Abel.

The Death of Cain after the manner of the *Death of Abel.* By a Lady. 1789. [Generally attributed to Mrs. Collyer. Revised and reprinted Oxford, 1814, with author's real name—W. H. Hall.]

The Creation, after the manner and as an introductory companion to the *Death of Abel.* By W. H. Hall. 1801.

Death, a Vision. By J. McGowan. 1776. (Printed with *Abel* and *Cain*, 1814.)

{*The Lamentations of Cain over Abel.*
{*The Death of Cain, intended as a companion to the Death of Abel.* Corrected and abridged by G. Stephens. Printed with *Abel* and Klopstock's *Adam*, Portsea, 1810.

Cain, the Wanderer. 1829.

The Wanderings of Cain. By Coleridge. 1798. (Planned and attempted in concert with Wordsworth, 1798. Only one canto written by Coleridge. First printed, 1828.)

Imitation of *Morning Hymn* in *Gent.'s Mag.*, XL. 39; 1770.

[1] This translation bears no name or date, and is not mentioned by Miss Reed. Brit. Mus. Cat. suggests 1780 as probable date. But Preface speaks of *Death of Abel* as having already gone through six editions, and seventh ed. of Mrs. Collyer's translation appeared in 1765. So date of this is more probably 1765.

[2] Miss Reed (p. 13) is wrong in giving date of this translation as 1761. She did not see a copy of the work. The only one I found is in Trinity College, Dublin. T. Newcomb (1675–1766) was nearly ninety when he made this translation. It is a remarkable production for a man of his years, but in itself it is only mediocre. Newcomb was author of several original poems. (See *Dict. of Biog. and Myth.*)

Appendix A

Idylls.

Rural Poems from Gessner. 1762.

Select idylls from Mr. Gessner's Pastorals. [By Anne Penny.] 1762.

New idylls by Gessner, with Letter on Landscape Painting. By W. Hooper, M.D. 1776. (Reprinted with some corrections, 1798.)

Select idylls or Pastoral Poems. By G. Baker. 1809.

Specimens of Idylls. By W. Taylor. *Hist. Surv.*, I. 208.

Several poems in Herbert's *Miscellaneous Poetry.* 1804.

Two idylls by " S," *Month. Mag.*, XXV. 329 ; 1808.

Selections from the Tales and idylls of Gessner. Translated into verse. Kerby. 1817.

Works.

Works of S. Gessner. [By Rose Lawrence (*née* d'Aguilar).] Liverpool, 1802.

Works of S. Gessner. By F. Schoberl. 1805.

Daphnis. Translated interlinearly, German and English. 1811.

Goethe

Dramas.

Götz.

(1) *Goetz von Berlichingen with the Iron Hand.* By W. Scott. 1799.

(2) *Goetz of Berlingen with the Iron Hand.* By Rose Lawrence (*née* d'Aguilar). Liverpool, 1799.

Clavigo. **Clavigo*, 1798. (Extracts in *Hist. Surv.*, III. 305.)

Stella.

(1) *Stella*, 1798.

(2) *Stella.* By B. Thompson. *Ger. Theatre*, VI. ; 1806.

Egmont. Act III., Sc. 1. By W. Taylor. *Hist. Surv.*, III. 3.

Die Geschwister. The Sister. [? By H. Mackenzie.] In *Dramatic Pieces from the German*, Edinburgh, 1792.

Iphigenie. Iphigenia. [By W. Taylor.] 1793.

Tasso. Tasso. By C. des Vœux. 1827.

Faust.[1] *Faust, a Drama. . . .* By Lord Leveson Gower. London, 1823.

Prose Works. Werther.

(1) *The Sorrows of Werter.* A German Story. Anon. 1779. [? D. Malthus.[2]] (Translated from the French *Les Passions du jeune Werther*, by Aubry.)

(2) *Werter and Charlotte.* A German Story. Anon. London, 1786. (From the German.)

[1] For partial translations before 1830 see Appendix to Hauhert, *The Reception of Goethe's Faust in England* (1909), and Carré, *Bibliographie . . . de Goethe en Angleterre*, pp. 78-96.

[2] A. E. Turner, *Mod. Lang. Rev.*, XVI. 164 ; 1921 suggests that the translation is by Richard Graves, tutor of D. Malthus. A *Sorrows of Werter*, Dublin, 1785, given by Carré as a new translation, is really a reprint of the above.

Prose Works (continued):

(3) *The Sorrows of Werter.* A German Story. Translated from the genuine French edition of Aubry by J. Gifford. London, 1789.

(4) *The Letters of Werter.* Anon. Ludlow, 1799.

(5) *The Sorrows of Werter.* Translated from the German of Baron Goethe by William Render, D.D. 1801.

(6) *The Sorrows of Werter.* Translated from the German of Baron Goethe by F. Gotzberg, assisted by an English gentleman. London, 1802.

(7). *The Sorrows of Werter.* A new translation by Dr. Pratt. ?1807. Second ed., 1809.

Wertheriana.

(1) E. Taylor. *Werter to Charlotte : a Poem.* 1784.

(2) *Eleanora*, from the *Sorrows of Werter.* A Tale. 1785.

(3) *The Letters of Charlotte during her connexion with Werter.* 1786. (Translated into German, French and Dutch.)

(4) F. Reynolds. *Werter : a tragedy.* London, 1802. (Performed at Bath, 1785; Covent Garden, 1786.)

(5) A. Francis. *Charlotte to Werter.* 1787.

(6) A. Pickering. *The Sorrows of Werter : a Poem.* 1788.

(7) J. Armstrong. *Confidential Letters on the Sorrows of Werter.* By Albert. London, 1790.

(8) Mrs. Farrell. *Charlotte : or a sequel to the Sorrows of Werter and other Poems.* Bath, 1792.

(9) *Werter and Charlotte : a pathetic story.* London. Sabine. (No year. B. M. Cat. gives 1800.)

(10) *Werter to Charlotte : a Poem.* London, 1812.

Dichtung und Wahrheit. Memoirs of Goëthe [sic]. 1823. (From the French.)

Wilhelm Meisters Lehrjahre. Extracts in *Month. Rev.*, XXVII. 543; 1798.

William Meister's Apprenticeship. By T. Carlyle. Edinburgh, 1824. (To end of chap. ix.).

Wilhelm Meisters Wanderjahre. Wilhelm Meister's Travels, or the Renunciants. By T. Carlyle in *German Romance*, IV., 1827. (Not complete.)

Wahlverwandschaften. Extracts in *Month. Rev.*, 1812.

Observations on the Laokoon. Month. Mag., VII., 1799.

Observations on L. da Vinci's Last Supper. By G. Noehden. 1821.

Poems.

Hermann und Dorothea.

(1) *Hermann and Dorothea* (blank verse). By T. Holcroft. 1801.

(2) *Hermann and Dorothea* (prose). 1805.

Palærophron and Neuterpe. A Masque. By J. C. Mellish. Weimar, 1801; and *Month. Mag.*, XI., 1801.

Grillparzer

Die Ahnfrau. Extracts by Gillies in *Black. Mag.*, VI. 247; 1819. Extract from Act III. by Sarah Austin, *Black. Mag.*, XVIII. 286; 1825.

Sappho. Sappho. By Bramsen. 1820. Extracts by Gillies in *Black. Mag.*, XIX. 404; 1826.

Das goldne Vliess. Extracts in *Lit. Gaz.*, May, 1821. Analysis and partial translation by Gillies in *Black. Mag.*, XXVII. 155-76; 1828.

König Ottokar. Analysis and partial translation by Gillies in *Black. Mag.*, XXII. 300-16; 1827.

Ein treuer Diener seines Herrn. Act I., Sc. i., by Gillies, *For. Quar. Rev.*, VI. 520; 1830.

Haller

Prose.

Usong. An Eastern Narrative. 1772.

Letters from Baron Haller to his daughter on the Truths of the Christian Religion. 1780.

Verse.

Die Alpen.

(1) *The Alps* (prose). By Mrs. Howorth in Poems of Haller, 1794.

(2) *The Alps. A Moral and Descriptive Poem of the great Baron Haller.* By Henry Barrett. 1796. (Extracts in *Crit. Rev.*, XVIII. 350; 1796.)

Poems of Baron Haller. By Mrs. Howorth. 1794. (Prose and verse.)

Doris.

(1) In above.

(2) By W. Taylor, *Month. Mag.*, XLIII. 46; 1817. And *Hist. Surv.*, I. 193.

German Literature

Herder

Prose.

A Tribute to the Memory of Ulric von Hutten. By A. Aufrere. 1789. (As by Goethe.)

Ideen zu einer Philosophie der Geschichte der Menschheit. Outlines of the Philosophy of the History of Man. By T. Churchhill. 1800.

Vom Geist der Ebraischen Poesie. Oriental Dialogues. 1801. (Abridged.)

Über den Ursprung der Sprache. Treatise upon the origin of language. 1824.

A Fragment on Shakespeare. By W. Taylor. *Month. Mag.*, LI. 409; 1821.

Verse.

The Cid. 1828.

Selections from *Volkslieder. Stimmen der Völker, Zerstreute Blätter, Blätter der Vorzeit*, etc. By W. Taylor. *Hist. Surv.*, III. 9 *ff*.

Klopstock

Messias. The Messiah. Bks. I.-X. (prose). [By J. Collyer.] 1763–71.

Part of Bk. VII. (prose), by A. B., *Gent.'s Mag.*, XXXIII. 570; 1763.

Extracts (prose) made from an Italian translation. *New Rev.*, VI. 321; 1784.

Part of Bks. II. and IV. (blank verse). *Anal. Rev.*, XIII. ii.; 1792.

Part of Bks. III. and XIV. (prose), by Sir Herbert Croft in *Letter from Germany*, 1797.

Part of Bks. II. and III. (heroic couplets), by J. M. Good, *Month. Mag.*, X. 1; 1800.

Extracts (hexameters). By W. Taylor. *Month. Mag.*, 1800–1, and *Hist. Surv.*, I. 270-8.

Elegant extracts from Messiah (prose). By G. H. Egestorff. Brighton, 1810.

The Messiah (Bks. I.-XIX., prose). By Collyer and Mrs. Meeke. 1811.

The Messiah (prose). By T. Raffles. 1814.

"The Death of Mary," from Bk. XII. By S. Candler. *Month. Mag.*, XXXIX. 389; 1815.

Part of Bk. II. (hexameters). By F. W. Cronhelm. (1820 ?).

Bk. I. (hexameters). By Δ. *Lond. Christ. Instructor*, 1821.

The Messiah (blank verse). By G. H. Egestorff. Hamburg, 1821–2.

Gethsemane (abridgment of *Messiah*). By Mrs. Montolieu. 1823.

The Messiah (blank verse). [By Miss F. A. Head.] 1826.

Appendix A

Dramas.

The Death of Adam. [By Robert Lloyd.] 1763.
Solomon. By Robert Huish. 1809.
Two choruses from the *Battle of Hermann.* By W. Taylor. *Hist. Surv.*, I. 295.

Odes.[1]

To Wingolf. *For. Rev.*, III.[2] 1829.
To Ebert. By Miss Smith. *Memoirs.* 1808.
To Ebert. By N. R. *Black. Mag.*, III. 416; 1818.
To Fanny. By Miss Smith. *Memoirs.* 1808.
Ode to God. By G. H. Egestorff, with *Messiah.* 1810.
Ode to God. *For. Rev.*, III. 1829 (verse x. to end).
To Bodmer. By Miss Smith. *Memoirs.* 1808.
The Lake of Zürich. By W. Taylor. *Month. Mag.*, VII., 1799, and *Hist. Surv.*, I. 246.
The Lake of Zürich. *For. Rev.*, III., 1829.
The Recantation (*Der Verwandelte*). By Miss Smith. *Memoirs.* 1808.
Ode to Young. By W. Taylor. *Hist. Surv.*, I. 250.
The Two Muses (prose). By W. Taylor. *Month. Mag.*, XLIX. 404; 1820, and *Hist. Surv.*, I. 246.
To Cidli, sleeping (*Ihr Schlummer*). Miss Smith. *Memoirs.* 1808.
To Mr. Schmidt. Miss Smith. *Memoirs*, 1808.
The Band of Roses. By Miss Smith. *Memoirs*, 1808.
The Band of Roses. By G. H. Egestorff, with *Messiah.* 1810.
Ode on his Recovery. By W. Taylor. *Month. Mag.*, VII. 1799, and *Hist. Surv.*, I. 252.
The Festival of Spring (prose). By W. Taylor. *Hist. Surv.*, I. 254.
The Solemnization of Spring. *For. Rev.*, III., 1829.
The Omnipresent. *For. Rev.*, III., 1829.
The Sea Course (*der Eislauf*). *For. Rev.*, III., 1829.
My Fatherland. *For. Rev.*, III., 1829.
Sacred Music (*die Chöre*). By W. Taylor. *Month. Mag.*, II. 249; 1796, and as *The Choirs*, *Hist. Surv.*, I. 257.
Lamentation (prose). By W. Taylor. *Hist. Surv.*, I. 260.
The New (prose). By W. Taylor. *Hist. Surv.*, I. 261.

Poems.

The Lesson. By A. B. *Black. Mag.*, I. 405; 1817.
Song: Lyda. By B. Beresford, *Ger. Poets.* 1801.

1 In verse where not otherwise stated.
2 These Odes in *For. Rev.* are between pp. 340-377.

Biography.

Memoirs of Friedrich and Meta Klopstock. [By Miss Elizabeth Smith.] 1808.

Klopstock and his Friends: Letters. By Miss Benger. 1814.

Some Letters of Klopstock. By W. Taylor in *Hist. Surv.*, I. 237 *ff*.

C. T. Körner

Dramas.

Rosamunde.

(1) Analysis and extracts by Gillies in *Black. Mag.*, VIII. 47; 1820.

(2) *Rosamond.* 1830.

Zriny.

(1) Analysis and extracts by Gillies in *Black. Mag.*, VIII. 543; 1820.

(2) *Zriny.* By G. F. Richardson in *Life and Selections from Korner*, 1827.

(3) Last scene by W. Taylor in *Hist. Surv.*, III. 430.

Joseph Heyderich. By G. F. Richardson. 1827.

Fiction.

Hans Heilings Felsen.

(1) *Hans Heilings Rocks.* *Black. Mag.*, VIII. 625; 1820.

(2) *Hans Heilings Rocks.* *Lond. Mag.*, III. 342; 1821.

(3) *Hans Heilings Rocks.* By G. F. Richardson. 1827.

Woldemar. The Harp.

(1) In R. Holcraft's *German Tales*, 1826.

(2) By G. F. Richardson. 1827.

[*Poems translated in:*

Lord Leveson Gower's *Poems and Translations.* 1824.

G. F. Richardson's *Life and Selections.* 1827.

R. Robinson's *Specimens of German Lyric Poets.* 1828.

Month. Mag., XLV. 537; 1818. *Black. Mag.*, III. 417; 1818. *Black. Mag.*, XII. 585; 1822.]

Kotzebue

Plays.

Adelheid Von Wülfingen.

Adelhaide of Wülfingen. By B. Thompson. 1798.

Adelhaide of Wülfingen. In *German Theatre*, II., 1801.

Armuth und Edelsinn.

(1) *Poverty and Nobleness of Mind.* By M. Geisweiler. 1799.

(2) *Sighs: or the Daughter.* Adapted from the above to the stage by P. Hoare. 1799.

Die Beichte.

The Confession. A Comedy in one Act. Anon. Philadelphia, 1820. (Possibly a reprint of an earlier translation of which I could find no trace.)

Die Beiden Klingsberg.

Father and Son. In *The New British Theatre*, III., 1814, etc.

Plays (continued):

Blind Geladen.

How to die for love. A farce in two acts and in prose adapted from the German. 1812.

How to die for love, in Cumberland's *British Theatre*, XL. 1829, etc.

Die Corsen.

The Corsicans. Anon. 1799.

Die edle Lüge.

The Noble Lie . . . being a continuation of the play *Misanthropy and Repentance, or the Stranger.* By M. Geisweiler. 1799.

Eduard in Schottland (frei übersetzt aus dem französischen von Dukal).

The Wanderer, or the Rights of Hospitality. Altered for the stage by C. Kemble. 1808.

Falsche Scham.

(1) *False Shame.* A comedy in four acts. Anon. 1799.

(2) *False Delicacy.* A drama in five acts. By B. Thompson. 1800.

False Delicacy. In *German Theatre*, III. 1801.

Graf Benjowsky.

(1) *Count Benyowysky, or the Conspiracy of Kamstschatka.* By W. Render. 1798.

(2) *Count Benyowsky.* By B. Thompson. In *German Theatre*, II., 1801.

(3) Adapted to the stage as *Kamstschatka, or the Slave's Tribute* at Covent Garden, 1811. (Never printed.)

Der Graf von Burgund.

(1) *The Count of Burgundy.* By A. Plumptre. 1798.

(2) *The Count of Burgundy.* By C. Smith. New York. 1800.

Die Hussiten vor Naumberg im Jahre 1432.

The Patriot Father. Adapted by F. Shoberl. 1830.

Die Indianer in England.

The Indians in England. By A. Thompson in *German Miscellany*, 1796.

The Indians in England, with new title *The East Indian*, 1799.

Johanna von Montfaucon.

Joanna of Montfaucon. Adapted from an anon. translation to the English stage by R. Cumberland. 1800.

Das Kind der Liebe.

(1) *Lovers' Vows, or the Child of Love.* Translated with biography of the author by S. Porter. 1798.

(2) *Lovers' Vows.* Adapted from an anon. translation by Mrs. Inchbald for Covent Garden. 1798.

(3) *The Natural Son . . . being the original of Lovers' Vows.* By Mrs. Plumptre. 1798.

Plays (continued):

Das Kind der Liebe (continued):

(4) *Lovers' Vows, or the Natural Son.* By B. Thompson in *German Theatre*, II., 1801.

(5) *Lovers' Vows.* Altered from (2) and (4) by J. Payne. Baltimore, 1809.

(6) *Lovers' Vows.* By W. Dunlap. New York, 1814.

Die Kreuzfahrer.

The Red Cross Knights. Adapted freely from Kotzebue by J. C. Holman. 1801.[1]

Also *Alfred and Emma: founded on the Red Cross Knights of Kotzebue.* Anon. 1806.

La Peyrouse.

(1) *La Perouse.* By B. Thompson. 1799.

(2) *La Peyrouse.* By A. Plumptre. 1799. Adapted to the English stage as *Perouse, or the Desolate Island* for Covent Garden by J. Fawcett. 1801.

(3) *La Peyrouse.* By C. Smith. New York, 1801.

Menschenhass und Reue.

The Stranger. Adapted by Sheridan from an anonymous translation. 1798.

Die Negersklaven.

The Negro Slaves. Anon. 1796.

Der Opfertod.

Self-Immolation, or the Sacrifice of Love. By H. Neumann. 1799. Adapted to the stage as *Family Distress.*

Das Schreibepult.

The Writing-Desk, or Youth in Danger. Anon. 1799. Adapted to the stage by Mrs. Inchbald as *The Wise Men of the East.* 1799.

Die silberne Hochzeit.

The Happy Family. By B. Thompson. 1799.

The Happy Family, in *German Theatre*, III., 1801.

Die Sonnen-Jungfrau.

(1) *The Virgin of the Sun.* By A. Plumptre. 1799. Adapted to the stage by Reynolds. 1812.

(2) *Rolla, or the Virgin of the Sun.* By B. Thompson. 1799.

(3) *The Virgin of the Sun*, with notes marking variations from the original. [By J. Lawrence.] New York, 1800.

Die Spanier in Peru, oder Rolla's Tod.

(1) *Pizarro* . . . taken from the German drama of Kotzebue and adapted (from a translation in MS. by M. Geisweiler) to the English stage, by R. B. Sheridan. 1799.[2]

[1] For account of the play at the Haymarket see Genest, VII. 454.

[2] Sheridan's adaptation was translated into German by C. Geisweiler, and appeared in Germany as *Pizarro, nach dem Drama des Herrn von Kotzebue für die englische Schaubühne verfasst von R. B. Sheridan.*

Plays (continued):

Die Spanier in Peru, oder Rolla's Tod (continued):

(2) *Pizarro in Peru, or the Death of Rolla.* By T. Dutton. 1799.

(3) *Pizarro, or the Death of Rolla.* By B. Thompson. *German Theatre*, I., 1801.

(4) *Rolla, or the Peruvian hero.* By M. G. Lewis. 1799.

(5) *The Spaniards in Peru, or the death of Rolla.* By A. Plumptre. 1799.

(6) *Pizarro in Peru, or the Death of Rolla.* By W. Dunlap. New York, 1800. (See Morgan, *Bibl. of Ger. Lit. in Eng. Trans.*, p. 306.)

Two imitations:

(1) *Pizarro. . . .* By a North Briton, 1799.

(2) *Pizarro, or the Peruvian Mother.* By Dr. Ainslie. 1817.

Der Taubstumme oder der Abbé de l'épée (übersetzt ans dem französischen.)

Deaf and Dumb, or the Orphan. By B. Thompson. 1801.

Deaf and Dumb, or the Orphan, in *German Theatre.*

Üble Laune.

The Peevish Man. By C. Ludger. 1799.

Die Verläumder.

The force of Calumny. By A. Plumptre. 1799.

Die Versöhnung.

(1) *The Reconciliation.* By C. Ludger. 1799.

Altered and adapted to the stage as *The Birthday* by T. Dibden, 1799. Printed 1800.

(2) *Fraternal Discord* . . . altered from Kotzebue by W. Dunlap. New York, 1809.

Der weibliche Jacobiner-Clubb.

The Female Jacobin-Club: A political Comedy. By J. C. Siber. Liverpool, 1801.

Der Wildfang.

(1) *The Wild Goose Chase.* By W. Dunlap. New York, 1800.

(2) *Of age to-morrow.* Adapted to the stage by T. Dibdin. 1800. Printed 1806.

(3) *The wild youth.* By C. Smith. New York. 1800. (See Morgan, *Bibl. of Ger. Lit. in Eng. Trans.*, p. 310.)

Die Witwe und das Reitpferd.

The Widow and the Riding Horse. By A. Plumptre. 1799.

Adapted to the stage as *The Horse and the Widow*, by T. Dibdin. 1799.

Fiction.

Ildegerte, Queen of Norway. By B. Thompson. 1798.

The Sufferings of the family of Ortenberg (*Die Geprüfte Liebe*). By Peter Will. 1799.

Fiction (continued):

The Escape. 1799.
The Constant Lover. 1799.
**The Pastor's Daughter and other Romances* (four vols.). 1806.
Novelettes from Kotzebue. 1807.
**Historical, literary and political anecdotes from Kotzebue.* 1807.

Biographical.

**The History of my Father*, 1798.
Life and literary career of Kotzebue. By A. Plumptre. 1800.
The most remarkable year in the life of Kotzebue. By B. Beresford. 1802. Reprinted in "Autobiography." 1827.
Travels in Italy. 1806.
Life of Kotzebue (from Kramer's *Lebensgeschichte*). 1820.
Beauties of Kotzebue. By W. C. Oulton. 1804.

Lavater

Physiognomik.

(1) *Essays on Physiognomy.* By Thomas Hunter. 1789–98. (From the French.)
(2) *Essays on Physiognomy.* By T. Holcroft. 1789.
  (*a*) *Physiognomy. . . .* By Samuel Shaw. 1792. (A bad abridgment of No. 2.)
  (*b*) *Essays on Physiognomy.* (Abridged from Holcroft's translation, 1792.)
(3) *Essays on Physiognomy.* By Rev. C. Moore. 1797. (From the French.)
  Lavater's Looking-Glass, 1800 (partly a compilation of Lavater's work).

Aphorisms on Man. By Fuseli. 1788.
Secret Journal of a Self-Observer. By Rev. P. Will. 1795.
On the Nature, Excellence and Necessity of Faith. By Rev. P. Will. 1805.
Letters of St. Paul the Apostle. 1805.

Lessing

Fabeln.

(1) *Fables.* By John Richardson. York, Etherington. 1773.
(2) *Fables and Epigrams.* London, Hunt. 1825.
(3) *Fables; in three books.* German and English. London, 1829.

Emilia Galotti.[1]

(1) By Benjamin Thompson. In *German Theatre*, VI., 1801.
(2) By Fanny Holcroft. *Theatrical Recorder*, I., 1805.

[1] Extracts (Act II., Sc. 7-12; IV., 5-7; V., 6-8) were translated in the *New Review*, IX., pp. 38-49 and 122-124, 1786. Readers were recommended to the French translation in Gunker and Liebault's *Théâtre Allemand*, 1785.

Appendix A

Minna von Barnhelm.

(1) *The disbanded officer: or the baroness of Bruchsal.* (As performed at the Theatre Royal in the Haymarket.) Altered from *Minna* by James Johnstone. London, 1786.

(2) *The school for honor, or the chance of War.* London, Vernor and Hood. 1799.

(3) By Fanny Holcroft. *Theatrical Recorder*, II., 1805.

Nathan der Weise.

(1) *Nathan the Wise. A philosophic drama.* By R. E. Raspe. London, 1781.

(2) *Nathan the Wise. A dramatic poem.* By W. Taylor of Norwich. Printed at Norwich, 1791. London, 1805.

Miss Sara Sampson.

(1) *Lucy Sampson, or the Unhappy Heyress,*[1] translated by a citizen of Philadelphia. Philadelphia, 1789.

(2) *The Fatal Elopement.* [By Eleanore H——], in the *Lady's Magazine, or Entertaining Companion for the Fair Sex.* 1799–1800.

Die Erziehung des Menschengeschlechts. The Education of the Human Race, by H. Crabb Robinson in the *Monthly Repository of Theology and General Literature*, I., 1806. (Including *Eine Parabel*, which was also translated as *Palace on Fire* in the *German Museum*, I., 1801.)

Faust: Fragment—included in Lord Leveson Gower's translation of Goethe's *Faust*, 1823.

A Critical Essay on Oil Painting. By R. E. Raspe. 1791.

Hamburgische Dramaturgie. A dissertation on the dramatic art. A notice with some translated extracts appeared in the *Literary Magazine* and *British Review*, II. 340; 1789.

A. Müllner

Die Schuld.

(1) *Guilt, or the Anniversary.* By R. P. Gillies. Edinburgh, 1819.

(2) *Guilt, or the Gipsy's Prophecy.* By W. E. Frye. 1819.

Der neunundzwanzigste Februar. The twenty-ninth of February. By Gillies in *Black. Mag.*, XCII. 331; 1820.

König Jugurd. Partial translation by Gillies, *Black. Mag.*, VII. 408 and 545; 1820.

Die Albaneserin.

Extracts by Gillies. *Black. Mag.*, XII. 218; 1822.

Extracts by Sarah Austin. *Black. Mag.*, XVIII. 291; 1825.

1 See Baker, *An Early Translation of Miss Sara Sampson*, *Mod. Lang. Notes*, XXII., 103. There is no copy in Brit. Mus. Todt, who had seen no copy, quotes from *Memoirs of D. Rittenhouse*, Philadelphia, 1813, p. 495. Morgan, *Bibl. of Ger. Lit. in Eng.*, p. 330, who had also seen no copy, gives date as 1797, quoting from Wilkens. *Early Influence of German Literature in America*, in *Amer. Ger.*, III. 2; 1899.

German Literature

J. P. F. Richter

Extracts from *Hesperus* in *German Museum*, II., 1801.

Extracts trans. by H. C. Robinson in *Amatonda*, 1811.

Specimens from *Flegeljahre*. [By De Quincey.] *Lond. Mag.*, IV. 606 ; 1821.

Analects from Richter. [By De Quincey.] *Lond. Mag.*, IX. 117 and 242 ; 1824.

The Dream of the Universe. [By De Quincey.] *Lond. Mag.*, IX. 117 and 242 ; 1824.

The Death of an Angel. From *Quintus Fixlein* in R. Holcraft's *German Tales*, 1826.

The Moon. From *Quintus Fixlein* in R. Holcraft's *German Tales*, 1826.

The Life of Quintus Fixlein. By T. Carlyle in *German Romance*, III., 1827.

Schmetzle's Journey to Flaetz. By T. Carlyle in *German Romance*, III., 1827.

Schiller

Dramas.

Die Räuber.

(1) *The Robbers*. By A. F. Tytler (Lord Woodhouselee). London, 1792.

(2) *The Robbers, a tragedy in five acts*. Translated and altered from the German as it was performed at the Brandenburgh House Theatre, 1797. London, 1799. (Largely based on Tytler's translation.)

(3) *The Robbers*. By W. Render. London, 1799.

(4) *The Robbers*. By B. Thompson in *German Theatre*, IV., 1800–1.

Adaptations :

The Red Cross Knights. By J. G. Holman. 1801. (Given at the Haymarket.)

The Gauntlet. By the Margravine von Anspach. (Given at Brandenburgh House.)

Bertram. By Rev. C. Maturin. 1816.

Lorenzo, the Outcast Son. By E. Gandy. 1823.

Die Verschwörung des Fiesco.

(1) *Fiesco*. By G. H. Noehden and J. Stodart. 1796.

(2) **Fiesco*. By Dr. Reinbeck. (Reviewed in *Blackwood*, XVI. 194 ; 1824.)

Adaptation :

Ravenna or Italian Love, 1823.

Dramas (continued):

Kabale und Liebe.[1]

(1) *Cabal and Love, a Tragedy.* Anon. 1795.

(2) *The Minister.* By M. G. Lewis. 1797.

Adapted for the stage and given at Covent Garden as *The Harper's Daughter.* 1803.

Don Carlos.

*(1) *Don Carlos.* Anon. 1795. (See *Biographia Dramatica,* II. 170 and *Monthly Rev.*, II. 311; 1795.)

(2) *Don Carlos.* By G. F. Noehden and J. Stodart. 1798.

(3) *Don Carlos.* Anon. [Symonds?] 1798.

(4) *Don Carlos.* By B. Thompson in *German Theatre.* 1801.

Adaptation:

Persecution, or Don Carlos. Anon. [Russell.] 1822.[2]

Wallenstein.

(1) *Piccolomini* and *Death of Wallenstein.* By S. T. Coleridge. 1798–99.

(2) *The Piccolomini* and *The Death of Wallenstein.* Anon. [George Moir.] Edinburgh, 1827.

(3) *The Camp.* By Lord Leveson Gower. 1830.

Maria Stuart.

Mary Stuart. By J. C. Mellish. 1801.

Mary Stuart. By Rev. H. Salvin. 1824.

Das Mädchen von Orleans.

The Maid of Orleans. By Rev. H. Salvin. 1824.

Wilhelm Tell.

William Tell. Anon. [Samuel Robinson.] 1825.

William Tell. Anon. 1829.

William Tell. By R. Talbot. 1829.

Historical Works.

Die Geschichte des Dreissigjährigen Krieges.

(1) *The History of the Thirty Years' War in Germany.* By Capt. Blaquiere. 1799.

(2) *The History of the Thirty Years' War in Germany.* By J. M. Duncan. 1828.

(3) *The Thirty Years' War; The trial and execution of Counts Egmont and Horn; Siege of Antwerp* in *Historical Works of Schiller.* By George Moir. Edinburgh, 1828.

Abfall der Niederlande.

History of the Rise and Progress of the Belgian Republic. By Thomas Horne. 1807. (Not complete.)

Essay of the effects of a well-regulated theatre and *The Legislation of Lycurgus,* in *German Museum,* 1801.

[1] A few scenes were translated by Ash in *The Speculator* of 1790.

[2] See G. Herzfeld: *Archiv. f. d. Stud. d. n. Spr.*, CXXII., 1909. Carlyle gives a long review of *Don Carlos*, and translation of Act I., Sc. 10 in his *Life of Schiller*, 1825.

German Literature

Fiction.

Der Geisterseher.

(1) *The Ghost-seer.* [By D. Boileau.] 1795.

(2) *The Armenian, or the Ghost-Seer.* By W. Render. 1800.

(3) *The apparitionist. A Fragment.* By T. Roscoe. *German Novelists*, III., 1826.

Der Verbrecher aus Verlorener Ehre.

(1) *The Criminal from lost honour.* By "F." *Ger. Mus.*, II. 344; 1801.

(2) *The Criminal become so from lost* [*sic*] *of honour.* By Lewis Wapler. Augsburgh. 1825.

(3) *The Criminal, or Martyr to lost honour.* By T. Roscoe. *Ger. Nov.*, III., 1826.

(4) *The Dishonoured Irreclaimable.* By R. Holcraft. *German Tales*, 1826.

Das Spiel des Schicksals.

(1) *The Sport of Destiny.* By W. Tooke in *Varieties of Literature*, II., 1798.

(2) *The Sport of Destiny*, in *Black. Mag.*, VIII., 1820.

(3) *The Sport of Destiny.* By T. Roscoe. *Ger. Nov.*, III., 1826.

Eine grossmütige Handlung aus der neuesten Geschichte as *Fraternal Magnanimity.* By T. Roscoe. *Ger. Nov.*, III., 1827.

Der Spaziergang unter den Linden as *Walk among the Linden Trees.* By T. Roscoe. *Ger. Nov.*, III., 1827.

A. W. Schlegel

Course of Lectures on Dramatic Art and Literature. By John Black. 1815.

Vorlesungen über die Theorie und Geschichte der bildenden Künste. Extracts in *Month. Rev.*, VII. 182; 1828.

F. W. Schlegel

Lectures on the History of Literature. [By J. B. Lockhart.] Edinburgh, 1818.

F. von Stolberg

Travels through Germany, Switzerland and Sicily. By T. Holcroft. 1796.

Poems.

Two *Odes.* By J. Six in *Gent.'s Mag.*, 1784.

Theseus. By W. Taylor. *Month. Mag.*, VII. 396; 1799. (Abridged.)

Several odes and ballads by W. Taylor in *Hist. Surv.*, II. 89*ff.*

[*Poems* (continued):

Hymne an die Erde.

(1) By Coleridge (1799).

(2) By Rev. J. Whitehouse. Bedford, 1800.

(3) (Part). Anon. *Lond. Mag.*, X. 512; 1824.

Lyrics in *Specimens of German lyric poets*, 1821; and J. Macray's *Stray Leaves*, 1827.

Odes trans. in *For. Rev.*, V. 124-53; 1830.

Translations and adaptations by Coleridge. [See *Poetical Works of S. T. C.* Oxford, 1912.]

Tieck

The Pictures. By Bishop Connop Thirlwall. 1825.

The Betrothing. By Bishop Connop Thirlwall. 1825.

Faithful Ekhart (1). By T. Roscoe in *German Novelists*, IV., 1826.

Aubern Egbert (1). By T. Roscoe in *German Novelists*, IV., 1826.

Faithful Ekhart (2). By T. Carlyle in *German Romance*, II., 1827.

The Fair Egbert (2). By T. Carlyle in *German Romance*, II., 1827.

The Runenberg. By T. Carlyle in *German Romance*, II., 1827.

The Elves. By T. Carlyle in *German Romance*, II., 1827.

The Goblet. By T. Carlyle in *German Romance*, II., 1827.

Ein Dichterleben—The Life of Poets. Leipzig, 1830.

Wieland

Der geprüfte Abraham. **The Trial of Abraham.* 1764.

Dialogen des Diogenes von Sinope. Socrates out of his senses or *Dialogues of Diogenes of Sinope.* By Winterſted. 1771.

Agathon. Agathon. [By John Richardson.] 1773.

Don Silvio von Rosalva. Reason triumphant over fancy. [By John Richardson.] 1773.

Die Sympathieen. The Sympathy of Souls. By Winzer (?1787). (From the French.)

Peregrinus Proteus.

(1) *Private History of Peregrinus Proteus the Philosopher.* [By W. Tooke.] 1796.

(2) *Confessions in Elysium.* (Abridged.) By J. B. Elrington. 1804.

Die Grazien. The Graces. By Sarah Austin. 1823.

Krates und Hipparchia. Crates and Hipparchia. By C. R. Coke. 1823.

Abderiten.

(1) Review with translated Extracts by "Germanicus." *Lit. Gaz.*, 1821, p. 21 *ff.*

(2) Extracts. *Black Mag.*, XVII. 673; 1825.

Araspes and Panthea : Socrates and Timoclea. Two Dialogues. [By John Richardson.] 1775.

Göttergespräche.

Nos. IX., X., XI., XIII. By W. Taylor. 1795.

Nos. V., VI., VIII., IX. and *Gespräche in Elysium.* [By W. Tooke.] *Varieties of Literature*, 1795.

Nos. I., III., V., VI., VIII. By W. Taylor. *Hist. Surv.*, II. 432 *ff.* 1828.

Charlotte Corday : eine Unterredung. By W. Taylor. *Month. Mag.*, XLVII. 308., 1819.

Some short pieces (from *Werke*, XXX.) in Tooke's *Varieties of Literature*, 1795. And **Selections from foreign periodicals*, 1798. (I. 330).

Two fragments from Wieland in W. Taylor's *Tales of Yore.* 1810.

Poetical Works.

Geron der Adelige. Geron the Courteous. By W. Taylor. *Month. Mag.*, LVII. and LIX., 1822 ; *Hist. Surv.*, II. 325.

Das Wintermärchen. The Winter's Tale. By W. Taylor. *Hist. Surv.*, II. 354.

Oberon.

(1) Bk. IX., 52-57 (ed. in 14 Bks.). By James Six. *Deutsches Museum*, II. 232 ; 1784.

(2) *Oberon.* By William Sotheby. 1798.

(3) Bk. I. 12-26. *Annual Rev.*, V. 499 ; 1806. *Hist. Surv.*, II. 408.

Rosamund. Concluding scene by W. Taylor. *Hist. Surv.*, II. 480.

Zimmermann

Über den Nationalstolz.

(1) *An Essay on National Pride.* 1771.

(2) *An Essay on National Pride.* By S. H. Wilcocke. 1797. (With memoir of the author.)

The influence of the knowledge of Jesus Christ. By Moses Browne. 1772.

Conversations with the King of Prussia. 1791.

Select views of the Life of Frederic the Great. 1792.

Über die Einsamkeit.

(1) *Solitude considered with respect to its influence on the mind and heart.* Dilly. 1791. (From the French of Mercier.)

(2) *Solitude, or the effects of occasional retirement on the mind*, etc. "Associated Booksellers," 1797.

(3) *Solitude, considered with respect to its dangerous influence on the mind and heart.* Dilly. 1798. (Sequel to No. 1.)

(4) *Solitude, or the Pernicious influence of a Total Seclusion from Society upon the Mind and Heart.* "Associated Booksellers," 1799. (Reprint of No. 2 and a second Vol.)

Appendix A

Reflections on Men and Things. 1799. (From the French of Zimmermann.)

Aphorisms and Reflections. 1800. (From the German of Zimmermann.)

Beauties of Zimmermann. By A. Campbell. 1804.

**Gleanings from Zimmermann.* By Mrs. Bayfield. 1809.

Dr. Zimmermann's Conversations with the late King of Prussia when he attended him in his last illness. Translated from the German. London, 1791.

Collections of Romances, Plays, etc., from the German

Popular Tales of the Germans. 1791.

Varieties of Literature. Tooke. 1795.

The German Miscellany. A. Thompson. 1796.

The German Museum. 1800–1801.

The German Theatre. B. Thompson. 1801–2.

The Juvenile Dramatist. 1801.

The Theatrical Recorder. T. Holcroft. 1805–6. (Including plays from the German.)

Tales of Terror. M. G. Lewis. 1800. (Adaptations from German.)

Romantic Tales. M. G. Lewis. 1808. (Adaptations from German.)

Tales of Yore. W. Taylor. 1810. (Translation from German.)

Popular Tales of the Northern Nations. 1823.

German Popular Stories. [Grimm.] 1823–4.

Tales from the German. R. Holcraft. 1826.

The German Novelists. T. Roscoe. 1826.

Specimens of German Romance. G. Soane. 1826.

German Stories. R. P. Gillies. 1826.

German Romance. T. Carlyle. 1827.

APPENDIX B

Chronological List of Translations

1752. Gellert : *Swedish Countess.*
1757. Rabener : *Satirical Letters.*
1761. Gessner : *Death of Abel.* By Mrs. Collyer.
1762. *Select Poems from Mr. Gessner's Pastorals.* By A. Penny.
Rural Poems from Mr. Gessner's Pastorals. By A. Penny.
1763. Gessner : *Death of Abel.* By T. Newcomb.
Klopstock : *Messiah.* By Mr. and Mrs. Collyer.
Klopstock : *Death of Adam.* By R. Lloyd.
1764. Gessner : *Death of Abel.* A new translation (?1764–5).
Schönaich : *Arminius.*
Wieland : *Trial of Abraham.*
1766. Möser : *Harlequin, or a Defence of the Grotesque.* By J. A. Warnecke.
1767. Bodmer : *Noah.* By J. Collyer.
1771. Klopstock : *Messiah.* By Collyer. Vol. III.
Wieland : *Dialogues of Diogenes of Sinope.* By Winterstted.
Zimmermann : *Essay on National Pride.*
1772. Haller : *Usong.*
1773. Lessing : *Fables.* By J. Richardson.
Wieland : *Reason triumphant over fancy.* By J. Richardson.
Wieland : *Agathon.* By J. Richardson.
1775. *Two Dialogues from Wieland.* By J. Richardson.
1776. Gessner : *New Idylls and Essay on Landscape Painting.* By W. Hooper.
Gellert : *Swedish Countess.* By a Lady.
Gellert : *Swedish Countess.* By Rev. Mr. N.
S. de la Roche : *Lady Sophie Sternheim.* By J. Collyer.
S. de la Roche : *Lady Sophie Sternheim.* By E. Harwood.
1779. Goethe : *Werther.* (From French.)
1780. Haller : *Letters to his Daughter on the Christian Religion.*
1781. Zachariae : *Tabby in Elysium.* By R. E. Raspe.
1786. Goethe : *Werter and Charlotte.*
1787. Wieland : *Sympathy of Souls.* By Winzer.
1788. Lavater : *Aphorisms on Man.*

Appendix B

1788. *Life of Baron Trenck.* By T. Holcroft.
Memoirs of Baron Trenck. By an Artillery Officer.
Life of Baron Trenck. Anon.

1789. Goethe : *Werther.* By J. Gifford.
Lavater : *Physiognomy.* By T. Hunter. (From French.) 1789–98.
Lavater : *Physiognomy.* By T. Holcroft.
M. Mendelssohn : *Phædon.* By C. Cullen.

1790. Brandes : *German Hotel.* By T. Holcroft.
B. Naubert : *Alf von Deulmen.* By Miss A. Booth.
B. Naubert : *Hermann von Unna.*

1791. Lessing : *Nathan.* By W. Taylor.
Zimmermann : *On Solitude.* (From French.)
Popular Tales from the German (of Musæus).

1792. *Dramatic Pieces from the German* (including Goethe's *Sister*). By H. Mackenzie.
Lavater : *Physiognomy* (abridged from Holcroft).
Schiller : *Robbers.* By Lord Woodhouselee.

1793. Knigge : *German Gil Blas, or Peter Claus.*
Goethe : *Iphigenia.* By W. Taylor.

1794. L. Flammenberg : *Necromancer* (*Der Geisterbanner*). By P. Teuthold.
Poems of Baron Haller. By Mrs. Howorth.
Lessing : *Emilia Galotti.* By Berrington.

1795. Klinger : *Modern Arria.*
Lavater : *Secret Journal.* By P. Will.
Schiller : *Ghost-seer, or the Apparitionist.*
Schiller : *Cabal and Love.*
Schiller : *Don Carlos.*
Veit Weber : *Sorcerer and Black Valley.* By J. Powell.
Tooke : *Varieties of Literature* (containing translations from Wieland, Meissner, etc.).

1796. Bürger : *Lenore.* Translations by W. Taylor, Scott, J. F. Stanley, W. Spencer and H. Pye.
J. Grosse : *Genius.*
J. Grosse : *Dagger.*
Haller : *Alps.* By H. Barrett.
Klinger : *Travels before the Flood.*
Stolberg : *Travels.* By T. Holcroft.
Wieland : *Peregrinus Proteus.*
Wieland : *Select Fairy Tales.*
A. Thompson : *German Miscellany.*

1797. Kotzebue : *Indian Exiles.* By B. Thompson.
Lavater : *Physiognomy.* By C. Moore (from French).
F. Schulz : *Maurice* (from French).

1797. Schiller : *Minister (Kabale und Liebe)*. By M. G. Lewis.
Zimmermann : *Essay on National Pride*. By Wilcocke.

1798. Goethe : *Clavigo*.
Goethe : *Stella*.
F. Kratter : *Maid of Marienburg*.
F. Kratter : *Natalia and Menzikoff*.
Kotzebue : *The Stranger*, and numerous other plays.
Lafontaine : two novels.
Nicolai : *Sebaldus Notdanker*.
Schiller : *Don Carlos* (anon.).
Schiller : *Don Carlos*. By Noehden and Stoddart.
Wieland : *Oberon*. By Sotheby.
Zimmermann : *On Solitude*. Two new altered editions.
Several anonymous *German Tales*.

1799. Goethe : *Götz*. By W. Scott.
Goethe : *Götz*. By Rose Lawrence (d'Aguilar).
Goethe : *The Letters of Werter*.
Iffland : *Bachelors*.
Iffland : *Forresters*. By A. Plumptre.
Iffland : *Lawyers*.
Iffland : *Nephews*. By H. E. Lloyd.
F. von Knigge : *Practical Philosophy of Social Life*.
F. von Knigge : *History of Amtsrath Gutman*.
Kotzebue : *Pizarro*.
Kotzebue : *Virgin of the Sun*. Numerous other plays and several novels.
Lafontaine : Several novels.
Lessing : *School of honour, or the chance of war (Minna)*.
Lessing : *The Fatal Elopement*. [*Miss Sara Sampsom*] in *Lady's Mag*.
Matthisson : *Letters*. By A. Plumptre.
Schiller : *History of Thirty Years' War*. By Blaquiere.
Schiller : *Robbers*. Anon.
Schiller : *Robbers*. By Render.
Zimmermann : *Reflections on Men and things*.
Zimmermann : *On Solitude*. Second vol.

1800. Herder : *Outlines of the Philosophy of the History of Man*. By T. Churchhill.
Kotzebue : Several plays.
Musæus : *Physiognomical Travels*. By A. Plumptre.
Schiller : *The Armenian, or Ghost-Seer*. By W. Render.
Schiller : *Wallenstein*. By Coleridge.
Vulpius : *Rinaldo Rinaldini*. By J. Hinklei.
Zimmermann : *Aphorisms and Reflections*.

1801. Beresford : *German Songster* (Berlin).
Goethe : *Hermann and Dorothea*. By T. Holcroft.

Appendix B

1801. Goethe : *Palærophron and Neoterpe.* By Mellish.
Goethe : *Werther.* By Render.
Goethe : *Werther.* By Pratt (?). (First ed. undated; second ed., 1809).
Herder : *Oriental Dialogues.*
Kotzebue : *Life and Literary Career.* By A. Plumptre.
Schiller : *Maria Stuart.* By Mellish.
B. Thompson : *German Theatre.*
  Goethe : *Stella.*
  Iffland : *Conscience.*
  Kotzebue : *Stranger.*
  Kotzebue : *Pizarro.*
  Kotzebue : *Lovers' Vows* and seven other plays.
  Lessing : *Emilia Galotti.*
  Schiller : *Robbers.*
  Schiller : *Don Carlos.* Other plays.
German Museum.
The Juvenile Dramatist, plays from Weisse and Engel.

1802. Gessner : *Works.* By R. Lawrence (d'Aguilar).
Goethe : *Werther.* By Gotzberg.
Kotzebue : *Most remarkable year.* By B. Beresford.
Lafontaine : *The Reprobate.*

1804. Lafontaine : *The Village Pastor and his Children.* New Moral Tales.
Herbert : *Miscellaneous Poetry* (some from German).
Beauties of Kotzebue.
Lafontaine : *Six novels.* By Mrs. Parsons.
Lafontaine : Other novels.
Wieland : *Confessions in Elysium* (*Peregrinus Proteus*). By J. B. Elrington.
Zschokke : *Abällino* as *Bravo of Venice.* By M. G. Lewis.
Beauties of Zimmermann. By A. Campbell.

1805. *Life and Lectures of Gellert.* By Mrs. Douglas.
Gessner : *Works.* By F. Shoberl.
Goethe : *Hermann und Dorothea* (prose).
Lafontaine : *Rudolf of Werdenberg.*
Veit Weber : *Wolf, or Tribunal of Blood.*
Holcroft : *Theatrical Recorder*, containing from German—
  Engel : *Affectionate Son* ;
  Gellert : *Tender Sisters* ;
  Lessing : *Minna* ;
  Lessing : *Emilia Galotti.*

1806. Kotzebue : *Travels.*
Kotzebue : Collection of Romances.
Lafontaine : one novel.

1806. Lessing: *Education of the Human Race.* By H. C. Robinson.
J. M. Miller: *Siegwart.* By M. L. Hawkins.

1807. Kotzebue: *Anecdotes.*
Kotzebue: *Novelettes.*
Lafontaine: one novel.
Schiller: *Rise and Progress of Belgian Republic.* By T. Horne.
Goethe: *The Sorrows of Werter.* By Dr. Pratt.

1808. Arndt: *Spirit of the Times.* By P. Will.
J. J. Engel: *Essays and Tales.* By T. Horne.

1809. *Memoirs of Klopstock.* By Miss E. Smith.
Klopstock: *Solomon.* By R. Huish.
Gleanings from Zimmermann. By Miss Bayfield.

1810. Klopstock: *Messiah.* Extracts in prose by Egestorff.
W. Taylor: *Tales of Yore.*

1811. Anton Wall: *Amatonda.* By H. C. Robinson.
Gessner: *Death of Abel.* By W. C. Oulton.
Gessner: *Daphnis.*
Klopstock: *Messiah.* By Collyer and Meeke.
Lafontaine: one novel.

1812. *German prayers and hymns.* By Miss Knight.
Kotzebue: One play.
Lafontaine: One novel.

1813. Lafontaine: One novel.
(Madame de Staël: *De l'Allemagne*, translated).

1814. Kleist: *Frühling* as *Vernal Season.* By Egestorff.
Klopstock: *Messiah.* By T. Raffles.
Klopstock: *Letters.* By Miss Benger.

1815. Goethe: *Faust.* Extracts by Shelley.
A. W. Schlegel: *Lectures on Dramatic Art.* By J. Black.

1817. *Selections from tales and idylls of Gessner.*

1818. Fouqué: *Undine.* By Soane.
Kotzebue: *Patriot Father* (*Hussiten vor Naumburg*). By F. Shoberl.
F. Schlegel: *Lectures on History of Literature.* By J. Lockhart.

1819. Müllner: *Guilt.* By R. P. Gillies.
Mullner: *Guilt.* By W. E. Frye.

1820. Fouqué: *Sintram.* By J. C. Hare.
Goethe: *Faust.* Extracts by Soane.
Görres: *Germany and the Revolution.* By J. Black.
Grillparzer: *Sappho.* By Bramsen.
Three *Tales from the German* (? Hamburg)—
C. de la Motte Fouqué: *Cypress Crown*;
C. de la Motte Fouqué: *Turn-Coat*;
P. Gottwalt: *Christmas.*

Appendix B

1821. Fouqué : *Minstrel Love.* By Soane.
Goethe : *Faust.* Part I, verse with connecting prose.
Klopstock : *Messiah.* By Egestorff.
Schiller : *Don Carlos* (anon. adaptation).
Specimens of German Lyric Poetry [Beresford and Mellish].

1823. *Memoirs of Goethe* (from French).
Gethsemane. By Mrs. Montolieu (abridgment of *Messiah*).
Faust. Extracts. By Lord Leveson Gower.
Schiller : *Song of the Bell*, etc. By Lord Leveson Gower.
Ravenna, or Italian Love (adaptation of Fiesco).
Wieland : *Graces.*
Wieland : *Crates and Hipparchia.* By C. R. Coke.

1824. A. von Chamisso : *Peter Schlemihl* (as Fouqué's).
German *Popular Stories* (Grimm). By E. Taylor.
C. de la Motte Fouqué : *Outcasts.* By Soane.
Goethe : *Wilhelm Meister.* By Carlyle.
E. T. A. Hoffmann : *Devil's Elixir.*
Kotzebue : *The Poachers* (adapted).
Schiller : *Fiesco.* By Dr. Reinbeck.
Schiller : *Maria Stuart.* By H. Salvin.
Schiller : *Maid of Orleans.* By H. Salvin.
Schiller : *Fridolin.* By J. P. Collyer.
Lord Leveson Gower : *Translations from German and original poems.*

1825. Fouqué : *Magic Ring.* By Soane.
Klinger : *Faust.* By G. Borrow.
Lessing : *Fables and Epigrams.*
Memoirs of M. Mendelssohn. By M. Samuels.
Tieck : *Pictures.* By C. Thirlwall.
Tieck : *Betrothing.* By C. Thirlwall.
Schiller : *Wilhelm Tell.* By S. Robinson.
(Carlyle : *Life of Schiller.*)

1826. Engel : *Lorenz Stark.* By I. Gans.
Klopstock : *Messiah. By Miss Head.*
Kotzebue : *Graf Benjowsky* (adapted).
Tales from the German. By R. Holcraft.
Specimens of German Romance. By G. Soane.
German Novelists. By T. Roscoe.
German Stories. By R. P. Gillies.

1827. *German Romance.* By T. Carlyle.
Fairy Tales from German of A. L. Grimm.
Goethe : *Tasso.* By C. des Vœux.
Goethe : *Wilhelm Meister's Travels.* By T. Carlyle.
Life and Works of Körner. By G. F. Richardson.
Lessing : *Laokoon.* Partial translation by De Quincey in *Edin. Mag.*

1827. Schiller : *Criminal from loss of honour.* By L. Wapler.
Schiller : *Wallenstein.* By G. Moir.

1828. Schiller : *History of Thirty Years' War.* By Marriot Duncan.
Schiller : *History of Thirty Years' War.* By G. Moir.
R. Robinson : *Specimens of German Lyric Poets.*
W. Taylor : *Historic Survey of German Poetry.* 1828–30.

1829. Lessing : *Fables.* In three Books.
Schiller : *Wilhelm Tell.* Anon.
Schiller : *Wilhelm Tell.* By R. Talbot.

1830. C. T. Körner : *Rosamond.*
Fouqué : *Undine.*
Tieck : *Life of Poets.* (Augsburgh.)
Schiller : *Wallenstein* (*The Camp*). By Lord Leveson Gower.

APPENDIX C

BIBLIOGRAPHY

Works Consulted

A. *General*

Allgemeine deutsche Biographie.

Americana Germanica.

Archiv für das Studium der Neueren Sprachen. (A.S.N.S.)

Biographica Dramatica. By Baker, Reed and Jones. London, 1812.

Dictionary of National Biography.

K. Goedeke: *Grundriss zur Geschichte der deutschen Dichtung.* Second ed., Vol. IV., third ed.

Genest: *Some account of the English Stage from* 1660–1830. Bath, 1832.

Jördens: *Lexicon deutscher Schriftsteller und Prosaisten.*

Journal of English and Germanic Philology.

Modern Language Notes.

Modern Language Review.

W. Scherer: *History of German Literature.*

W. Taylor (of Norwich): *Historic Survey of German Poetry.* Three vols. 1828–30.

H. G. Fiedler: *Deutsche Literatur in England : das literarische Echo.* März, 1909.

J. L. Haney: *German Literature in England before* 1790. *Amer. Ger.*, No. 2, pp. 144-54; 1902.

J. Harris: *The First Printed Translations into English of the Great Foreign Classics.* London, Routledge. 1909. (V. incomplete.)

Georg Herzfeld: *Zur Geschichte der deutschen Literatur in England. A.S.N.S.*, vol. 110; 1903.

Emil Koeppel: *Deutsche Strömungen in der Englischen Literatur.* Strassburg, 1910.

Max Koch: *Uber die Beziehungen der englischen Literatur zur deutschen in achtzehnten Jahrhundert.* Leipzig, 1883.

Ernst Margraf: *Einfluss der deutschen Literatur auf die englische am Ende des achtzehnten und im ersten Drittel des neunzehnten Jahrhunderts.* Leipzig, 1901.

German Literature

B. Q. Morgan: *A Bibliography of German Literature in English Translation.* Madison, 1922.

O. Seidenstücker: *The Relations of English to German Literature in the Eighteenth Century. Poet. Lore,* II.

R. Singer: *Einige englische Urteile über die Dramen deutscher Klassiker.*

Leslie Stephen: "The Importation of German" in *Studies of a Biographer,* II., 1898.

F. W. Stokoe: *German Influence in the English Romantic Period.* Camb. Univ. Press., 1926.

T. Süpfle: *Beiträge zur Geschichte der deutschen Literatur in England im letzten Drittel des achtzehnten Jahrhunderts. Koch's Z. f. vgl. L. G.,* VI. 305-28; 1893.

F. H. Weddingen: *Geschichte der Einwirkungen deutscher Literatur auf die Literatur der übrigen europaischen Völker der Neuzeit,* Leipzig, 1882.

T. Zeiger: *Beiträge zur Geschichte des Einflusses der neueren deutschen Literatur auf die Englische. S. z. vgl. L. G.,* Bd. I., Heft 2 and 3. and Berlin, 1901.

B. *On Particular Authors*

GESSNER.

Berta Reed: *The Influence of Solomon Gessner on English Literature.* Philadelphia, 1905.

GOETHE.

Goethe Jahrbuch (1882).

Publications of the English Goethe Society.

Publications of the Manchester Goethe Society. (For particular articles see footnotes to Chapter V.)

J. M. Carré: *Goethe en Angleterre.* Paris, Plon-Nourrit. 1921.

Bibliographie critique et analytique de Goethe en Angleterre. Paris, Plon-Nourrit. 1921.

HERDER.

Herder in England and America. By M. D. Learned. *Ger. Amer. Annals,* II. 9; 1904.

KOTZEBUE.

Kotzebue in England. Ein Beitrag zur Geschichte der englischen Bühne und der Bezeihungen der deutschen Literatur zur englischen. By Walter Sellier. Leipzig, 1901.

LESSING.

Lessing in England. By W. Todt. 1912.

Lessing in England. By S. H. Kenwood. 1914.

Appendix C

SCHILLER.

Schiller's dramas and poems in England. By Thomas Rea. London, 1906.

For Bürger's *Lenore* see—

A. Brandl : *Lenore in England*, in Erich Schmidt's *Charakteristiken*, II., p. 244 ; 1886. (Incomplete.)

W. W. Greg : *English Translations of Lenore. Mod. Q. of Lang. and Lit.*, V., p. 13 ; 1899.

G. Herzfeld : *Zur Geschichte Bürger's Lenore in England. A.S.N.S.*, Nr. 314, 1901.

W. B. Colwell : *An Eighteenth-century Translator of Bürger's Lenore. Mod. Lang. Notes*, XXIV. 254 ; 1909.

A. R. Hohlfeld : *Scott als Übersetzer. Studien zur vergl. Lit.*, 1903.

C. *Memoirs, etc., of English Writers interested in German Literature*

Life, Writings and Correspondence of George Borrow. By W. Knapp. Two vols. 1899.

G. Herzfeld. *A.S.N.S.* Bd. CVII. 62 ; 1901.

C. Shorter. *George Borrow and his Circle.* 1913.

T. Carlyle, 1785–1835. By J. A. Froude. 1882.

Early Letters of T. Carlyle, 1814–1826, ed. Norton.

Carlyle's Stellung zur deutschen Sprache und Literatur. By Krager. Anglia, vol. 25.

Carlyle als Vermittler deutscher Literateur und deutschen Geistes. By W. Streuli. 1895.

A. Brandl : *Coleridge und die englische Romantik.* Berlin, 1886.

Letters of Coleridge. Heinemann, 1895.

De Quincey's Life and Writings. By H. H. Yapp. 1890.

W. Dunn : *T. de Quincey's Relation to German Literature and Philosophy.* Strassburg, 1901.

Memoirs of a Literary Veteran. By R. P. Gillies. Three vols., 1851.

Memoirs of the late Thomas Holcroft. 1816. Republished abridged in "Travellers Library," 1852.

Life and Correspondence of M. G. Lewis. 1839.

Memoir of Rev. Thomas Raffles, D.D. By T. S. Raffles, 1864.

Diary, Reminiscences and Correspondence of H. C. Robinson. By T. Sadler. 1869.

K. Eitner : *Ein Engländer über deutsches Geistesleben im ersten Drittel dieses Jahrhunderts.* Weimar, 1871.

J. M. Carré : Several articles. *Vide* Chap. X.

Lockhart : *Life of Scott.*

Life of Shelley. Medwin.

Life of Shelley. E. Dowden. Second ed.

Die Belesenheit P. B. Shelleys. A. Droop. Weimar, 1906.

Life and Correspondence of Robert Southey. 1849.

Memoir of William Taylor of Norwich. By J. W. Robberds, F.G.S. 1843.

G. Herzfeld: *William Taylor von Norwich. Eine Studie über den Einfluss der neueren deutschen Literatur auf die englische*. Halle, 1897.

Life of Wordsworth. By W. Knight. 1889.

D. *English Periodicals between* 1750–1830.

Analytical Review. 1788–1799.

Annual Review. [A. Aiken.] 1802–1808.

Anti-Jacobin. 1797–1798. (Lasted eight months.)

Anti-Jacobin Review. 1798–1821.

Blackwood's Edinburgh Magazine. 1815– .

British Critic. 1793–1826. Reunited with *Quarterly Theological Review*.

Critical Review. 1756– .

Edinburgh Review. 1802– .

European Magazine and London Review. 1782–1825. New series, 1825– .

Foreign Review and Continental Miscellany. 1828–1830.

Foreign Quarterly Review. 1817– .

Gentleman's Magazine. 1750– .

Lady's Magazine. 1770– .

Literary Gazette. 1819– .

London Magazine.

Monthly Register and Encyclopedean Magazine. 1802–3.

Monthly Magazine. 1796–1826. New series 1726– .

Monthly Mirror. 1795–1806. *New Series*, 1806–1810.

Monthly Review. 1750– .

Monthly Repository of Theological and General Literature. 1806–26. New series, 1826– .

New Review (Maty's). Nine vols. 1782–86.

Quarterly Magazine (Knight's). 1823– .

Quarterly Review. 1809– .

Westminster Review. Continued as *London Review*. 1824– .

INDEX

Index

 Z

Index